A Caribbean Poetics of Spirit

A Caribbean Poetics of Spirit

Hannah Regis

The University of the West Indies Press

Published by The University of the West Indies Press
7A Gibraltar Hall Road, Mona
Kingston 7, Jamaica
www.uwipress.com

© 2024 by Hannah Regis
All rights reserved. Published 2024
A catalogue record of this book is available from
the National Library of Jamaica.

ISBN: 978-976-640-945-6 (paper)
978-976-640-943-2 (ePub)

Cover image by Hannah Regis with artistic rendering courtesy of
Lisa Marie Ford.
Cover and book design by Robert Harris
Set in Scala 11/1.5 x 24

The University of the West Indies Press has no responsibility for the persistence
or accuracy of URLs for external or third-party Internet websites referred to in
this publication and does not guarantee that any content on such websites is, or
will remain, accurate or appropriate.

Printed in the United States of America

Contents

Acknowledgements   *vii*

1   Anchoring Spiritual Memory in the Pre- and Post-Atlantic Caribbean World   *1*

2   Indigenous Cosmovisions and Postmemory in the Fictions of Wilson Harris   *37*

3   Haunted Histories: Spectres of the Middle Passage in M. NourbeSe Philip's *Zong!* and Grace Nichols's *I is a Long Memoried Woman*   *63*

4   Re-Architecting Freedom: Myth, Ancestors and Ritual in George Lamming's *Season of Adventure* and Erna Brodber's *The Rainmaker's Mistake*   *86*

5   Writing the Absent Presence: Locating Discourses of the Unspeakable   *109*

6   Tracking Signposts to a Caribbean Poetics of Spirit in Wilson Harris's "Arawak Horizon" and Derek Walcott's *Omeros*   *136*

Afterword   *171*

Appendix   *175*

Notes   *177*

Bibliography   *205*

Index   *219*

Acknowledgements

THIS BOOK OWES ITS COMPLETION TO THE MANY individuals who have contributed to my growth over the years. I would like to thank Erica Johnson and Nadi Edwards for their fierce support, meticulous comments and gracious conversations that impressed on me the immense value of spirit worlds. I pay tribute to Paula Morgan, mentor and guardian of my destiny, who took the time to carefully read several versions of this work and provide detailed comments. I salute the legacy of Gordon Rohlehr who taught me the value of creative criticism. My heartfelt gratitude is due to Elizabeth Jackson for years of unwavering friendship, encouragement and generosity of spirit. I must acknowledge the unstinting support of Elizabeth Walcott-Hackshaw who helped to clear obstacles in the way and went beyond the call of duty to offer major assistance on my journey. A special thanks to Jean Antoine-Dunne, who initially inspired me to pursue this project. Particular mention must be made of Anita Lundberg whose warmth and support I deeply value. I thank Christine Randle, the director of the UWI Press for her unfailing professionalism, efficiency, patience and courtesy, which is worth emulating everywhere. I gratefully acknowledge the *Journal of West Indian Literature* and *Caribbean Quarterly* for permission to incorporate reworked material from two of my previously published articles: "Myth, Ancestors and Ritual," in *Journal of West Indian Literature* 27, no 2 (2019): 29–38 and "Not Fit to be Mentioned: Ghosts and Narratives of Criminal Intimacies in Selected Short Stories from *The Haunted Tropics: Caribbean Ghost Stories*," in *Caribbean Quarterly* 66, no 2 (2020): 117–94. I wish to acknowledge with gratitude, Lisa Marie Ford, for her contribution in crafting the cover image for

ACKNOWLEDGEMENTS

this book. Finally, I pay tribute to my beloved mother, Martha, who – as far as I can remember – has maintained that the spirit world is the real world. I also acknowledge with immense reverence, my late father, who I miss every day. Thanks to Aaron, Tenille, Joshua and Jonathan for their unqualified love. I extend my deepest gratitude to my Creator and also to my husband, Kyron, whose wisdom and love inspire me daily. The merits of this book belong to all above.

CHAPTER 1

Anchoring Spiritual Memory in the Pre- and Post-Atlantic World

A PREAMBLE ON CARIBBEAN SPECTRALITY

In the Caribbean, where societies have been built on collective loss and rupture – as in the persecution of the First Peoples, chattel slavery, indentureship and the host of other atrocities in the region – ghosts and spirits have become a common phenomenon. Spirits are not simply the sort of vaporous visage floating about, but are intimately associated with aspects of the supernatural, psychological hauntings, hallucinations, the undead which reveal themselves in the present, a shadow of the mind, the energy or special feel of a place and the immaterial aspects of human experience. They accord to them specific temporal, historical, social, ideological and cultural circumstances. In the wake of the Caribbean's grievous colonial legacy, a discursive style of narrative was invented to question the relationship between the material and immaterial world. My concern is with the nature of this connection and the ideological issues that are subsequently provoked. Surviving the catastrophic collisions with empire, the *'geist'*[1] – or breath – of the region's first inhabitants was lodged in time, space and the natural world. Teetering between the thresholds of life and death, presence and absence, spirits can be defined by their liminal status. Their shape dovetails with the holes or gaps in reality that coincide with colonization and its aftermath, the impact of which continues to seep into every dimension of the postcolonial world.

Martin Munro makes a useful observation in his introduction to *The*

A CARIBBEAN POETICS OF SPIRIT

Haunted Tropics: Caribbean Ghost Stories in which he recognizes the circuit of relations between the material and immaterial:

> Every island of the Caribbean is the site of a deep haunting. Before Columbus, the various indigenous peoples – the Arawaks, the Caribs, the Tainos – lived in relative harmony with the land, the sea and each other. Everything changed in 1492: the Amerindian people quickly were decimated, their presence erased by disease, wars and overwork. These are the Caribbean's oldest ghosts, almost invisible in history yet still present in the form of place names, fragments of language, ancient foods and pockets of descendants speckling the islands. Following Columbus, the islands saw some of the most brutal systems of work in all human history. The Atlantic slave trade . . . must have felt like death. To be a slave was to be a kind of ghost, living a half-life in a foreign land, an existence that denied the African's humanity, making the slave a kind of non-being.[2]

By placing the reader in the shadow of the manifold violences of the colonial world, Munro provokes feelings about the nature of spiritual memory and its legacy in contemporary times. Much like the many drowned bodies that drift on the floor of the Atlantic, there is also the reality of the First Peoples, whose memory can be traced in the landscape, language, images and indeed in *writing*. The environment also lends itself to be a receptacle of other-worldly energies.

The quest to recuperate and give epistemic saliency to these often unacknowledged *presences* has found its way into literary pursuits. And, it is in this sense that I turn to literature to hone what is fundamentally a social issue into a research problem. Narrative should not be read as a neutral enterprise that is detached from life. Rather, it should be utilized to produce new analytical insights and meanings of the world. For a long time, Caribbean critics have been engaged with the importance of temporality, the plural unity of the past, present and future and its signifying functions in language. This book embodies this ethos and probes a range of perspectives relevant to Caribbean spirit worlds with a focus on Indigenous, African-Caribbean and mixed heritage through fiction produced between 1960 and 2015. More specifically, the selected works of Marlene NourbeSe Philip, Grace Nichols, George Lamming, Erna

Brodber, Shani Mootoo, Maryse Condé, Gisèle Pineau, Patricia Powell, Derek Walcott and Wilson Harris demonstrate the extent to which a spectrum of writers have thematically and conceptually deployed spirit presences to theorize and address the complex ideological, cultural, social, ethical and political issues that pertain to the region. By adopting a decolonial position, these writers have turned attention to a species of submerged knowledge that are brought to the surface through an innovation in fiction that reshapes form and content. Before unpacking the contours of these innovative structures, it is useful to trace the effects of colonial literary trends that denied and divided as opposed to reconcile the hybridity of cultures and beliefs in the Caribbean universe.

THE PROBLÉMATIQUE OF WESTERN MATERIALISM

Prior to the imposition of colonial thought, the Caribbean universe, with its mythic layers of cultures, ancestral wisdom and environmental diversity, was a locus of cosmological dynamism and relational ways of being-in-the-world for the First communities. However, the machinery of imperialism produced a taxonomy of the self that erased ideas of mutualities, the belief in parallel time, mythologies and ancestral faiths. Historical materialism was arguably the bedrock by which European capitalism thrived and expanded. Governed by an unchecked desire to rule and conquer, empire levied its forces to claim absolute dominion of the New World. The subsequent compartmentalizing of spaces and peoples found its way into literary writing. Colonial literary trends – with its rigid polarities – produced the effect that the social world operated in accordance with binarity and material (realist) conventions.

In his text, *Realism,* Damian Grant explains that the language of realism, which pivots the one-dimensional plot or storyline and the omniscient narrative perspective, seeks to define the mortal world as one that subsists within strict mono-linear coordinates.[3] This account of reality ignores the creative power of plural universes, hybridity and spiritual intermedialities that afford metamorphic processes. It was not until the early and mid-twentieth century that Caribbean writers and cultural architects began to overtly experiment with the fragments of memory, the creativity of myths and the fluidity of time and space in an effort to defy the forces of assimilation. The imperative to engage memory, testimony and belated hauntings emerged in an innovative craft and genre which maintained both liberatory focus and theoretical rigour.

TOWARDS AN ANTI-COLONIAL PRAXIS

The indictment against European colonization is unmistakable in Frantz Fanon's scholarship, in which he broadly maintained a space for a radically altered sense of Caribbean self and territory. Fanon's de-colonial thought informed the discursive debates on black ontology, consciousness and freedom. He underscores some of the most profound philosophical questions about Caribbean ontology in *Black Skin, White Masks*,[4] where his thesis confronts the psychological ramifications of systemic racial discrimination on Afrosporic persons – the result of which is an interstitial subjectivity that is ambivalently negotiated between complex cultural and racial imperatives. He imagines that the nervous conditions left in the wake of empire must be worked out through the construction of a radically new subject who will refuse to replicate Western protocols. However, Fanon's divergent socially-oriented order garnered criticism and he was accused of excessively promoting violent resistance and opposition to (neo)colonial forms of power, which resulted in a re-exposure to and reciprocating of Western biases. Nonetheless, it remains indisputable that his intellectual cultivation of black and Antillean consciousness has broadened the very foundation of Caribbean existential phenomenology[5] and self-reflexive capacities for Caribbean ways of being in the world.

Interestingly, Fanon's disposition towards myth and syncretism was one of skepticism and ambivalence. In *The Wretched of the Earth*, he refers to acts of conjure as "exhausting" and "fanci[ful]".[6] This incertitude is most apparent near the end of *Wretched* when he asserts, "Since 1964 we have drawn the attention of French and international psychiatrists in *scientific* works to the difficulty of 'curing' a colonized subject correctly."[7] This statement is resonant with a call to address the insidious nature of colonial wounding through the parameters of socialist methodologies, which do not readily account for the metaphysical conditions of colonial violence that endure and erupt as propitiating vengeful duppies of history in modern times.

One is thus constrained to search out other strategic readings of Caribbean metaphysicality readily located in the oeuvre of Édouard Glissant. In his magisterial philosophizing on the diversity of Caribbean space, history, time and culture, Glissant submits that Antillean history is one of "shock, contraction, painful negation, and explosive forces. This dislocation of the continuum, and the inability of the collective consciousness to absorb it all, characterizes what I call a nonhistory".[8] These multifaceted and "explosive forces" did not appear in tranquility or neat lines, but are encapsulated in a highly evolving and spiritually interconnected temporality and language that are expressed in the process of creolization. The principle of creolization is linked to the idea of suturing sedimented cultures and mythologies across a wide, spiritual region. Embedded in Glissant's definition of creolization is the concept of syncretism[9] – or the merging of knowledges which embraces circuitries, psychic spirals and spiritual values that debunk the idea of Europe's totalizing presence functioning as the architecture of Caribbean reality.

This turn in Caribbean criticism accommodated processes of aesthetic reinvention that dovetails with the insights of Edward Baugh, who suggests that the diversity of Caribbean experience in literature was not merely found in concrete "geographical sites" but is mapped on the heart.[10] According to Baugh, the substratums of Caribbean humanism are inextricably linked to a syncretic creativity, which produces a new logic that transgresses processes of Western acculturation.[11] This new logic that embraces a multidirectional memory would assert a most radical intervention in the idea of how history is shaped, driven and sutures the divide between action and being.

On this ground, this book asks: How does Caribbean literary discourse, through the construction of spirit presences, conceive alternative ways of being that are vigorous enough to withstand the impacts of (neo)colonialism? What intellectual spadework has been designed to effectively accomplish this? The subsequent and arguably the most pivotal questions are, therefore: Why have these presences erupted? Do these unspoken histories forcefully extend their tentacles into our future? If the latter proves true, it begs the questions: How do literary representations of Middle Passage spectres demonstrate the extent to which its terms of interaction have persisted in contemporary times? How have Caribbean writers deployed spirit presences to embody troubled histories and reflect evolving subjective social positions and complex forms of personhood? And more specific to this enquiry is: How are representations of spirit presences in West Indian Literature connected to literary evocations of therapeutic interventions that are rooted in ancestral, ritual practices? Significantly, this book explores the implications of the rise of a Caribbean poetics of spirit and asks, how can fictional engagements with spirit presences emerge as a prospective model for a Caribbean aesthetic? I am therefore, concerned with the major operative categories of spirituality for the shared purpose of forming (i) a crucial counter-archival history through which the voices of the oppressed find articulation and belonging, (ii) a mode of historical and contemporary redress to societal woundedness, (iii) a repository or index of cultural, psychological, affective expressions that are linked to the unfinished business of history and (iv) therapeutic interventions to the effects of social and cultural injustices architected by imperial and neo-imperial systems.

Before proceeding to explicate on the history of thought, it is imperative to note that in this project, I investigate a selection of Anglophone Caribbean writers with the exception of Maryse Condé and Gisèle Pineau (Francophone writers) whose respective ghost stories, "The Obeahman, Obeahed," and "The Voyage of the Centipede," are used to glean insights into the overarching nature of Caribbean haunting. The comparison of Anglophone and Francophone literary traditions requires an acknowledgement of the ethnic, culture-specific, linguistic and socio-historical complexity of each practice while emphasizing their inter-relatedness. More specifically, the terms, 'Anglophone' and 'Francophone' refer to communities of English and French-speaking countries globally, which were respectively colonized by Britain and France. While this book adopts an interdisciplinary approach towards an examination of Caribbean spectrality, I am cautious to not over-generalize or produce reductive synthesis between both literary fields. Although an appraisal of the key differences between the French and British post-colonies is useful, an extensive investigation into the distinctions between the Anglophone and Francophone literary traditions will certainly require an altogether different project. For all intents and purposes of this work, I provide a brief analysis that distinguishes the respective traditions that comprise the Anglo and Francophone literary worlds.

The Francophone Caribbean was arguably constrained to Martinique, Guadeloupe, French Guiana, Haiti and the French-speaking part of St. Martin. Naturally, the French Caribbean was smaller in size than the large and diverse British colonies. Among other differences, is the argument that while the French-speaking islands were governed centrally from France, the Anglo-speaking colonies were supervised by Great Britain through a variety of legislative bodies.[12] With the implementation of governors in the English-speaking Caribbean, there was greater autonomy for the population than was the case in the French colonies, which were governed by an unyielding set of arrangements from the metropole, including the approved language usage from the Académie Française.[13] A provincial management of the French-speaking territories, which were seized during the mid-seventeenth century, provided the premise for the gallicization of its Caribbean colonies. This exercise meant that the French colonizers attempted to fashion Antillean culture in accordance with Parisian standards by establishing a rigid political and judicial administrative system, the regularizing of writing and speaking in erudite French and other forms of control with ensured French enculturation.

This implementation has deeply influenced the relationship between the French overseas departments and France. Contrastingly, the autonomy of the Anglophone Caribbean in the mid-twentieth century can, in part, be referred to as an amalgamation of efforts including the existence of self-sufficient local governments and the autonomy that Anglophone Caribbean writers, cultural workers, linguists and major calypsonians exercise/d via their free-wheeling engagement of Creole as a literary language. In the Anglophone world, movements towards literary independence involved, in part, a steady pioneering of the Creole by the Caribbean Voices and later the Caribbean Artists Movement during the 1960s and early 1970s. The founding members included Edward Kamau Brathwaite, Andrew Salkey and Henry Swanzy.[14] This observation does not elide the important work of performers in the Anglophone Caribbean such as Paul Keens-Douglas, Alfred Pragnell, Black Stalin and David Rudder, whose careful lyrics, humour and picong reflect the expressive systems and local varieties of English. Notable linguist, Richard Allsopp observes that West Africans brought to the New World a complex network of sub-Saharan languages and expressions that led to patterns of idiomatic deep structure which gave rise to the formation of Caribbean Creoles.[15]

Despite the many divergent historical, linguistic, theoretical[16] and cultural contexts between the Anglophone and Francophone traditions, the prevailing theme of fragmentation in the postcolonial world and the complex issues it gives rise to, comprise important structural connections that allow for a meaningful dialogue between Anglophone and Francophone literary traditions. By exploring the *haunting effects* of contemporary forms of violence and abuse in relation to gender, I propose that Condé and Pineau open their narratives to discussions about power and hegemony, which transcend distinct cultural contexts. Through a close reading of both short stories, the writers interrogate the human concerns of female suffering and the trauma of secret abuse, which give rise to a discrete set of hauntings insofar as it becomes manifested through psychic hurt and affective agency. Caribbean literature is a naturally comparative one, particularly within the context of a diasporic audience and the world at large. Given that the selected writers investigate a vast range of transnational and historical terrains, a greater degree of participation and affective understanding of Caribbean identity is afforded from all manner of audiences.

THE RISE OF A CARIBBEAN POETICS OF SPIRIT

It is also useful to discuss the process of reasonings and aesthetical configurations of 'spirit' by Caribbean thinkers who assume responsibility for recuperating submerged selves and constructing viable epistemologies. Paget Henry traces the development and evolution of African syncretism in literature amidst the peripheral forces of imperial history. Henry engages the interdisciplinary dimensionalities of Caribbean ontology, spirituality and metaphysicality to offer a composite assessment of Caribbean consciousness.[17] He submits that Caribbean philosophy encompasses alternative ways of knowing that are congealed from Caribbean space. Caribbean reasonings therefore underwent "a seismic shift in orientation"[18] that co-opted some of the signifying practices of ancestral, religious ceremonies and syncretic belief systems. African Caribbean magico-religious practices became one of the primary "lenses through which the consciousness of a racialized and colonized existence was articulated" and re-negotiated.[19] Caribbean critics like Sylvia Wynter, Wilson Harris, Édouard Glissant and others actively determined adaptive responses to the social conditions of plantation society which embraced the pathways of pre-Columbian knowledges and African-Caribbean syncretism. Henry submits that the tableaux of Indigenous communities, with its streams of associations into archetypal maps, range of ritual and vast landscapes provide a polyvalent literary horizon through which systems of knowledge about Caribbean being could be assembled.[20] Yet, despite the existence and vibrancy of this repository, there were pervasive and insidious colonial forces, which sought to undermine any emerging sense of Caribbean being-ness.

Early writers of fiction wrestled with intense seasons of colonial brainwashing[21] – a dilemma which fertilized and ensued in a distinct style of writing. Edward Kamau Brathwaite traces this tradition and identifies the colonial forces which combined to stifle the folkways and syncretic traditions long after emancipation. These included white missionary work, colonial education and legislation, which labelled African Caribbean religions as devil-worship.[22] Territorial expansion in the region eventually imposed colonial protocols with forceful impositions of measure and division. New types of historicization followed a bureaucratic system in which absolutist ideas elided ancestral and local realities. Truth was thus governed by strict socialist criteria, which dismissed oral histories. The post-emancipation assemblies eventually passed laws banning religious gathering and other elements of African Caribbean syncretism evoked in the legacies of Obeah,[23] Voodoo, stick fighting and Carnival.

Even though Caribbean writers would, in time, recuperate the spiritual equilibrium of folk-based practices, there was an in/advertent contribution to the colonial enterprise of distancing the literary canon from the spirituality of the folk masses. Some of the late nineteenth and early twentieth-century Caribbean mimics modelled Europe's devaluation of a Caribbean spirit universe. It was an era of mismatched absolutes. Cynric Williams's novel, *Hamel, the Obeah Man* comes to mind.[24] *Hamel*, which was first published in 1827, presents the reader with ambivalent attitudes and images of African syncretic spirituality. Although the sorcerer, Hamel is distinguished by his superiority of conduct over the vileness of Roland (the white Methodist missionary), syncretism is associated with devil worship, primitiveness and delusion. This is apparent quite early in the text when Roland asks Combah, "Are you too leagued with the Prince of Darkness?"[25] The association of Obeah with grave-digging, dirt-eating and self-cutting thematizes the shunning attitudes of many of the planters in the West Indies and their supporters in Britain. According to Diana Paton, repressive laws were justified by beliefs that linked Obeah to child sacrifice and cannibalism.[26] Given its association with the occult, superstition and African-ness, the practice was widely viewed as "backward". Interestingly, very little is known of Cynric Williams. Critics like Eugenia O'Neal have speculated that he was a Jamaican slave owner.[27] It is therefore no surprise that his text invites a complicity and coercion into (mis)labelling African spirituality as barbaric and primitive.

Similarly, Herbert de Lisser's pernicious depiction of African ceremonies as "black magic" in *The White Witch of Rosehall*, exposes his quasi-embarrassment about Caribbean religious syncretism.[28] In this 1929 novel, de Lisser makes creative use of the fearsome legend of Annie

Palmer whose story begins with her childhood in Haiti – a territory that De Lisser describes as the "stronghold of devil-craft".[29] When Palmer moves to Jamaica, her combined power of whiteness and knowledge in Vodun makes her a monstrosity to the politicians and houngans alike. In this story, magico-religious rituals are evinced towards the harm of the African enslaved community and there is panic of being "obeahed" by the white witch. De Lisser's overt Eurocentric anxieties resulted in his condescending rendition of Caribbean spirituality in which supernatural activities are wielded by a satirical imperial mother to quell and terrorize the masses. The distortion of Caribbean spirituality by writers who misunderstood the importance and value of spiritual phenomena continued to perpetuate Eurocentric associations between blackness and devilry. Christian missionaries were too eager to label Obeah as devil-worship and did their best to erase it. African derivations of magic in the New World remained uncharted, and tales of the bogeyman and wild women of the forest were closely orientated with savagery.

The misrepresentation of syncretic spirituality in literature and popular culture continued to fuel hegemonic agendas and elide the pragmatic effects of alternative traditions. Edgar Mittelholzer's work is of similar interest; for while Mittelholzer is celebrated for his intuition and transgressive use of the Carib bone flute, his over-identification with Europe circumscribes the scope of his work. His view toward Obeah and Shango, for example, exposes an undermining of the Shango-Obeah complex:

> Travel-writers from the north have taken pains to highlight the "superstitions" of the natives, giving such practices as voodoo and obeah far more importance than they deserve. So far as I am aware, only in Haiti is voodoo strongly rooted. In other territories obeah is heard of as, in England or America, the average citizen would hear of, say, quack spiritualists or fortune-tellers. Only a few ignorant peasants believe in it seriously, and even among these the obeah-man has been exposed for what he is – a man who wants to make an easy living by pretending that he can work magic, cure illnesses, or wreak evil on an enemy for a "small fee". He is no more a primitive than any of the practicing crystal-gazers or spirit-mediums in

Britain or America. The police are always on his track, for obeah is an offense punishable by imprisonment.[30]

Mittelholzer's attitude towards magico-religious syncretism is not atypical of middle-class communities in Trinidad who remained ambivalent to the social functions of Shango, Obeah, Vodun or Revivalism. The Guyanese writer certainly occupies an intriguing disposition, often falling back into an imperialist bias which he tries to distance himself. Significantly, Mittelholzer's conservatism, by way of a close affinity with the Romance and the Fantastic[31] purports conformity to the British Gothic where a fantasy world is created in order to conceal a perceived violent colonial reality. One therefore had to wait for Wilson Harris's *Palace of the Peacock*[32] to apprehend the vestiges of the submerged Caribbean unconscious, which carry vast potentialities of ceremony, plural meaning and instruction.

The experimental stages with Caribbean spirituality by early Caribbean writers reveal the surrounding anxieties of empire and the influence of a hegemonic reading of Caribbean space and people. Projecting beyond this critique, I offer a revised indexing on the functionalities of spirit presences as one that redeems a sense of Caribbean being and metaphysicality from its distorted misrepresentations and submergence. This introduction sets out to respond to the core questions on the facets and potentialities of the inter-relationship between the immaterial and the human worlds that has existed for eons. The following sub-categories which are offered delineate the derivatives of Caribbean spectrality as represented in the selection of literature and interrogate the stakes of such an inquiry.

THE CARIBBEAN MYTHIC IMAGINATION AND VESTIGIAL PRESENCES

Unlike Williams, de Lisser and Mittleholzer's ambivalent engagement with questions of Caribbean ritual and metaphysicality, Wilson Harris, in his creative and philosophical enterprises, was devoted to illuminating Caribbean space as alive rather than inert. Harris refers specifically to the womb of space that seethes with ancestors, ghostly traces, living fossils and spirit-imbued conduits. It is a viewpoint that puts forward the idea that a vibratory, incorporeal world coexists on an equal footing as the material. Harris felt the inadequacies of the novel of realism with its emphasis on the 'individual' as opposed to the collective unconscious, its proclivity to the singular point of view as opposed to a polyphonic perspective, its emphasis on the one-dimensional world as opposed to the nebulous connections that palpitate in the West Indies.

The novel of consolidation, Harris tells us, has a vested interest in linearity, judgments and moralities.[33] Pointing the way out of European obscurity, he offers the (Caribbean) novel of fulfilment. In the essay, "Tradition and the West Indian Novel," he outlines a tapestry of paradigms including, but not limited to, the mythic imagination, ancestral sages/ totems (whose particular functions serve to warn, instruct, bless and curse), the signifying practices of African limbo and Haitian Vodun, the scale or drama of consciousness, the symbolic or formulaic function of the Amerindian bush-baby, metamorphosis, shamanism and rain-making vestiges that reside in the world of the living.[34] These paradigms translate into formal literary tools in Caribbean writing through which the reader is able to perceive traces of the spiritual. Harris also provides the utility of the mythic imagination that is manifested via language. The mythic imagination incorporates the register of New World cosmologies and is a vehicle for theorizing ideas of Caribbean being, simultaneity, existence and metaphysics.[35] Literature, therefore, becomes a threshold or gateway through which the wreckage or vestiges of colonial history are manifested. The narrative of this kind is vast in scope as it gives voice to the hidden tongues and eloquence of the earth and space – rocks, rivers and ocean. The intrusion of deity, ancestor and the ghosts of history into a mode of modern literature contributes to the elucidation and validation of the existence of simultaneous worlds.

Harris is, however, castigated by scholars such as Sylvia Wynter for having a theoretical blindness to the materiality of the social world. Yet, quite contrary to the allegations that label Harris's work as arbitrary and escapist,[36] Harris, in fact, grounds his investigations in particular elements of regional differences, ceremonies, rituals and community-specific epistemes. His range of mythic structures does not negate his concern with distinct cultures, but functions as deliberate epistemological strategies and choices for reinterpreting the vastness of Caribbean history and its relation to Caribbean being. Barbara Webb asserts with similar conviction that mythic codes illuminate the cross-cultural resources that are available to the creative imagination, and which equip one with the skills of critical reasoning outside the ground of received Western models. Caribbean myth, then, can be engaged as an analytical tool that bridges the sacred and the secular as well as temporal and spatial chasms. It is the cement that binds the worlds of the living with the dead. Webb postulates that the imagination is not a solipsistic function of the subconscious but is a critical resource in the construction of meaning.[37] The potentialities of the mythic imagination include a recuperation of the suppressed qualities of Caribbean being which yield profound moments of self-awareness and creativity.

This reinvigorating of Caribbean criticism by Harris and Webb carries connections with Édouard Glissant, whose methodology of relation involves an inclusion of myths towards a process of self-recovery and self-actualization from the wreck of history.[38] In the context of narrative relationality, Glissant asserts, "[E]very poetic intent leads straight to a narrative of the world, for which this narrative is not a [static tale] but a state of relatedness".[39] By placing emphasis on the circuits of relation in his wider oeuvre, Glissant rejects the closure of reading the 'stable' self that is embalmed by materialism. An excessive attention to material domains, which ignores the opacity and spiritual density of (Caribbean) experience, inhibits true self-fulfilment. Rather, the relationality – or seepage – of one entity to another, which is stimulated by states of historical rupture are transformed into illuminating gateways. Glissant conceptualizes the wounds of history as a fissure, hole or opening which unites wo/man and spirit in a secret bond. It permits the accretion of time through simultaneous layers of history and provides freedom to the creative imagination. This functioning and positionality of the Caribbean universe as a vessel of energy is further illuminated through the techniques of haunting and ghostwriting.

SUPERNATURAL GHOSTS AND HAUNTING

In *Caribbean Ghostwriting* Erica Johnson offers a meditation on the historical dynamic of the region, whereby the past returns through ideas of haunting.[40] Haunting, in the Caribbean world, as argued by Johnson, takes the form of repeated and intrusive, uncanny encounters, arguably because of trauma that has been repressed, ancestors who were not remembered, things lost and debts unsettled. Johnson notes, "The ghost is by definition a witness to events from an individual's life or from a collective past that have been repressed either willfully or unconsciously".[41] She posits an intimate connection between the unjust and painful atrocities of colonial experience and the subsequent phantoms which return to monitor the present world. Acts of historical torture, mutilation, plantation nightmares and journeys are connected with contemporary forms of restlessness and dis-ease. "Ghostwriting" in many ways takes into consideration the ontology of subalternity. That is, writers who become conduits for other voices are aware of what cannot be reconstructed. Gaps and silences are emphasized as much as what can be known; thus, the writing is characterized as spectral.

Johnson also tells us that ghosts carry a complex set of cultural associations. She references Jenny Sharpe's arguments regarding the continental African-derived belief that the spirits of those who die an unnatural death or did not receive proper burial rites remain in the mortal world to perpetuate havoc.[42] The restless soul is, therefore, connected to that which seeks a *reckoning*. The ghost may not manifest itself in any strict, chronological sense, but operates on a labyrinthine temporality which enables useful explorations in the quest to eventual self-discovery. In deploying the geography of the Caribbean islands as a palimpsestic tool, Johnson shows how layers of the past are inscribed and razed through a ghostly temporality. This is identified in an articulation of inward movements into the unconscious, excursions into memory and repressed trauma, the fashioning of interior monologue as a simultaneous flow of experiences and re-enactments of loss. She draws on Michelle Cliff, Maryse Condé and Dionne Brand's use of memory as a tunnel, images of isolation and

A CARIBBEAN POETICS OF SPIRIT

gaps to define this emerging narrative field of ghostwriting. Johnson demonstrates how testimonies from beyond the grave are insurgent as they cross and displace boundaries between literary, documentary and autobiographical realms. The materialization simultaneously dispenses justice and underscores the role of uncanny rhetoric in disrupting the repetitions of violence.

However, the representations of Caribbean spirit activity in literary writing encompass more than just a return to and suturing of haunted memories. I am therefore interested in the *mutations* of spirit, which include, but may not be limited to, the appearances of duppies, boloms, revenants, possessed humans, ancestral belief systems and veneration, processes of transcendence and hallucinations, fevered imaginations, time-travel, coven gatherings, shape-shifting and anthropomorphized landscapes. Emphasis is therefore placed on investigating how spirit is deployed as a tool of revelation, a source of communal memory, a receptacle of cultural symbols, an expression of psychic trauma, societal woundedness, a symbol of unfinished business, a trope that enables one to reconnect time and consciousness, and a modality used to challenge the effects of social and historical wrongs impelled by imperial and neo-imperial systems. A deeper review of these constituent parts will hopefully achieve the dimensions I wish to identify with each mode of Caribbean spirit presences in the selected literary works. Naturally, all the items that make up this tradition cannot be adequately interrogated in one text, but this introduction provides a representative sample to familiarize the reader with the exigency that gives rise to these mani-festations in the first place and the subsequent role of this tradition in the affirmation of Caribbean being and identity.

RITUAL AND ANCESTRAL VENERATION

Ancestral veneration forms a critical modality of spirit that comprises liturgy and ceremonies to summon the spirits of deceased elders who serve as divine guides in the natural world. Ancestralization speaks to the performance of religious ritual practices (mostly) at the completion of a life cycle. It is not simply an alternative way of knowing from afar, but is a metaphysical principle that is evaluated against totalitarian understandings of death as a finite and static state. The definition of an ancestral presence is broadened to include a force outside of immediate blood relations that is connected to a spatially-expansive or communal history. Carolyn Cooper, in "Something Ancestral Recaptured: Spirit Possession as Trope in Selected Feminist Fictions of the African Diaspora," compares the ways in which creative writers in the African Diaspora (in the Caribbean and elsewhere) re-appropriate old magic to resurrect identities and communal energies.[43] According to Cooper, ancestors are generational presences and powerful communal gatekeepers who are integral to self-construction and historical transformation. Through an exploration of the fictions of Paule Marshall, Erna Brodber, Sylvia Wynter and others, Cooper catalogues the mechanisms that may be deployed to summon their appearance. She signposts myalism, drum rhythms, herbalism, shrubs and vines, stones and crystals and articles of clothing or ornaments, through which the spirits materialize to dispense healing.[44]

The potentialities of ritual and possession are explored in chapter four of this work, particularly in the context of George Lamming's *Season of Adventure*. In *Season*, Lamming grants insights into the ritualized union of the peasant community and the spirit world to promote acts of self reengineering, autonomy, healing and transcendence. The Ceremony of Souls makes communication with ancestors a continuous, dynamic and intimate practice. It is induced by dance and the participant's rhythmic movement to the bold pulse of the drum beat in honour of the powers and spiritual force that will be evoked. The general atmosphere of excitement, clapping, continuous drumming, prolonged spinning and falling to the ground encourages spirit possession. In Lamming's text, the *hounfort* is a zone where spirit is able to touch spirit in the quest for the power to retell an unspeakable history. In principle, ancestral veneration enables ancestors to spatially coexist with the living and become influential in their daily lives. Their return undermines any complacent image of the self and knowledge-making in the material world.

A CARIBBEAN POETICS OF SPIRIT

The idea of Caribbean space as containing ancestral energy and memory is also echoed by Kamau Brathwaite, through his concept of the 'geo-psyche'. In *Word Making Man: Poem for Nicolás Guillén*, Brathwaite writes of "[t]he sea between us [that] yields its secrets" and which permits the scattered islands to communicate in a most uncanny way where "together we say wind/ & understand its history of ghosts/ together we say fire/ & again there is a future in those sparks".[45] Brathwaite's acceptance of a living landscape is concretized by his own admission to encountering ghostly forces in Barbados. In an interview with Joyelle McSweeney, he recalled an experience with a presence from beyond the grave whom he identified as Namsetoura.[46] The poet described a visionary incident in which the ghost of Namsetoura appeared to him at his home in Cow-Pastor, Barbados. She charged the poet not to leave his island, which had been exploited by the government and systems of ecocide. As the ancestor rose up from the earth, Brathwaite received a stern rebuke for his cowardly demeanour, which, she asserted, instigated no change to modern systems of warfare and territorial dispossession. By the ghost's chastisement, Brathwaite had trespassed into sacred territory, as signified by the Anansi's web which he first encountered. Anansi is the custodian between the lands of the living and dead. Brathwaite's assertion, it seems, is that Caribbean space is a vast memorial as it houses the vestiges of every ethnic migrant culture. This poetic style certainly distinguishes itself from Western rationalist thought structures that positioned the material and the spiritual as mutually exclusive.

There is also something very spiritual about Brathwaite's inspired term for Caliban's language and video style. To enter fully into Brathwaite's poetry, it is necessary to understand his texts as works of conjure and magic in a real sense, since Caliban seeks to answer to the old colonial landlord (Columbus/Prospero). Sycorax, Caliban's powerful mother (who is the ghost in Brathwaite's computer) is the muse and the typeset that inspires his work. This is not simply an experimentation with shapes and font, but a deep acknowledgement that for generations, African peoples have relied on extra-human networks and spiritual powers for redemptive measures. Something ancestral is retained in the power of

Sycorax who is the anti-colonial matrix of creativity and who energizes the written word with orality. She is also present in the Shango spirituals and train songs, in the possession of the poet during the composition of his volume *Barabajan Poems 1492–1992*, and in the African forms of New World jazz. Similarly, ancestral energies seep into Brathwaite's poem "Caliban", which first appeared in his 1968 volume, *Masks*. An assumed identity is invoked and it is one that frees the person behind the mask to access and express the buried parts of their own identity. As Caliban dances the limbo, "down/down/down" with "knees spread wide",[47] the power of old African gods manifests as an underlying presence and transformative power. The dance, as Wilson Harris also contends, delivers the possibility of regenerated myth, the myth a people can turn to in order to resist erasure and forms of disempowerment.

FOLKLORE, TRICKSTERS, CONDUITS AND MEDIUMSHIP

Another category of *spirit presence* includes those beings born out of the stressful contexts and torturous violence in the colonial Caribbean world. These are not necessarily summoned through rituals but are powerful gods, guides, tricksters, avatars, legends and folkloric creatures who subsume shapes in seasons of distress. In Walcott's *Omeros*, for example, there is the premise that Achille suffers sunstroke. Whether Afolabe (his ancestor) literally appeared before Achille, or figuratively visits him because of his fevered senses, is determined by the reading audience. The materializing of a spectral presence because of a frenzied subconscious state may signify that repressed fears and desires are surfacing. Of equal significance to the idea of cultural exchange, is the legend of Nanny, the Jamaican Maroon warrior.[48] In *Ghosts of Slavery*, Jenny Sharpe examines the factual reports and oral accounts of Nanny, the leader of runaway slaves in Jamaica known as the Windward maroons.[49] Embedded in the myth of Nanny is an alternative science tradition, particularly those anchored in the belief that an individual can acquire and exercise magical abilities with the aid of products, enchantments and spells. Rumoured to have been able to channel spiritual liberatory tactics via spell-casting, the memory

A CARIBBEAN POETICS OF SPIRIT

of Nanny delivers a generative myth about the survival of Africans in the New World and the reassurances about the capacity of Caribbean peoples to resist oppressive forces. Not unlike Afolabe in *Omeros*, Nanny is a boundary crosser and facilitator of healing processes. The emphasis is on the power of interconnection. Brathwaite's Legba figure is another useful example to reflect on the ways in which deities and gods appear in works of literature. In *Islands*, Legba – the persona – invites the reader to "[L]ook, [at] his rags,/. . . crutch and . . . satchel".[50] Brathwaite suggests that the deity can be invoked through myriad ways: the oral traditions such as hailing and chants, by journeying (via crossroads), iron-making, blood sacrifice, weeping and local gatherings. Although Legba represents processes of negotiation and accommodation, he embodies the horrific realities of colonization, which is most evident in his crippled disposition. He is, therefore, mandated to become the wound that speaks, while imparting a worldview of reinvention in the wake of a grievous history.

LIMINALITY AND LIMBO

In reading the betwixt spaces teeming with supernatural beings, there is the critical relevance of liminality to the discussion at hand. This is probed in relation to ideas of hybridity in postcolonial criticism and its further applicability for the texts on which this book is based. Liminality emphasizes the position of being caught in the in-between, unavoidably connected to two worlds and states of being. The theoretical formulations of Homi Bhabha are asserted particularly through the "unhomely", which marks a series of movements by people whose crossing of thresholds generate a flow of memories and cultural traditions. The motif of the migrant in transition concurs with the elements of spirit passages, interstitial perspectives and engineered zones of resistance.[51] Within the interstice, threshold or gap, the imagination is utilized as a mechanism for calling up immortal presences that unsettle the hubris of a human-centred cosmos. To this degree, Bhabha's third space takes on new, contextual meaning that encompasses explorations of the supernatural. This is engaged as an aesthetic sensibility to de-centre and transcend reductive ways of knowing. It finds expression in Derek Walcott's, *Omeros*[52] and Wilson Harris's short stories in *The Sleepers of Roraima*,[53] which contain hybrid universes that are populated by threshold beings such as ancient gods (Afolabe in *Omeros*), sorcerers/border-crossing figures (Ma Kilman in *Omeros*), magicians (Yurokon's uncle in Harris's "Yurokon"),[54] mystical totems (the lizard in "Couvade"),[55] and spirit messengers (the sea-swift in *Omeros*).

The concept of liminality is also characterized through the African inflected rite of being in limbo. Limbo, as posited by Harris, is a physical and spiritual site of dislocation. It is epitomized in the limbo dance.[56] Unlike Brathwaite's invocation of spirit guides, Harris deploys the image of art as a portal through which the past and the present maintain a plastic relationship. Thus, the limbo imagination facilitates a new architecture by combining the body with language. As stated by Harris, the activation of a limbo sensibility relates directly to a mode of survival; it is a coping mechanism for 'getting through' a (conceptual and physical) restricting space. The limb that is severed from Africa remembers the place of its origins via the limbo dance, which becomes a ritual enactment of that dismemberment.[57]

The limbo aesthetic is positioned as a curative process through which the newly transplanted Africans shape new relationships by a perfor-mance of being locked within the belly of the ship. The dance of bending backwards to negotiate a pole held horizontally at the lower abdomen invokes the many-limbed spider, Anansi. It designates the space of the in-between as a site of resistance through a fusion of the numinous and material life. In the dance and space of limbo, there occurs an activation of "sleeping resources of dismembered gods".[58] These "sleeping resources" are reflective of creative activity and energy that are capable of imparting and establishing new meanings. Thus, the limbo aesthetic reflects "a certain kind of gateway or threshold of a new world and the dislocation of a chain of miles".[59] We can think of limbo as a methodology for nego-tiating the tensions between survival and liberation; and it is a prospect of unending potential since it carries ideas of transformative resilience. It is a spatial technique that is engaged as a locus for remaking identity

CULTURAL MEMORY, AFFECTIVE FILIATIONS, PSYCHOLOGICAL PHENOMENA

under the pressures of social forces by subsuming the energies of lost traditions in the unconscious.

On this point, cultural memory is invoked as a carrier and facilitator of spirituality. Apart from psychic processes, memory is preserved in other traces: embodied personalities, monuments, runes, family lore, the archive, feelings, symbolic writing, formulaic rites and sacred texts. These conduits are carriers of cultural knowledge. Erica Johnson explains in *Cultural Memory, Memorial and Reparative Writing* that cultural memory in literary discourse refers to the textuality of repressed history through which transhistorical consciousness, cultures and identities function as a structuring and informative matrix.[60] This heralds the correlation of affect criticism and cultural memory studies. The actual and socio symbolic impact of histories of loss, displacement and their eruptions into personal histories is immortalized in collective memory. In other words, by re-interpreting memorial sites or historical landscapes through experimental writing (symbols, tropes, metaphors or representational themes), the cultural critic acquires new knowledge regarding the value of shared experience outside of normative modes of reading.

Through the symbolic practice and ethics of memory work, absent presences begin to surface in affective traces. This is spatialized for example, in *Zong!*, where the greyness of the font, the presence of a waterlogged archive and the metaphors of the decapitated black bodies overwhelm the reader. This materializing disallows forgetting as ghosts travel down the corridors of time. Christian Lundberg defines affect in literary work as "the set of forces, investments, logics, relations, and practices of subjectivization" that invade the consciousness of the reader, who in turn, enacts a visceral and emotive exercise in meaning-making.[61] Although the concept of affect far exceeds the scope of this book, its reparative underpinnings and bent to new lines of inquiry prove valuable. That affect becomes a palimpsest of encounters traversing the ebbs and swells of unarticulated, psychic intensities that pass from human to human, it encapsulates the potential for realizing a world that exceeds the horizon of the norm. Thus, through a sensitivity to a style of writing that preserves connections between ideas, values, bodies, objects, temporalities and events, affect criticism proves useful in exploring the underlying psychic (and emotive) engagements with a phenomenon under scrutiny. Since affect criticism stitches together different temporalities, it is a valuable resource to process a deep and painful past. Indeed, a series of meaningful contact between bodies, objects, signs and energies are evidential in several of the texts selected for this project.

Philip's enterprise in *Zong!* finds especial significance, since she takes on the task of not only self-archiving or indexing the repressed knowledge of the 1781 Massacre, but is actively perceiving and transmitting the emotional tensions and pain that underlie the formless presence of its history, which comes out into the open through a manner of literary exorcism.[62] Her innovative strategies impel the reader to grapple with the incomprehensibility of the case and to enter experientially into a story which she explains cannot be told. The sheer power of her response to the 1781 mass killing of some one hundred and thirty-three living Africans has stirred up an affective register of feelings that not only identify the historical backdrop of sugar, servitude and racism, but reflect the unfolding imprint of systemic racial oppression in the contemporary world. All of these strands of meaning – historical, political, sociosymbolic, mythic and cultural are relevant for decoding the repetition of signs. The sensory and emotional registers of language which Philip deploys to excavate human experience are fully explored in chapter three.

The persistence of memory and unarticulated grief are also evoked in Gisèle Pineau's short story, "The Voyage of the Centipede", and Patricia Powell's novel, *The Fullness of Everything.*[63] In these narratives unresolved generational hurt gives rise to a discrete set of hauntings insofar that, like spirituality, it asserts psychic and affective agency over its subject. More specifically, the troubled psyches of characters are projected by way of the phantoms they encounter. These ghosts can be read as hallucinations brought about by a traumatized state of mind and a tide of past emotions that still haunt in the modern world. The difficulty of grasping the enormity of old and new traumas at the point of their convergence brings both numbing belatedness and intrusive memory in touch with each other, insofar that the subconscious mind catapults it into conscious states, thus repeatedly demanding that it be confronted and addressed.

POSTMEMORY

The manifestation of submerged and unspeakable traumas – in part – constrains a reckoning with transgenerational pain whether within the context of familial or social relations. The concept of postmemory reveals a state of being connected to a past "although not actually mediated by recall".[64] The "post" in "postmemory" describes the relationship that a generation after a historically tragic event occurs may come to feel. These experiences are transmitted so deeply and affectively that they seem to constitute memories in their own right. Postmemory also refers to memories that are passed to the second generation in myriad ways – through stories, photographs, private and collective reminiscences, testimonies and embodied knowledge. According to Marianne Hirsch, this process involves an unconscious participation in history via "imaginative investment, projection and creation".[65] Hirsch's transgenerational connection to the Jewish Holocaust influences her research pursuits whereby she conceptualizes a theory of vicarious traumatization which can be (unknowingly) passed down and inherited by descendants. This living connection between ancestor and descendants may be felt through dreams, memories and overwhelming feelings of displacement and disease that defy coherent narrative reconstruction. Postmemory, therefore, illustrates the unassimilated nature of whatever returns to haunt the survivor later on. Hirsch argues that this form of haunting has the power to draw from a storehouse of familiar and unexamined cultural images that intervene between thought and emotional impulses.

This is realized in several of Harris's short stories, but is most evident in "Couvade" and "Yurokon." Couvade's reaction to his orphaned existence is mediated by an uncanny recall of events that preceded his birth. The forbidden actions of his parents, which altered the fortune of the tribe, affect him so deeply that he must voyage into history through shamanistic rituals to reconcile the displacement and fragmentation he feels. Couvade is not physically present at the moment of his community's genocide but he assimilates their experiences all the same. What's even more perplexing is that the memories that he inherits from several characters in the text have an underside to them which dictates the severity of his grope towards healing and understanding. Couvade's postmemories are often concurrent with shame, guilt and overwhelming responsibility. Similarly, in "Yurokon," generational transmissions are not closed off but ensnare the mind and body of the protagonist, and unsettle his existence. The focus on haunting signifies a developing interest not only for circumventing the viciousness of the past but working through ancestral hurts in order to create a viable present – and future – for subsequent generations. Memory, therefore, becomes possessed of agency that is akin to spiritual practice through which the unknown becomes vital in self-determining acts of meaning-making and modalities of healing.

SPECTRAL PRESENCE

Concealed pain is thus explored and unraveled in many ideas that are connected to spectrality. Yet, while the term spectre is mostly associated with the return of the dead, it is also deployed as a conceptual vehicle to realize another mode of absence. The definition of the spectre, as qualified in chapter five of this book, dovetails with the elided or concealed ontologies of those alive/undead human beings who are marginalized and disregarded from prevailing discourses and culture. Place, person and interior schisms unfold as 'absent presence' and become more complicated against events such as migration and self-imposed exile. Thus, while a spectre may symbolically relate to ideas of immateriality, I argue that they equally encompass particular groups of persons who are marked by forces of subalternity, invisibility, constant displacement and movement, negation, absence and liminality. The term is therefore engaged to re-conceptualize social maps in relation to sites and experiences of

A CARIBBEAN POETICS OF SPIRIT

struggle in the modern world. This pattern of association between the frames of reference as it pertains to ghost, spectre, spirit and haunting persists throughout this work, but in some cases, the crises and issues they provoke are quite distinct. Spirits should, therefore, not be read as a homogenous entity since they serve different functions in the contexts by which they appear in the narratives.

MAGICAL SPACES AND ANTHROPOMORPHIZED SCAPES

While embodied personalities operate seamlessly within communities and society at large, I also submit that presences are resident in the Caribbean land and sea world. Elizabeth DeLoughrey and George B. Handley, in their introduction to *Postcolonial Ecologies: Literature of the Environment,* describe the symbiotic relationship between nature and humanity to articulate that the environment is an agent of knowledge. They assert that an innovative, critical approach to interpreting Caribbean space, "must reckon with the ways in which ecology does not always work within the frames of human time and political interest, [thus] the definition reflects a complex epistemology that recuperates the alterity of both history and nature."[66] DeLoughrey and Handley's definition of a resurging human-environmental overlay in the Caribbean resonates with the complexity of Caribbean space. The land, in this case, is not an unliving setting but is a narrator. It has existed through various epochs as a being with its own rhythms, memories and longing. The material-spiritual quality emerges from the folklore that the Caribbean landscape is a latent cemetery in which many enslaved groups were interred on the land itself. In *The Lessons of Nature in Mythology,* Rachel McCoppin notes that in pre-Columbian communities there was no demarcation between soil, animal and human realms (including the vegetal world). She affirms, "[T] he Earth was . . . a place where the ancestors went. As seeds are broken and give use to shoots, so new life came from the underground realm of the dead" (22).

This sentience of the earth also holds true to the Afro-Caribbean diaspora. Lizabeth Paravisini-Gerbert and Margarite Fernandez Olmos in

Creole Religions of the Caribbean: An Introduction from Vodou and Santería to Obeah and Espiritismo, have traced sediments of continental African cosmologies and spiritualities that are resident in the topography of the New World. They determine that during the transatlantic slave trade "the flexibility . . . and malleability of African religions allowed practitioners to adapt to their *new* environment, drawing [and imparting] spiritual power from wherever it originated" (3). Paravisini-Gerbert and Olmos underscore the livingness of Caribbean space with specific reference to "Ochosi, the [African] deity of forests and herbs" (1). As such, to read the Caribbean natural world, is to read the landscape as encryptions of ancestral faiths and energies. This process dovetails with Katherine McKittrick's concept of "Plantation Futures" where the plantation is a site to procure alternative worldviews of liberation, resistance and survival. One therefore finds that while the landscape bears the memory of colonial torture and violence, it is equally sustained as a powerful receptacle of other-worldly presence that shapes everyday interactions with the natural world.

In "Novel and History, Plot and Plantation", Sylvia Wynter opines that the plantations were the "superstructure of [Caribbean] civilization; and the plot was the roots of culture".[67] Wynter continues, "But there was a rupture between them [as] the superstructure [began to] respond to the demands of external shareholders and metropolitan markets".[68] Taking a lead from Wynter, one notes the manner in which localized agrarian folkways were undermined by pervasive capitalist markets and systems of monopoly. The idea of ecological imperialism seems appropriate to the discussion at hand, since it theorizes the invasion of foreign forces into localized ecosystems. Biopiracy, for example – which is the taking of resources from the native land and the substitution of local life with imported products – subsequently created another dimension of colonialism. This concern is evoked in the poetry of Olive Senior who has unfailingly grappled with the theme of environmental equity. Senior engages the metaphors of cultivating and nurturing the wounded landscape to advance multivalent Indigenous cultural forms with the power to heal and revitalize the human psyche.[69] Similarly, in his 1992 Nobel speech, Walcott, recalling the performance of the Indian epic, the *Ramleela*, in

A CARIBBEAN POETICS OF SPIRIT

Trinidad, re-envisions the role of nature within collective articulations of identity, belonging and ritual passage. The poet remembers:

> We had to . . . go through the creeks of the Caroni Swamp, to catch the scarlet ibises coming home at dusk. In a performance as natural as those of the actors of the *Ramleela*, we watched the flocks come in as bright as the scarlet of the boy archers, as the red flags, and cover an islet until it turned into a flowering tree, an anchored immortelle.[70]

The routine flight of the red ibis is integral – both literally and metaphorically – to the entire conceptual shape of the West Indian collective unconscious as it yields the birth of metaphor itself. Here, a metaphor is conceived on the swampy terrain, where the poetic mind is entangled with the material world as the islet comes to be written over by the physical scribbling of birds only to appear as a tree. It is a performance of the uncanny and non-human energies that feed into Walcott's poetic reflections. Couched in the interpretive framework of the Indian ancestral ritual (the Ramleela) is a recovery of lost, cultural traditions, which are activated through an encounter with the landscape and transmitted via the Caribbean literary imagination. It is an example of experimental writing that reveals alternative strategies for excavating the deeper essences of the natural world and Caribbean identity.

The idea of the landscape as repository and living entity correlates with the formulations of Wilson Harris, who has unfailingly argued that to enter into the Guyanese tropics means to step into a whole universe of multiple temporal pockets where stones, trees, bushes, birds and rivers thicken time. A.J. Bundy describes Harris's advocacy for cultural ecology via the use of myth in West Indian literature:

> Harris sensed that the conventional novel, especially as it came to be realized in the nineteenth century, did not altogether fit, [and] that other resources were called for . . . Harris experienced the interior of Guyana as a river and land surveyor in the 1940s. The interior speaks through a music of silence, a language of silence. The interior is also a *living organism*, an organum of forest, rocks, rivers and cataracts. The experience of the interior brought home to Harris the picture we hold of reality, and its reification in the conventional novel.[71]

Harris, consequently, developed a parable of the Caribbean self "that is to be found in the music of living landscapes, seascapes and skyscapes".[72] This is expressed through the deployment of natural motifs and animist landscapes, which present an alternative way of measuring time. This approach prevents the permanent destruction of life and allows the possibility of regeneration. The palpability of nature is also echoed in Edwidge Danticat's assertion that the Caribbean cane field is a "farming of bones".[73] By implication, spectres reside on the foothills of the Caribbean landscape.

Brathwaite also pays homage to cosmic forces in the woodland territories of Barbados and Jamaica. Through a symbolic journey into a dark forest as recounted in, "The Black Angel", the persona asserts: "It was as if my spirit was waking up in the middle of/a very dark night/as if I was alone in a wood of presences and powers/vague enraged personalities I could not see or name".[74] These obstinate spirits, desperate to speak and mingling in the ears of the speaker, revise a grammar that exists in the submerged Caribbean unconscious. By virtue of memory, their voices become part of a time-space continuum that is effected via language. Their knowledge is released, perceived and developed in the explosive and vibratory force of images, complex narrative structures and the conventions of flashback that concretize their experience.[75] Nature holds the energies of the dead as a calcified memory.

Apart from the landscape, the Antillean Ocean has also come to function as a potent shifting and fluid graveyard. Caribbean writers like David Dabydeen, Fred D'Aguiar, Grace Nichols and Marlene NourbeSe Philip have turned to the sea, which awakens memories of the Middle Passage. The many millions of lives that have sunk below the surface beg for answers to questions which remain unanswerable. Paul Gilroy reads the transatlantic journey as an interstitial, liminal space in which free men and women were transformed into forced and later voluntary workers.[76] The symbolic voyage to a presumably new life upon distant shores expresses the dual idea of this crossing as a passage that is at once the death of one cultural identity and the formation of another. Gilroy alludes to the forging of identity amid traumatic conditions and the implications of this

A CARIBBEAN POETICS OF SPIRIT

violent syncretism.[77] This theorization of Caribbean super syncretism retains a sense of recurring tensions of movement, settlement, closeness to and distance from generations of family members and communities. This materializes in Grace Nichols's collection of poems where the long-memoried persona psychically wrestles with ancestral memories and mutating forms of domestic servitude on the plantation.

Moreover, Derek Walcott's, "The Sea Is History" presents the ocean as a living keeper of history. It is both a mediator and an entity that vibrates with pain and memory.[78] Like Walcott, Glissant references the aquatic residue of life and calcified bones of Africans that refuse to transition into another world, because of a lack of justice. In "The Open Boat", he states: "[T]hose who [went] straight from the belly of the slave ship into the violent belly of the ocean depths . . . did not die; [they] quickened into this continuous/discontinuous thing."[79] The presences imagined to be pacing the ocean's floor seek reparation and retribution. Brathwaite's concept of tidalectics is also edifying at this point.[80] The optics of the ocean underscore a circular movement through a pattern of language that is synonymous with the ebb and flow of the tides. This circuitous movement between communities and territories imbibes the process of Caribbean becoming that is spatialized via an experimental artistic form, where meaning is constantly sought from various encounters outside of time and space. In *Sun Poem*, something emerges from suppressed collective memory: "It had happened a long time ago said the cattle wash boys longer ago than uh nevvah remember when the *loa* came out of the sea the sun shining down and everything peaceful when they lifted themselves loudly heavy and darkly out of the water."[81] The idea of the Igbo giants emerging out of the deep at Bathsheba on the east coast of Barbados demonstrates a high level of spirit receptivity. The Atlantic, and more specifically, water become an important paradigm for addressing the spiritual essence of Caribbean communities. It speaks of the necessity to enter the grey tombs within the depths of the ocean with a creative audacity that will fill the gaps and holes in history with new knowledge while delivering the possibility of regenerated myth. This radical search and rediscovery of Africa within the seascape functions as a means of bridging the disarticulation encountered in European social science methodologies. The thrust to locate alternative methodological devices for arriving at a culturally relevant way of gathering data and applying it to the lived experience of African diasporic peoples is similarly evoked in the concept of polyphony.

POLYPHONY

Melvin Rahming notes in his thoughtfully-conceived essay, "Towards a Critical Theory of Spirit: The Insistent Demands of Erna Brodber's *Myal*", that the "fusion [of spirit and body] through the narrative technique of polyphonic and polyvalent associations . . . adds to the mystery of combined entity [. . .]. [It is] a conceptual act that blurs the line between human and [non-human] consciousness and challenges, consequently, Western ontological paradigms".[82] Rahming contends that the activation of non-human voices through speech enacts a preemptive strike against the colonial formulations of the submerged West Indian subject. Through the activity of language and the resonances that emanate from it, there is the force of breaking through rigid codes and syntax. This is exemplified in Erna Brodber's *Myal*. The myalists who heal Ella O'Grady from her septic pregnancy and spirit thievery are literal and spiritual. Mas Cyrus, in whose balm yard Ella is healed; Ole African, the necromancer who drives away Anita's duppy; Miss Gatha, the Kumina leader; Dan Simpson, the Baptist preacher; and Maydene Brassington, White Hen, all embody spiritual characteristics. This is Brodber's signature polyphonic structure as we learn through disrupted and disruptive pieces that the characters who comprise this group are embodiments of spirits who have travelled to Jamaica from Africa. They have been in communication with each other for several hundred years. This coven of spirits communicates through telepathy and jerky cryptic statements. Language thus becomes repossessed as it is fused with the vestiges of memory. Through a transgressive poetics, time is re-positioned and the subject is refashioned. Brodber is here signposting a literary effort to

A CARIBBEAN POETICS OF SPIRIT

reach for a diction and symbology that will reframe temporal angles and simultaneous experiences to break through sterility and impotence. The use of multiple voices is posed as a culturally relevant way of gathering data and reconciling the disparateness of individual history.

I am reminded of Wilson Harris's author's note to *The Whole Armour*, in which he concludes that the first step to a New World artistic modality begins with an inclusion of "the very old or eclipsed, buried material of [Caribbean] consciousness which cries out for relief".[83] Harris's remarks illustrate the potential of recalibrating all the main registers of the Caribbean, which promises a re-assemblage of history that is geared towards the deeper essences of the self and human freedom. The polyglottic and moving life of the Caribbean are themes that are threaded throughout this project. As illuminated in the many ways/routes in which spiritual practice is elucidated, one notes the multifarious composition of Caribbean space and identity.

This analytic approach to apprehending diverse ways of knowing via a deployment of various philosophical trends in the Caribbean certainly destabilizes hegemonic relations and subverts the operations of cultural imperialism. A preliminary summary of these methodologies includes George Lamming's Ceremony of Souls and the backward glance as signifying practices of ancestral veneration;[84] Gordon Rohlehr's aesthetic continuum and metaphor of possession as a re-interpretation of language that elucidates the submerged and socially repressed self; Kamau Brathwaite's nation language, which intimates the fragments and ghosts of history through repetition and the developing line of a new creole aesthetic;[85] Derek Walcott's twilight poetics as a movement through which spectres move between the veils of day and night, death and life, open and close;[86] and Édouard Glissant's fissures of history as an architectural response or portal through which the past and the present maintain a plastic relationship.[87] Naturally, these paradigms are oriented towards an eclectic ethos that transgresses codes of privilege with the effects of producing new ways of understanding Caribbean being. This sense of Caribbean praxis conceptualizes and converges with the multiple ethnicities, cultures, languages and spiritualities that comprise the region. It is, therefore, integral to the theme of plentitude that is born of a history of endurance and survival.

The concept of plentitude is embodied in the complex life of the tropics, that is, its rhythmic exuberance, double talk, manoeuvering between a series of spaces (hinterland vs city life) and oscillation through several layers of time (past and present). This dynamic is reinforced by the idea of polyphony. The entanglement of voices that are raised to the surface in the narrative milieu in each text encompasses the echoes and groanings from beyond the grave, which takes concrete shape through ceremonies, totems, seers and spirit guides. Barbara Lalla fittingly observes that the "polyphonic narrative in [Caribbean] fiction includes intercepting voices not only of different personae but also of the fragmented individual consciousness that reaches back to the past [. . .]. [This] re-membering involves an integration of voices" from across time and space.[88] Indeed, NourbeSe Philip's *Zong!*, Grace Nichols's *I is a Long Memoried Woman*, Wilson Harris's *The Sleepers of Roraima* and *The Age of the Rainmaker*, George Lamming's *Season of Adventure*, Erna Brodber's *The Rainmaker's Mistake* and Derek Walcott's *Omeros* constitute a cacophony of expression that connects with Harris's concept of the phantom limb, which offers the possibility of thinking about freedom through a movement into psychic space and consciousness.

In keeping with the broad characteristics of Caribbean spirit activity and the wide-angled approach that the selection of texts allows, one is able to discern trends and patterns. In consequence, qualitative content analysis is useful since it provides the base for a deep study across multiple texts through the identification of thematic units. Hsieh and Shannon define qualitative content analysis in the Humanities as an approach of controlled analysis for the interpretation of the content within a text.[89] This may be accomplished through a systematic classification and process of coding recurring content patterns. Yet, this research strategy goes beyond counting themes to an examination of language with the intention to acutely classify recurrent topics that procure fresh and complex meaning. Within the principles of this methodology, reparative reading techniques are also engaged to locate and recuperate with care, the repressed knowledges that attend to human agency. The term "reparative," travels in myriad ways but is largely associated with the work of Eve Kosofsky Sedgwick, who suggests that a reparative reading practice is one that resists the temptation of hegemonic/definitive (or what she calls "intellectual baggage") interpretations of culture, which locks one into fixated modes of perceiving the world.[90] In place of monopolistic and paranoid reading tendencies, Sedgwick's accretive framework of reparative criticism opens up connective approaches and affiliations to a given context. To this extent, each chapter focuses on multiple texts which display evolving concerns about Caribbean being and belonging from the vantage point of spirit activity in the Caribbean world. The texts are explored not just in terms of their content but in relation to contemporary theoretical discourses that intersect with the elucidation of how the subject of "spirit" is depicted in the context of each narrative. Glissant's poetics of relation holds true to the task of constantly fashioning and constructing meaning with great awareness of the Caribbean theoretical traditions. It is a method that is used to orchestrate the arrangement of the chapters. While the selection of texts can be seen as providing ten different perspectives on spirit, they can be grouped in terms of their relation to particular socio-cultural, geographical and historical contexts. This divides the book into six interrelated sections. As the subsequent chapter overview demonstrates, the texts thrive on the similarities and echoes as well as their counterpoints and distinctions.

Chapter two, "Indigenous Cosmovisions and Postmemory in the Fictions of Wilson Harris", is a critical starting point since Harris, through his allegorical handling of the Guyanese tribal narratives, explores how the ideologies and ontological uniqueness of the First Peoples influenced perceptions of a spirit-imbued Caribbean universe. This chapter provides a strategic beginning for examining the instructional power of mythic forms and figures through an engagement with Marianne Hirsch's concept of postmemory. The third chapter, "Haunted Histories: Spectres of the Middle Passage" is devoted to examining the creative labour of NourbeSe Philip in *Zong!* and Grace Nichols in her poetic collection, *I is a Long Memoried Woman*, which involves a deconstructing of the imperial archive and its haunting ramifications in the African diaspora. Through an experimental and technical poetic form that is evident in polyphony, edgy images of bone fragments and disintegrated words, the writers create a compelling New World aesthetic and counter-archival work in an attempt to make peace with ruptured spaces. This chapter also provides a demonstration of the way that Nichols draws upon the tropism of the female body and shows how memory operates as an agency which comes over characters through the power of syncretic practices. The analysis construes cultural memory as a spiritual performance which is coalesced and fertilized to produce creative syncretism. In this sense, Philip and Nichols are dedicated to the ideological power of experimental writing. The articulation of such power, albeit in different contexts, resonates in the works of Lamming and Brodber.

The fourth chapter is suitably entitled, "Re-Architecting Freedom: Myth, Ancestors and Ritual in George Lamming's *Season of Adventure* and Erna Brodber's *The Rainmaker's Mistake*". It considers how Lamming and Brodber's novelistic handling of freedom moves beyond materialist representations of the Caribbean's social composition during seasons of emancipation and independence. Focus is given to how the texts stand in interface with folk-based activities within a quest for agency and self-discovery while working through complicated social, economic and existential questions. This chapter submits that in undercutting pedagogies of materialism, Brodber like Lamming, re-engineers portraits of the self and represents humanity through metaphysical understandings of origins.

The interpretation of the self who struggles with seasons of social death and complex forms of personhood is also developed in chapter five, "Writing the Absent Presence: Locating Discourses of the Unspeakable." Here, I critically analyse a selection of short stories from *The Haunted Tropics* (Condé's "The Obeahman, Obeahed", Pineau's "The Voyage of the Centipede" and Mootoo's "The Bonnaire Silk Cotton Tree") and Patricia Powell's novel, *The Fullness of Everything*. In this chapter, the dynamic of spirit involves more than just a backward glance as explored in the previous chapters. Violent memories erupt as a discrete set of hauntings, insofar that, like spirituality, they assert affective force over its subjects. The deleterious consequences of being culturally tabooed and "bastardized" also cohere in this section and gesture into Julia Kristeva's category of the abject. Ideas of closeted abuse map onto Abraham and Torok's concept of the cryptophore, which is aptly illustrated in Patricia Powell's novel, *The Fullness of Everything*, where the characters' inner dead spaces are construed as tombs in which deep family hurts and betrayals are buried.

Recourses to transformation and empowerment are afforded through the simple but signifying moments of confession and sensuous touch, which cancel the grip of phantoms in the mind. To recognize the many ways in which Caribbean spectrality has been negotiated is also to acknowledge that the reconstruction of the self certainly facilitates new modes of symbolization. The reader is, therefore, compelled to contemplate the seismic shifts in the Caribbean imagination that facilitate alternative modes of seeing and being.

I posit that Walcott's *Omeros* and Harris's "Arawak Horizon" – examined in the final chapter – provide some responses since the texts enable a mimetic patterning of literature, through which the residues of hurt and exclusion, as well as methods of therapeutic interventions and metamorphosis, become immanent.

CHAPTER 2

Indigenous Cosmovisions and Postmemory in the Fictions of Wilson Harris

IN HIS ESSAY, "THE SUBJECTIVE IMAGINATION", WILSON HARRIS describes the haunting phantasmagoria of Indigenous ancestors lost in the Caribbean's violent past.[1] According to Harris, their deathways have been largely fossilized and elided from mainstream literary discourse, turning into what Gordon Rohlehr terms, a culture of terminality. [2] Part of Rohlehr's assertion, like Harris's, is to evince the livingness of ancestral tradition and its contemporary relevance through critical research. By this articulation, I look to a selection of the fables in *The Sleepers of Roraima* and the novel, *The Whole Armour,* in which Harris grapples with the nature of generational haunting, while advancing the significance of the landscape as a mover in fulfilling humankind's previously eclipsed potentials. Marianne Hirsch's theory of postmemory is critical in this regard. Hirsch defines postmemory as the phenomenon through which history persists in a transgenerational form whether through a familial or social context. She asserts, "Postmemory's connection to the past is thus not actually mediated by recall but by imaginative investment, projection and creation".[3] Reflecting confluences with Harris's idea of intergenerational transmission, Hirsch contends that the latent existence of traumatic memory erupts as an unexplained presence in the descendants of previously enslaved and besieged populations, even though the former never lived through the event.[4] The temporal gap between historical processes of genocide and intertribal conflict, and its effect on subsequent generations, is evidence of intergenerational (traumatic) latency.

A CARIBBEAN POETICS OF SPIRIT

This temporal flow of memory in relation to the Indigenous[5] holocaust in the Caribbean disallows forgetting as the group's representations travel down the corridors of time. The belated and embodied persistence of angst, grief and self-imposed exile are echoed in the short stories, "Couvade" and "Yurokon" and the novel, *The Whole Armour*. Harris makes meaning from a space of extreme loss and conceives an instrumental modality of healing and self-fashioning rooted in metaphors of community, storytelling, shapeshifting and psychic mediation. The short story "Couvade" is an apt example where the young protagonist derives significance and individual worth only when he begins to confront the psychic hurts of his orphaned existence. This is accomplished through acts of servanthood and apprenticeship to the tribe's clever man who facilitates self-affirming processes through complex ritual rites, telepathy and storytelling.

As Couvade tries to make sense of the angst that he feels, he sets out to correct the faults in his lineage. Harris highlights the idea that, quite apart from the pathology of European conquest, the First Peoples also share responsibility for the breakdown of their community. The participation in an infinite rehearsal of the past emerges from the uncertainties that lie in the background of Couvade's personal history. This imaginative participation in ancestral history is also pursued in "Yurokon", whose apparition appears to his ancestors at the time of their defeat by Spain. Yurokon reflects the haunting conscience of the clan since he was one of the Carib bush-babies sacrificed in the Guyanese savannah. In Yurokon's undying spirit, Harris incorporates many of his common themes, including the possibilities of rebirth from conflicting situations and reconciliation through ritual and metamorphosis.

Another text poetically interpreted within the parameters of Indigenous mythic connections is *The Whole Armour*. Locating the sequence of events in the Pomeroon hinterlands, Harris depicts the organic concept of community through the interrelatedness of the characters' consciousness; the absence of a fixed boundary between the living and the dead; and the community's growing need to grasp the nature of the legacy of the "dead" within themselves. Cristo is only truly free from the excessive control of his mother, Magda, after he encounters what Harris calls the "compassionate alliance of [his] dead" forbearers whose spirit-dance in the forest incurs a needful reinterpretation of history and self.[6] Similarly important, is the critical standpoint that Magda embodies ideas of metensomatosis and Amazonian queenship. She vacillates between the roles of seer, temptress, tigress and an archetypal mother whom the villagers secretly worship. She is a shape-shifter since she wields her skin and body in creative ways to keep Cristo from harm.

The binding thread among the three narratives is a preoccupation with the re-writing of Caribbean history using the script of Indigenous mythologies. Harris, it seems, is instituting new symbols that can act on the literary imagination to probe a highly structured pattern of associations between contemporary Caribbean society and the protagonists in each tale. His critical frameworks of the mythic imagination, the womb of space and limbo instrumentalize and stage an empathetic identification with survivors of genocide, and who approximate these original experiences with their contemporary realities. The fictional emphasis on Indigenous art, warfare, tactics and daily communal methods, reacquaints the reader with the intelligences that have become, as Rohlehr asserts, "terminal".[7] For Rohlehr, it is through "the indigenization . . . of the content of our curriculum, [which] grounds our cultures in the affirmative energy of our ancestors that we can generate within ourselves the force of identity [. . .] we need to survive the continuous onslaught of negative and corrosive cultural influences".[8] This statement resonates in the works of Harris and reflects an imperative to transmute objects and settings of suffering into sites of recovery.

"Couvade" is a tale of intertwined histories and tribal war. In this narrative, the hidden memories of race and myth are uncovered. The story's title is derived from a lived custom among the native people connected with the birth of a child, male or female. After the birth, the father takes the child to his hammock and receives the congratulations of his friends while the mother continues with her domestic routine. This practice of couvade is a foundational trope in the design of the narrative. Harris opens the story with a personal note:

A CARIBBEAN POETICS OF SPIRIT

The Caribs have virtually disappeared as a people though their name is attached to the islands of the Caribbean Sea and remnants of their mythology can be traced deep into the South American continent. This story is based on their little-known myths – the myth of *couvade*. The purpose of *couvade* was to hand on the legacy of the tribe – courage and fasting – to every newborn child. All ancestors were involved in this dream – animal as well as human, bird as well as fish. The dust of everything . . . [was] turned into a fable of history – the dream of *couvade*.[9]

The ritual is largely based on a belief in the existence of an uncanny connection between the child and its father. However, the plot becomes even more complex when the child is swiftly made an orphan because of the untimely disappearance of his parents who defied the sacred law of eating what had been forbidden during a season of fasting and seclusion. It echoes the always present temptation and unchecked impulses of humankind, which complicate seasons set aside for deep sacrifices.

The dilemma of parental abandonment cuts to the heart of the narrative. Couvade is informed through a story his grandfather tells, that on the night of his parents' transgression, the entire community was attacked and his parents were never again seen. Eventually, the child's grandfather discovers the six-week-old baby (Couvade) at the mouth of a cave. By locating his parable within the safe setting of the cave, the old man can delicately divulge to the boy the most painful stories of abandonment and wartime violence. It suggests a moment of a transactive process (a necessary sign of initiation) through which the past is internalized by the listener. The wise elder continues his creative account of how this particular episode of defying the ancient custom of couvade precipitated the endless game of hunter and hunted, which all descendants must thereafter endure. It is here that Harris divulges the manner in which the Caribs became the infamous "huntsmen of the night" who must "conceal" themselves from their enemies, whatever the cost.[10] The theme of Carib cannibalism is also introduced through Harris's visual language as in "flesh and blood",[11] "skeletons", "fishermen of . . . our enemies",[12] "hunter and hunted",[13] and "prisoner of the tribe".[14] He also gives emphasis to time as a cycle by activating the landscape as a divine presence through which the protagonist must traverse. The process is one of penetration into the layers of Carib-being.

Although Couvade's quest for his individuality seems to corroborate the legend of the predatory huntsmen, he discovers that his greatest enemy is his own, unbridled nostalgic longing to reunite with his missing parents, which blindside him from discerning friend from foe. This conundrum provides narrative space for the exposure of the similarities between the human bondage of pre and colonial slavery and individual freedom. To this extent, the action of the narrative moves forward on several levels of myth and reality. In Couvade's ancestral lineage lurks the ghost of the past, and the more he strives to unify the traditions of his people, the deeper he sinks into a world of hallucinations. The long-term noxious, psychic woundedness that he feels, on one level, reads as a metaphor for the dislocation and dismemberment of the Indigenous inhabitants of the Caribbean regions who were open targets for the artillery warfare from European invaders. Through the archetype of Couvade, Harris portrays the Indigenous community as having developed a strong consciousness through which they claim communal responsibility amid the conditions of European conquest. This is evident in the exposition of Couvade's grandfather's parables about war and leadership. His goal throughout the complicated plot is to teach Couvade the dangers of revenge, pride and fickle urgencies, which bring about the divisions of humankind and community. The adventures that they both embark upon are riddles and lessons on the need to be adaptable, which yield creative strategies for avoiding generational errors. For these reasons, Couvade must himself become the living image of the new Caribbean man. He must cross the entryway between dream and reality and wear the tribal robes of humility, which are passed on to him.

As the plot progresses, the elder tells an old tribal story that initiates the ten-year-old child into the secret of his name and the mystery of the clan. History is absorbed in the intimate exchange of ritual storytelling and ancestral dreaming. Dreams are used in Harris's fables as vehicles of spiritual revelation. The link to one's ancestors is re-activated through trance-like reconnections or ceremonious dream time. On this account,

A CARIBBEAN POETICS OF SPIRIT

dream ritual is employed as a narrative strategy to break the symmetry of linear time and to create a hybridization of forms and realms where humans are connected to other energies and presences. True to its mythic nature, boundaries which are erected between family members who are separated by time and space are removed so that Couvade is able to catch the shadows of the past and return to the present illumed.

In the first phase of his hypnosis, he returns to the cave where he was abandoned as a baby. Here, he has reentered the womb of earth, which is symbolic of the questing modern man seeking spiritual regeneration through an encounter with his first mothers and fathers. On the walls of the cave, Couvade sees a curious coexistence of various species – birds, fish, men and women who were half-bird, half-fish.[15] The creatures step out of the walls and a pool of water separates the boy from them. What follows is a series of questions and creative possibilities on how to cross the bridge of souls:

> He would change himself into a fish . . . Half-boy, half-fish. On the other hand, if he changed into a bird—half-boy, half-bird—he could fly across the river and approach the two birdlike figures [his incarnated parents] —listen to their conversation [. . .]. He decided he would . . . do what he had first thought of—turn himself into a fish and swim . . . He had reached about halfway when he was beaten back again by the water of fear.[16]

Several ideas emerge at this point. The bridge is wielded by Harris as a useful gateway through which the natural and supernatural domains intersect in the mythic imagination. This sets in train expressions of personal transformation and healing pathways for Couvade. The gateway between realms that is embodied in the image of the bridge presents the landscape as a psychic resource.

Unsurprisingly, Couvade becomes fully ensconced in the river, which signifies the deep connection he feels with nature. As he immerses himself in the river, he hears many voices and swims in its generational music. The landscape offers a fertile environment with many possibilities for metamorphosis and spiritual power. The sites of untold trauma and loss become a rich receptacle of knowledge. By traversing the bridge,

Couvade is presented with the opportunity to intuitively sense the pain and grapple with the incomprehensibility of his ancestors who stand on the other side. He seeks to creatively morph into a wraith-like presence in an attempt to touch them. His circumstance gives rise to a dilemma between his present existential state and the meaning he seeks. However, he finds that his attempt to penetrate the gulf that exists between himself and his dead parents is more complicated than he anticipates, and his odyssey ceases as he becomes transfixed by the fear of the waters that stand in his way. Like the various absent presences in the narrative, Couvade's parents have no voice, but they provide a silent, emotional backdrop to the mysterious tale in which he is inscribed. Perhaps, in the frame of Couvade's character, Harris is establishing a dialogue between strength and weakness, responsibility and recklessness. Not until Couvade becomes fully aware of the real textures of his individual and communal history, and admits to the traumatic memories of his childhood, is he able to transcend the betrayal inherent in his lineage.

Disappointingly, he finds that his ancestors are not at the other end of the bridge when he finally arrives. Instead, he enters into an illusion of a forest where the enemy held their camp. His conversation with the talking lizard reveals that he has fallen into the trick of his adversary, which is fundamentally to lock him into charmed circles of unconscious ruin and violence. The lizard is revealed as Couvade's grandfather's totem or spirit companion who keeps watch over the young boy. In another phase of his dream, Couvade and his grandfather escape the enemies who were waiting to attack them at the illusionary scene of the cave. Their escape is made possible through camouflage and shape-shifting. In a ritual enacted to cross the body of water, Couvade learns the lesson that the only enemy to fear is the enemy of one's self. At this point, the child protagonist is confronted with the responsibility of searching for clear understanding amidst the chaos of deception and illusion. Here, Harris raises the urgent need to redefine a viable Caribbean identity which transcends cultural and racialized stereotypes of Indigenous barbarity and inhumanity. Although the narrative is set in Guyana, this revelation of Caribbean Indigenous ontologies speaks to all of humanity with equal force and urgency. This is inscribed, for example, in Couvade's assertion: "It was like a curious initiation into the secret names [and] masks" of the region's cross-cultures.[17] Harris's structural dynamic becomes clearer at this point. "Native" or Indigenous, in this regard, is not at all a pejorative term nor does it refer only to a particular group of people. For the writer, this encounter may be scalable to anyone whose connection to the land is so deeply visceral that they embrace the layered nature of Caribbean reality. Through Couvade's imaginative involvement with his submerged history, Harris is illuminating the potential of confronting masked codes of behaviour and the subsequent processes available to the modern man willing to rehearse and excavate the buried knowledge, which frees him from stasis.

The story is suitably shaped with overlapping potentials as evident in the creative use of doubling. There is the eerie feel of a shadow that leaves the present, returns to the past to inspect it and brings news back. In "Couvade," it is not just the ghost of another person who is traversing realms; there are ghosts of civilizations. Interestingly, Harris uses circular structures that function as a pool of reflections "on which concentric circles and horizons appear",[18] thus providing Couvade with a source of reflection. Through this circular design, Harris is outlining an instructive illustration of the womb, globe or egg of creation as a natural symbol, which contains the genesis of all life. Couvade thus experiences time in cycles or in chain-like moments, which girdle him. In his psyche, he intuits the emotions and ancestral temptations, all of which influence his choices. However, in genuine Harris style, it is through these loops or magical rings that Couvade begins his absorption, metamorphosis and reinvention.

He eventually learns to take the position of listener in the testimonial chain of stories that his grandfather tells. In one of these fables, the elder describes the ways in which the ancestors would camouflage themselves as stilts while crossing the "bridge of the aged"[19] and would secretly enter into the village of the enemy. His fable clearly demonstrates the processes for victory through acts of invention and submission. While telling his narrative, the elder applies the scales of a fish to the boy's head. Particular

INDIGENOUS COSMOVISIONS AND POSTMEMORY IN THE FICTIONS OF WILSON HARRIS

focus is given to Indigenous healing rituals as a way to mitigate cultural trauma, pain and loss. The wise man's ritual of cladding the boy's eyes with fish scales, while "sprinkling the dust of the . . . toucan upon his . . . head"[20] stands as a belief system dependent on ceremonial invocations and charms. The application of these practices dovetails with modalities of spirituality, sorcery, magic, spells and healing for various purposes. With his extensive training in earth-magic, the clever man continues to usher Couvade into the special quality of mind or knowledge necessary to serve the spirit of the tribe. He becomes a guide and companion in the child's journey into an uncharted land – a journey the survivor cannot traverse alone.

One of the last tasks which Couvade must perform entails crossing the bridge of deception where figures "appeared to be both enemy and friend".[21] To do this, he is instructed to wear the "camouflage of nothing".[22] In this riddle, there is the simple but evocative truth that one's vulnerability is life-giving, and what Couvade feels at this point is no longer a reaction to the pain of his past but a responsibility to his tribe. As he proceeds with this understanding, his courage becomes a pivotal and symbolic field of power that summons the magic of the moon, which moves across the galaxy to conceal him as he makes his crossing. A grand constellation of stars forms an arc that dazzles the enemy and blocks their view until Couvade is safely on the other side.

He awakens to find himself standing radiantly on the bridge of dawn. He learns, through the series of adventures that he is able to deliver the much-needed healing of the imbalance in the cosmos by restoring a broken link in his lineage. He is finally able to understand "life as a sacrifice," and can answer the question that has haunted him all his life, "Why did you give me this name?"[23] Through telling, retelling and novelizing his story, he ultimately fulfils his name's meaning – "Couvade – sleeper of the [Carib] tribe".[24] As Couvade traverses the frontlines to protect his interconnected community, he is inevitably righting the balance, naming and confronting the apparatus that steals life. Ultimately, he emerges as a keeper of the Carib legacy which is embodied in his personal trajectory of dispossession, loss, triumph and final fulfilment. His story provides the argument that it is necessary to forge stronger, affective links with ancestral cultures that have historically been ignored, despised, and suppressed. Theirs are the drumbeats to breathe to, the leaders worth our collective attention. Interestingly, one can read Couvade's reaction to his grandfather's instructive stories as an example of postmemory, for as Hirsch notes, to be "dominated by narratives that preceded one's birth . . . is to risk having one's own life stories displaced".[25] The elder's storytelling and guidance signpost particular methods of intergenerational transfer, which eventually function as instruments of repair and redress. It is through Couvade's commitment to ceremonial passages and willingness to resist generational temptations, that he transcends the faults in his lineage. His journey is one of natal homecoming that honours the grief of his predecessors and channels them into breath, force and movement.

The narrative also explores, explains and in some cases subverts stereotypical representations of the First Peoples. Harris's Carib trilogy does not embody generalizations of the group's reputation for fierceness or the racialized discourse which posits that the only real Caribs are the pure Caribs. On the contrary, Harris's explorations border upon the reserves of cross-culturality and knowledge that is transmitted transgenerationally. He creates a credible view of Carib being to unravel patterns of human culture and behaviour that demonstrate the seepage and vestigial traces of history. Through the writer's processes of imaginative reconstruction, the cultural critic is presented with new pathways for understanding the sense of a living connection with the past. This, Harris proposes, are the real vestiges that haunt the modern world. This series of explorations persists in the story, "Yurokon", where Harris apprehends the fragments of myth by unravelling the ritual performed on the Carib bush babies. He accomplishes this through an interrogation of the dualities between inner and outer domains and the creative ambiguities or twinship that arise within the protagonist. The text presents an interplay of traumatizing catalysts which multiply with the identities assumed by the protagonist. It is an experience that facilitates rebirth and reconciliation. The pervading themes in the story include generational guilt, the recuperation of native traditions (including cannibalism), the myth of the bone flute and reconciliation through reunification with the Guyana landscape. The narrative symbolizes an age of renascence where perspectives into the past reopen afresh. Yurokon is a Carib bush baby whose death comes from being thrown into a blazing furnace in the Guyana savannah. He is the last Carib who identifies with his sixteenth-century namesake and with the bush baby spectre which appeared among his ancestors at the time of their defeat by Spain. His death is an allegory for the virtual extinction of the tribe whose presences fade into the natural world. As detailed in the essay, "Amerindian Legacy," the figure of the bush baby is linked to a sacrificial act of infanticide to safeguard the health of the tribe.[26] Structurally, Harris returns his reader to sites of physical and psychological torture. Yurokon's death is represented in the realm and language of ritual. He reflects on his dying moment and laments that it was, "the fiercest savannah of living memory".[27] The narrative originates out of a need to reconstruct a lifestory that is punctuated with gaps, holes and sudden displacement. However, the searing flame of the fire in which he burns hardens him and he becomes a fearless warrior. As Yurokon's body begins to flower out of the flames, he flies through the air. It is a symbolic image of the seed of genesis that is a common trope in Harris's fiction. In this cleansing ritual, Yurokon emerges as a timeless and immortal spirit. He eventually soars "like a ladder into the sky" and into immortal existence.[28]

The spatial metaphor of the ladder sustains a frequency of communication between incorporeal, cosmic energies and earthly beings. It is a major expression of the plural realities and parallel universes that operate throughout the text. Just as Couvade discovers himself in the cave of ancestors, Yurokon also experiences a leap or flight in the imagination as revealed in the images of the ladder and kite. The concept of the steps that connect earth to sky and the image of a half-man, half-god, climbing the staircase, render a sense of numinous intercourse that occurs in Caribbean space and time. Technically, the symbol of the ladder provides an apparatus for establishing a dialectical relationship between heights and depths, not simply in content but in form. It presents a new method of re-conceiving representations of character, community and space.

Yurokon's position as demigod foregrounds him with a dual conception that is embodied in the child of the vessel outlined by Harris in the essay, "The Schizophrenic Sea".[29] It is a concept that dovetails with the sacredness of Indigenous artefacts or pottery vessels, which are shaped out of the dirt from the savannahs that contain the spirit of the Carib infant. In the myth of Yurokon, Harris shapes a fissure or – to use Édouard Glissant's term, "fold" – that contains the indestructible or immortal spirit of the title character. Glissant's formulations of the "folds" of relation as first referenced in his 1957 essay, "Le romancier noir,"[30] represents "the infinite capacity for slippage that exists between reality and consciousness".[31] The aesthetic of layering or overlap encapsulates a deterritorialization of space and states of consciousness. The metaphor of "folds" carries the potentiality of moving in tangled trajectories which are especially figured in images of the sea, the wind and the current.[32]

These ideas of interchange and simultaneity take on further meaning as epitomized in the movement of waves that crash upon many shores of origin at the same time. The "fold", according to Glissant, enables a meeting on all sides of realities and serves as a useful tool in mediating between a search for origins and a need to fill the void of history. In this networking of entities, time itself becomes interiorized and opposites converge into a sacred space. Since origins are no longer connected to one root, but rather meet and are traced through lines of flight, the idea of becoming is linked to unending possibility and to ongoing difference. In the story, Yurokon's wraith seeps simultaneously into the natural elements that move into the air and "into the leaves of wood [. . .]. He was the child of legend and the lore of creation and his paper or map, kite or globe, was a magical witness of curious survival, the terrifying innocent play of a timeless element [manifested] in all places and things".[33] As such, the story is an expression of Harris's interest in the many possibilities of rebirth from conflicting situations. This is also corroborated in the actions of Yurokon who morphs into various personalities according to the context. In such a manner, Harris's narrative illuminates the cycles of life or reincarnation trope. This approach is akin to the animism of Caribbean Indigenous cultural pathways, where the environment acquires a life of its own.

At the narrative opening, Yurokon is depicted as a presence that emerges from the smoke of the campfire:

> His uncle was expecting him and though he barely discerned the spiral of smoke like twine coming up out of the pot on the fire, he felt the sting of fire [. . .]. The unwritten symphony of the windy unwritten spark of the wind, made him bark [. . .]. His uncle stared at the bristling dog of the fire, fire break, fire bark . . . magic; he smacked his lips and the roast of Yurokon's bark subsided [. . .]. Yurokon saw himself aloft in the cauldron of fire as a dog-kite; the twine connecting him to earth.[34]

This is a manifestation of the convergences among the natural elements (earth, wind, fire and water) which are imbued with otherworldly energies. The child's apparition whips up a gust of wind as he emerges out of the flames. He then soars into the wind, which is deployed as a device to transport his spirit from the earthly to the stratospheric plane. Harris, it seems, is seeking to identify a hitherto invisible Indigenous presence in the Caribbean, whose sign is the wind. Despite the many imperial invasions, the Caribbean woodlands, forests and cosmos continue to replenish and are witnesses to the layered, connective histories projected onto them.

The cosmos was, for Harris, an inexhaustible metaphor. The metaphor of space is used to coalesce matter and spirit into one reality. Language is specifically suited to express this interrelatedness of all creation. In the collection of essays edited by DeLoughrey, Hena Maes-Jelinek notes that Harris's cosmic and nature-based themes, enable him to *"visualize . . . a* counterbalance between rape or devastation and implicit freedom [that equalizes] extinction with a renascence . . . of lost cultures whose vestiges and imprints" are awakened with many possibilities for moving through the wound of history.[35] This creatively connects with the observations of Paget Henry, who postulates that Harris's experimentation with nature achieves its power because of its elasticity: "For Harris, nature is neither a dead nor an organic materiality. On the contrary, for him all nature

A CARIBBEAN POETICS OF SPIRIT

. . . *signifies*, speaks . . . and is alive with meanings that *include* us [. . .]. Consequently the . . . *symbolic activity* often speaks very directly to the lives of the [Amerindian] people and cultures that are inscribed in [our] subconscious processes of representation and meaning production."[36] The environment is therefore a mystical cradle for humankind to reflect on their own unconscious state and ancestral past. Harris is cultivating a praxis of radical listening – of tuning in to the sound, vibrations and rhythms of the earth. Movements between different worldviews provoke new ways of seeing beyond received ideologies.

This interactive awareness and responsibility are echoed in Yurokon's confrontation with his uncle as he protests the community's amoral acts of cannibalism and infanticide. He cries, "'Once upon a child . . . you ate me.' [. . .] Yurokon was the scarred urchin . . . victor-in-victim; over the centuries he remained unageing (ageless) as a legend, a curious symptom or holocaust of memory."[37] His nervous exhaustion functions as a double-edged sword as he channels both the rage of the conquistadors and the savannah infants who were burned to their deaths. Here, he is at once the undying, rebellious spirit of the tribe as well as its growing conscience. It is useful to note that his ability to shape-shift exemplifies the relation between body, spirit, survival and creativity born of necessity. This duality is concretized when he becomes "an immortal dog of war".[38] That he can mutate or remake himself into his tribe's archetypal enemy points to the deep-seated responses to his unresolved psychic repression. Yurokon becomes the wound that cries out a pain and reflects a groping for ways to shake off the entrapment of a grievous history.

In an effort to bring release to the boy's wheel of confusion, his uncle renders visions of the past and the future through a cauldron. In the bubbling pot, Yurokon sees himself as the twine that connects earth with sky and spy with native.[39] He notices a floating morsel of flesh plucked from the enemy's body and asks:

> "Are we really huntsmen of bone?" Yurokon asked, looking down at his uncle and through the sky as he sailed in space [. . .]. "We became huntsmen of bone when we ate our first Spanish sailor," his uncle replied to the intricate sticks of the sky. "For that reason we are sometimes called cannibals"

[...]. "How can you say such a thing?" Yurokon cried, descending from kite to earth in a flash and stopping dead, riveted now to the ancient trunk of man.[40]

The idea that his identity is linked to the horror of cannibalism is re-introduced through the spiritual practice of flesh-eating. According to Harris in "The Schizophrenic Sea", a limb of the slaughtered enemy was "brought back to the settlement [...] which would then be cooked so as to get the flesh more easily off the bone; a flute was made out of this".[41] Symbolically, the flute contains the living spirit of the dead and is a source of prophecy. Having been a figure of exploitation himself, Yurokon repurposes the bone shaft as a confessional organ to invoke a vision of ritual cleansing and rebirth.

When the melody is played, a "robe of mercy"[42] falls over the Guyana landscape and the forest is charmed. We are told that the sound was "a sad yet vibrating melody of space. All at once he could hear...an unwritten symphony: the dark roots in the past of that tree – a strange huddle of ancestral faces attuned to quivering wings".[43] One begins to sense an equation between the melody of the dead, Yurokon's relationship to the natural world, and a remedy for healing. Furthermore, the lullaby of the bone-flute is a seismic lament, which has to do with a memory of conquest and the ruins of a tribe. In fact, the flute can be read as a symbol of the psychological cleavage and dualities that Yurokon embodies. Fashioned out of the bones of the enemies, the flute exemplifies the tensions and horror of colonialism. However, this vestigial reminder of war forms a bridge between cultures and allows Yurokon to thrust towards his community with a possibility for regeneration. Importantly, this transgenerational memory connects with a responsibility of properly mourning the pain of past civilizations while maintaining political peace for future generations. The myth of Yurokon facilitates a vision of grace, forgiveness and acceptance.

Through this complex network of relations Harris asserts that it is not impossible to overcome the ills of colonialism. The constant temptation that Harris guards against is the need to adhere to what appears to be absolute. Yurokon deploys the therapeutic interlude of the flute and re-crafts capacities for mending a broken reality. His ascent to growth

A CARIBBEAN POETICS OF SPIRIT

and maturity through a series of new undertakings is an example of the potentialities of the intuitive imagination. Many ideas of spirit are embedded in the metaphor of the bone-flute and are worthy of critical attention. The technicality of the music unlocks a portal through which presences pour. And the interiority of the tones provides a language that allows communication with the world of spirit. Without fail, it sets in motion the remaking of the self in question where the melody produces an alchemy which transmutes rage, disorientation and disempowerment into a powerful form of cultural resistance. The flute, then, becomes a dual symbol of the displaced past as well as the splendid creation of the present. Another example of its duality and potentiality emerges from the image of the shaft which is obviously a male component while also containing the shape of a womb, which is typically associated with a female regenerative sound. A process of rebirth is thus facilitated. The flute, therefore, illuminates the melding of figures and spaces which Harris presents in a quiescent form.

"Yurokon" offers penetrative insights into the social and cultural dynamic of the First Peoples and the powers that are implicit in their expressions of faith. Like Couvade, who creatively reworks his loss and personal angst, Yurokon emerges from the flames of death to bring reconciliation and benediction to the land and his community. At the end of the story, he occupies a supreme position in the Carib heartland and stands as "a magical witness of curious survival [. . .] in all places and things".[44] The final melody that he plays synthesizes the contradictions between the native and the conquistador. In this collection of stories, Harris fuses the actual and metaphorical to promote memory as an interpretive framework that dislocates the dangers of one-sided notions of reality. The narratives reflect Harris's creative attempts to rescue shattered worldviews in the aftermath of colonial trauma.

His use of the mythic imagination and overlapping spatial and cultural histories are also identified in *The Whole Armour*. Set on the Guyana coast, the tension revolves around the inhabitants of the Pomeroon Village who are unable to fruitfully cultivate the land. Their living is difficult as they alternate between seasons of drought and flood. On a symbolic level, the villagers' ignorance of the instability of the land reflects their own spiritual limitations. Cristo, the emblematically named protagonist, is despised by the community because he is different and educated. Ironically, it is only through him and his unborn son that a thriving future can become possible. When Cristo is willing to accept personal responsibility and the burden of guilt imposed by the community, he finds peace for himself and offers an ethical example for others to follow. However, his journey – not unlike Couvade's and Yurokon's – is not without difficulties. His voyage and discovery in the hinterlands reveal that the Pomeroon landscape and community are not what they seem. Harris is advancing the themes of illusions, masquerade, boundary-convergence, doubling, and embodiment.

The text symbolically opens with Abram's dream of his impending death and the fall from the tree of community with its roots in the sky (not in the earth). It is possible that Harris may be alluding to the Amerindian myth of the Milky Way and Orion legend.[45] By using the metamorphic framework of the creation bridge between sky and earth during a season of inter-tribal war, Abram's dream is at once a vision of his imminent death and a portent of the metaphysical overlay in the narrative. In the original myth, the Arawaks would seek refuge among the trees from their enemies. However, the adversary would set the trees on fire, and the spirits of the slain natives would rise into the stars and become permanent watchmen over the territory. The myth is a motif that runs throughout *The Whole Armour* as the Pomeroon people crumble because of their resistance to change. It is only through Cristo's self-sacrifice that they can attain revelation and self-perception. The convergence of boundaries between illusion and reality, the cosmos and the earthly, and the circuit of primordial relationships embedded in Abram's vision are materialized in the plot, setting and characters.

Throughout the sequence of events, there are fluid personalities and bodies which signpost Harris's transmutative intent. The character of Magda is of interest as she is perhaps one of the most evocative and necessarily metamorphosed figures in the novel. She is a terrifying tyrant who can make others do as she desires. Her power is demonstrated when she forces Cristo to steal Abram's clothes and identity. She challenges Cristo to, "[t]ake off all your gab, Boy, quick. Nobody want to spend their . . . life in this vicinity. Quick!"[46] She attempts to use her promiscuity to persuade the sergeant to save her son once more at the end of the novel.

Magda's body represents many things to the Pomeroon people. She is a warrior woman, sorcerer, fierce matriarch and a highly sexualized figure as indicated by her first appearance in the novel. Her bewitchment of the villagers is vividly realized in the frenzied possession of the crowd at the wake and the manner in which the villagers are transfixed by her beauty. In her character, Harris offers an Indigenous face to ancient mythologies and monstrosities. He describes her voice as having "a diabolic edge", and her smile is a grimace.[47] Her skin tone is depicted as a "black fantastic mood of mahogany" and her eyes are narrow and slit-like.[48] Her physique seems to rehash the myths and enchanting beauty of the Amazonian queens, who moved seamlessly between the magical and physical domains. It comes as little surprise that in Magda, the villagers recognize their "true mother" and are prepared to secretly worship her as their "goddess of identity".[49] While it is not clear whether or not Magda is of Indigenous ancestry, Harris's description of her as sorcerer and warrior woman is evidence of her magisterial countenance. At the wake, the villagers are enthralled, for example, by "the dark bloom of her skin [which] was adorned by a royal purple gown [. . .]. It enfolded her, making her look like a queen wishing to make a magnificent and enigmatic gift of herself to a hungry crowd, the more mysterious because gratuitous and barbaric; the column of her neck and her arms were bare, and her naked feet were planted squarely on the ground."[50] These layers of references to her "queenly" disposition are allusions to her demigod role and female tyranny. A creative thread can thus be joined between the cultural icon of the Amazonian warrior queen archetype and Magda, to contextualize the latter's South American, goddess-like resemblance, which lends to the agency and interest in her character.[51] Indeed, she embodies the concepts of domination, sudden strength in the face of danger, beauty and unearthly agency.

Her life is a succession of scandals because of her liaisons with many men whose advances she indifferently rejects. Her alluring characteristics are directly linked to masquerade and performance where her body is deployed as a costume and skin is wielded as a medium. A ritual occasion like Cristo's wake encourages her to enter a place of spontaneous invention and improvisation. This establishes the themes of deception and illusion as the action takes place within the backdrop of an eerie night. Importantly, the villagers' pride hinders their sensitivity to Magda's guile. Their need to constantly cast blame imprisons their conscience and restricts true spiritual freedom and clarity. The presence of the tiger that roams the dense hinterlands is indicative of the villagers' fears, anxiety, dread and hazy consciousness. They have selected as their sacrifice Peet, who leads the search party for the notorious tiger that snatches the child from the village. In Peet, the villagers have found a scapegoat; however, he fails in his enterprise and his failure is perceived as his own.

Interestingly, Peet's sexual dalliances with Magda are used as a device to further identify the illusory atmosphere at work in the narrative. During his physical struggle with her, she is recognized as a hybrid creature, who is half-woman, half-beast. Peet's vision of the tiger is a spectral manifestation of Cristo. Gregory Shaw observes that like Magda, the tiger is an "[u]ntamed and primordial creature [that] prowls the frontier between human settlement and unexplored interior, a shadowy region populated by fantasy and imagination".[52] Both the tiger and Magda epitomize a present-day threat to the Pomeroon folk. Susceptible to her charms and promiscuity, Peet, is unsurprisingly emasculated. Unlike Shaw, Mark McWatt asserts that Magda's sexual aggression is a manifestation of her unspoken pain created by the changing face of power structures that have transmogrified into neo-colonial and cultural injustices. According to McWatt, "Magda . . . has internalized the exploitation and violation contained in the conquistador's view of the need to plunder, possess and subdue".[53]

To this degree, her role as a hypersexualized seductress and dreaded sorcerer traffics in the representational politics of both her race and gender. In other words, she is an archetype of the painful and neglected residues of history that have been imprinted on the body and mind. Attention

A CARIBBEAN POETICS OF SPIRIT

must be given to her coping strategies that border on manipulation and seduction. At the wake, for example, Peet is invited to recognize the deception that she has concocted to protect Cristo. However, he is too morally weak to challenge her conspiracy, and Magda, who is ever aware of his fleshly desires wields her body as an expressive energy to stifle the knowledge that he discerns. It is indeed this very lack of perception, which has prevented the Pomeroon people from seeing in themselves the subjective or intuitive community for which they are longing. When Magda rejects Peet's sexual advances, he becomes grossly bitter. He returns to the enchanted villagers and shouts to Mattias, "I shall kill you".[54] His rage is a clear demonstration of the rejection that he feels.

Shades of deception and psychic manipulation are also discerned in Magda and Sharon's exchange. Throughout Sharon's confrontation with the old matriarch, she (Sharon) is urged to identify her own guilt for the violence she has provoked. Within the upper chamber of Magda's abode, the two women consummate their relationship. Rape and intercourse become a bridge in this scene. On a metaphoric note, it corresponds with the rape of the Indies by empire – an event that re-circuited the foundations of Caribbean identity.[55] This metaphor is sustained in the character of Sharon, whose bodily penetration becomes a threshold or limbo gateway through which colonial relationships are exposed and transformed. Amidst this intense and intimate struggle, Harris re-purposes the forces that meet in this interval and makes possible an alternative future in which the walls of power are broken down.

During her encounter with Magda, Sharon is teleported into another act of intercourse with Cristo. Through this leap in the imagination,[56] Harris is prompting his reader to alter their boundaries of perception and recognize the possibilities of paradoxes and contrasts. This pluralism emerges from acts of assemblage. When the white-skinned Sharon and the brown-hued Cristo conjoin, a dimension of psychic healing is bestowed to the consciousness of the Pomeroon people. Their relationship produces a cosmic and physical harmony that affects historical, social, cultural and spiritual relations. The process that Harris seeks to map leads to a form of depersonalization and a movement to community. Activism can therefore be viewed as an encounter with the other in all the forces of space and time. As Sharon reunites with Cristo, a shared communality is expressed. After they consummate their relationship, they are described as people who live on the moon. There is a very apt analogy to be found here between Harris's creative explorations and Indigenous mysticism, where the moon receives the soul of the dead before their second death and rebirth.[57] Through her affirmative intimacy with Cristo and spiritual journeying across the mystical hinterlands, Sharon is able to shed her protective *kumbla* of whiteness and embrace an instructive, cross-cultural and multi-ethnic past.

Equivalently significant is the design of boundary convergence and the mystery of Magda's more-than-human powers,[58] which work together to disintegrate boundaries and alter each character's experience. Her sorcery and power carry all the symbology of the Caribbean mythic figures of the la diablesse and the soucouyant. The la diablesse is the quintessential beautiful woman who hides her corpse-like countenance and cloven hoof. In Caribbean folktales, she conceals her malicious intentions and appearance by wearing a wide-brimmed hat, an exquisite blouse and a long skirt. She would appear at village social events to charm and lure men into distant cane fields where a horrific fate awaited. Both Magda and the la diablesse possess an untamed and irresistible seductive sexuality. That their magical power is rooted in their sexualized bodies, says much about the danger they may impose.

This is gestured in the cruel death of Mattias. Like the soucouyant who slips out of her skin at night, Madga is associated with nocturnality, defiance, creative interpersonal exchanges and performativity. Harris's deployment of disguise and metamorphosis maps onto his preoccupation with creative appropriation. For him, the synthesis of language, traditions and forms (oral and scribal) makes increasingly possible a process of narrative transformation that takes as its first principle the shards of cultures. In other words, the idea of collective identities encourages new thought on the markers of survival and the cultural dynamics of Caribbean peoples.

The tropes of illusion and masquerade are also discerned in the role of

A CARIBBEAN POETICS OF SPIRIT

Cristo, who appears in the guise of Abram. As an unintentional gateway, he is complicit in the drama of Magda's creative tale of death, murder and escape. As Cristo moves through the Pomeroon wilderness, he becomes a living dead who must enter a process of mental metamorphosis (not unlike Couvade and Yurokon) to reconcile the betrayal that he feels. During those forty days, while he was thought to be dead, he discovers the reverse side of reality including the death of his ancestors: "'There's a whole world of branches and sensations we've missed, and we've got to start again from the roots up even if they've looked like nothing. Blood, sap, flesh, veins, arteries, lungs, heart, the heartland, Sharon. We're the first potential parents who can contain the ancestral house'".[59] The trees of the forest become extensions of archetypal presences, and the flora and fauna of the heartland bring deep self-reflection and rejuvenation to Cristo's imagination. The woodland is given a central position of a limbic space where one cannot tell whether it is day or night, dusk or dawn. The timelessness borders on images of shadows, spirits and presences that rise out from the darkness. It is a space of remembrance. Cristo's vision of a primordial and un-reclaimed part of the community is worth quoting at some length:

> The Arawaks I saw belonged to two or three centuries ago. As far back as that, I would swear [. . .]. It was around here – Pomeroon to Moruca – that the Arawaks and the Caribs last clashed. A ferocious war it was. . . . [T]he Arawaks won the war because their healing medicine-men knew how to restore the dead. Their fighting strength therefore never diminished [. . .]. I saw the first member of a band. A degenerate profile and crew. They were Caribs, I knew. God knows where they were coming from. Their skins were dyed, I tell you. Almost naked. Tattooed. They wore a yellowish muddy dye as if they had been rolling on the ground. Parrot feathers – bright macaw too – framed their heads. Some, no head-dress at all [. . .]. I swore they'd do me in. Couldn't understand where in God's name they'd come from. And then I realized they took me for one of themselves [. . .]. One of [them] . . . glared into his crystal . . . I was ripped to tatters . . . Just torn to shivers . . . That's when I got this . . . he pointed to the long bitter scar on his face [. . .] The thought laid hold over him. [He had] belonged to the carnival as well as the tragical spirit of place, ancient and modern masquerade.[60]

What Cristo recounts to Sharon is, in fact, his journey to becoming his own person, and the emptying of the psyche. In his meeting of the indigenes within one space, he is able to deduce parallel meanings without the illusion of his mother.

This encounter is largely spiritual as evidenced in the images of initiation rites and corporeal scarring that he endures to attain psychic purification. Cristo's radical metamorphosis is not unlike Couvade's, who, in his crossing of borders, also traverses treacherous landscapes to unite with his ancestors. It is through his experience with the first mothers and fathers of his native land that Cristo discovers the potential embedded in the intricate folds of experience. His engagement with a supernatural universe provides a safe terrain for the stripping of the roles imposed on him by Magda. Embedded in this scenario, is the larger socio-historical event of the legacies of conquest that seek to dominate the modern world. In Harris's literary representation of the spectral presences of the First Peoples, there is a meaning-system for the articulation of evolutionary thinking, change and release from a violent past. Cristo's world, under Magda's control, was indeed decrepit and filled with ruin. However, through this immaterial encounter, he acquires new grounds for self-empowerment that is attained through social action.

While critics like Hena-Maes Jelinek have explained the encounter with the native spirits as a sign of guilt imposed on Cristo,[61] there is another interpretation to be had. Cristo's body becomes a vessel of change that is loaded with symbolic potential. In his interaction with the shamanic figures, he stands outside of time and space and reaches towards a renewed consciousness. This identification with the original inhabitants of the Pomeroon region enables him to tell Sharon, "We've begun to see ourselves in the earlier grassroots [. . .]. We're born into the oldest native and into our oldest nature."[62] Its true impact is a re-sensitized perspective of the community. Consequently, he is willing to make a sacrifice to reaffirm the possibility of communal harmony. Following this experience, Cristo actively seeks to demolish the walls of control his mother had imposed on him. He accomplishes this through a symbolic wrestle with the man-devouring and castrating tiger of death: "It was here that Cristo

A CARIBBEAN POETICS OF SPIRIT

had found himself [. . .]. He had followed and tricked the beast, inviting her in a dark blinding moment of pure reflex, daring impulse and instantaneous perception. It was a . . . narrow escape Sharon mused. Her nail had ripped one cheek from eye to mouth. Cristo bore the mark of all the tiger's sinister intent [. . .]. Fear died within him as it died within her."[63] The tussle for individuality is depicted through mythic images. Cristo's near-death experience and physical scarring, for example, dovetail with Amerindian iconography. This is figured in Gregory Shaw's assertion that Cristo's scar "resembles the tribal scar of initiation testifying to courage, a badge of maturity and manhood found in Amerindian . . . practices".[64] The space of this intense tussle that carries the movements of dips, cutting and combative attacks mirrors Caribbean history which was shrouded in exceeding violence and martyrdom. Symbolically, the tiger is an avatar for Magda, hence Harris's overlay of violence and the theme of mismanaged power.

Magda's character, however, is grounded in the earthly pain of single motherhood and the need to safeguard her only child, albeit at the high premium of deception and manipulation. She also weathers the territory's racial and physical exploitation to sustain self-love and power. In this sense, her subaltern reality recalls the tense, colonial past that continues to haunt the present circumstances in Harris's text. In this light, Magda's narrative becomes an emblem of the unrecorded and sacrificial past in the context of single motherhood. Ultimately, the idea of spiritual freedom that Harris posits, is inseparable from a mature understanding of individual responsibility. As a result, self-sacrifice involves a surrendering of all pretenses. Cristo's submission to psychic dismemberment in the forest embodies this emptying of self and rebirth. It is a journey that allows his moral victory over the tiger of his soul that domesticated him all his life.

Unsurprisingly, when he returns to the village, Magda's "magical identity and heredity had departed".[65] He notes that she is no longer the village's enigmatic idol and her powers are bound. It prompts the idea that her strength was indeed rooted in her physical control and manipulation of her son. He observes, "Something had drained out of him, blood or sap, and in passing out of him it has also served to reduce all her fantastic compelling ardour and frustration into powerlessness and petulance."[66] When her façade crumbles, she is but a desperate and powerless mother, who, for the last time, urges Cristo to escape upon seeing him. The falling of her mask reveals the immorality that breeds behind humankind. However, Cristo chooses to sacrifice himself so that a new vision of life and responsibility may prevail. Spiritual freedom and communal cohesiveness are presented in humankind's accountable actions. His choice to die is an attempt to defy the historical ego that has been imposed on him by both his mother and the community. As a sign of his renewed morality, the abnormal drought that plagued the Pomeroon Valley ceases. In this interface between the metaphysical and the material worlds, Harris sees the redeeming nature of sacrifice and ritual rebirth. Cristo symbolically represents the absorptive capacity of humankind, which provides him with a moral advantage through which he finds himself.

The pieta-like scene at the end of the novel is emblematic as it shows Cristo sitting with his head on Sharon's lap, listening to their child growing at the moment of his execution a year hence. The police surround the house but Cristo feels that "No one could intervene and trap the essential spirit."[67] Cristo's decision to remain resolute within his own skin and choices propounds the internal unity needed for the struggle against new forms of conquest, and injustice. This cultural vision, in fact, has its roots in the transformative participation in collective memory that affords connections between similarly oppressed peoples. Moreover, Harris argues that the alleviation of injustice and its consequences require collective social action. In other words, transgenerational intervention is required to expiate historical transgression and to disrupt its violent, present-day manifestations. Indeed, the short stories, "Couvade" and "Yurokon" and the novel, *The Whole Armour* are instructive fictions, which envision new patterns for interpreting the principles of nation, family and individuality.

The constellation of narratives that Harris creates serves as meridian forms of mapping flight and return: away from settler innocence and a carceral state, toward free-flowing decolonial futures. The emphasis is on

A CARIBBEAN POETICS OF SPIRIT

the power of interconnection. This project also looks to the Afro-Caribbean diaspora and the ancestors of this community, who were the engine and moving force within the colonial plantation economy. The interpretation of their sea journey and land experiences, through the dimensions of myth and spirit, is the focus of the next chapter.

CHAPTER 3

Haunted Histories

Spectres of the Middle Passage in *Zong!* and *I is a Long Memoried Woman*

FOR ALMOST FOUR CENTURIES, IN EXCESS OF ELEVEN MILLION Africans were stolen from the shores of Africa by European slave dealers and coercively transported over the Atlantic Ocean to the New World. The Middle Passage evokes the worldwide commercialization and abuse of a racialized people group. The correspondences between time past as well as the present, and the ethical stakes of the transatlantic slave trade continue to rebound in the present. The ghosts of slavery still haunt the present perhaps because there is still a search for an escape from the prison of the past. In *Zong!* and *I is a Long Memoried Woman*, Marlene NourbeSe Philip and Grace Nichols have respectively re-conceptualized the trajectory of this haunting event in an effort to lift the shroud of silence that surrounds this memory. Through an experimental and highly technical poetic form that is evident in polyphony, splicing, recording, dissecting and fragmenting words, the writers create a circulation of themes such as the importance of memory, the probing of generational traumas, quarrying the sea as a graveyard and the problematizing of mythical time to commemorate a discursive memorializing of this historical grief.

The imperial archive, with its many exclusions, constitutes a significant point of reference for those who continue to contest it through fiction and other creative means. As Jean Wyatt observes, many black lives that journeyed through the Atlantic died "midway between a place in African

A CARIBBEAN POETICS OF SPIRIT

history and a place in the history of [Caribbean] and American slavery" and thus "never made it into any text".[1] The desire to confront these specific, archival gaps and ideological failures finds materiality in both Nichols and Philip's oeuvres. It is telling that these women writers seek to bridge the gap between a submerged account of what transpired by symbolically assuming responsibility for the dead. Philip builds a bridge over the water for the drowned dead to make their voyage and their grievances known. Similarly, Nichols takes on the task of procuring new avenues of remembrance as groundwork for the consideration of reparations. The writers' interventions into the colonial archive reflect an ethos of affective capital that encompasses a collective feeling of responsibility for mitigating the woundedness of 'unknowing' and 'un-belonging' that linger in the diaspora. This residual woundedness is evident in the relentless repetition of anti-black violence in the modern world, social wars and deep cultural alienation. Like an unpleasant dream during a troubling sleep, history haunts in present and altered forms, arguably because of its aversion, neglect and denial. Ron Eyerman argues that trauma is a culturally and generationally transmitted phenomenon. Its submergence and lack of articulation continue to tear apart the social fabric that affects an entire group of people whose history remains largely dismembered and unaccounted for.[2]

The literal brokenness of *Zong!* evokes, rather than simply describes, the frames of reference to the Middle Passage which the reader is forced to negotiate. The archive is not necessarily a place to discover the past, as it is a way to engage with some of the haunting legacies, epistemes and traumas that emerge in the present. By way of implication, Philip's highly experimental and difficult poetry is stripped of binaries and normative modes of the 'human'. Her use of embodiment, intermediality, ancestral cosmologies and ritual within the broader context of black haunting is geared towards the principles of reckoning, re-memory and testimony. *Zong!* is a ceremony plate and liturgic memorializing of the pain of the memory of the 1781 Zong Massacre while demonstrating a commitment to filling the holes or gaps in history through a mode of wake-work that apprehends the names and presences of lost lives. Philip closes the gaps and erasures of the violent sea voyage with groping for the meanings of what Erna Brodber terms in *Myal*, "the half" which has "never yet been told".[3] According to Paula Morgan, "The half that is subject to incapacity to fully articulate is as heavily infused with meaning as the half which finds its way into some measure of uneasy articulation."[4] This is actualized in the poet's re-purposing of words that extend beyond the British law in an effort to negotiate and emancipate the dis-membered lives that still haunt the Atlantic Ocean. Philip is, in effect, crafting an affective response to a grievous historical experience through divination, song, ritual and liturgy.

The atrocity embedded in the *Gregson vs Gilbert* case of 1783 is probed and stylistically spatialized, as it was (at the time) the only remaining document to record the insurance dispute that resulted from one hundred and thirty-three living Africans being thrown overboard the *Zong* vessel to perish in the ocean en route to the Caribbean. The decision to discard human passengers was the solution for offsetting physical and financial losses incurred during an extended sea voyage. Philip grounds this public historical event in a range of philosophical and cultural worldviews to re-assemble with care the essence of a horrific experience that elides any clear meaning. The sea becomes a repository of memory. Philip initially proposed the term "exaqua",[5] which is a technique deployed to unbury those dispossessed lives from the Antillean Sea. In an interview with Patricia Saunders, she describes the necessity for remembering the horror and the task that awaits her to ceremonially resuscitate this memory. When she says that she "want[s] the bones",[6] she does so on the premise of an affective investment that will be made in the absence of the actual, material objects. Together with the poet, the reader is drawn into a collaborative exploration of the holes and spaces in the case.

The reading community is gathered to actively explore and reconstruct the fragments that are left in the wake of a failing archive. A ritual song is made as the poet and reader alike enter into a metaphoric mortuary. Saidiya Hartman aptly notes, "Commodities, cargo and things don't lend themselves to representation, at least not easily. The archive dictates what can be said about the past and the kind of stories that can be told about

A CARIBBEAN POETICS OF SPIRIT

the persons catalogued, embalmed, and sealed away in box files and folios. To read the archive is to enter a mortuary."[7] To begin her enterprise of cataloguing the anonymous dead and entering the mortuary, Philip returns to the one-page summary of the 1783 case. Formally trained as an attorney, she decides to dismember or slice apart the language of the official archive. This is performed, in part, to deconstruct the inequitable juridical and political understandings of certain groups of people and the relations it informs.[8]

The paucity of names cannot be apprehended easily, however. The excessive presence of the spectral captures this immense loss of life and the way that the first experience escapes our grasp. The section that is polemically deployed to begin the task of articulating the identities of those who perished during the journey is, "Os" (Latin for bone), which consists of twenty-six poems. It is depicted through an index of phrases and words that Philip refers to as the skeletons of the project. For example, within the main body of the text, there is a thin black line below which is a handful of names: "Masuz Zuwena Ogunsheye Ziyad Ogwambi Keturah"[9] and "Kesi Modele Mtundu Ibukunle Adeyemi".[10] The poet is here grappling with how to counteract an epistemic violence that has relegated a people to an afterthought.

Later in her notation of the collection, she indicates that "Os" reflects a forensic impulse to trace and identify from the liquid tombs, the bones of the murdered dead which are required for her performance and enactment of mourning. The desire to sound out the names reflects the kinds of cultural observations that are predisposed to traversing submerged knowledge with care and devotion. By continuing to recuperate the suffocated history of the voyage, the poet strategically situates the repetition of the phonemes, 'w' 'a' 't' 'e' 'r' across the opening pages of the collection.[11] Water's double meaning echoes the layered violence at the heart of the text, where Captain Collingwood took advantage of an approaching storm to dump the human cargo into the ocean. Philip indicates:

> I mutilate the text as the fabric of African life and the lives of these men, women and children were mutilated. I murder the text, literally cut it into

pieces, castrating verbs, suffocating adjectives, murdering nouns, throwing articles, prepositions, conjunctions overboard, jettisoning adverbs: I separate subject from verb, verb from object – create semantic mayhem, until my hands bloodied, from so much killing and cutting . . . and like some seer, sangoma, or prophet who, having sacrificed an animal for signs and portents of a new life, or simply life, reads the untold story that tells itself by not telling.[12]

The massacre and the intense violation of human life are embodied in the scattering of words across the page. It is an attempt to break and enter into a hegemonic version of history through violence and fracture. The word bank is divorced from any shared code of meaning, much like the floating corpses tossed off the *Zong*. It is an archaeological work that involves the unearthing of submerged memories.

True to this mode of wake-work, "water" is used as a reparative entry point and concurs with the washing away of hurts. It also emblematizes the resuscitating value of the currents of movements that is afforded through liturgy. Interestingly, *Zong!* is a near cryptonym of "song." The haunting symphony of the poet's musical arrangement of words invites a melancholic reflection and affective connection to anyone touched by the tragedy. The onomatopoeic effect in sounding out the graphic representation of syllables expresses a visually wide space and a hole appears in the middle of the graphemes. What persists is the image of the brooding sea which dovetails with the sensation of being at a loss. The readers themselves are very likely to experience this when grappling with the text. The metaphor of absence is a wider thematic operation in the text. It demonstrates the importance that absence and loss distil the attendant reality of disembodiment.

One hears not only the English language but also the water, human song, groaning and suffering. Through a song that is hummed for the dead, the ghosts are invoked and their collective presence takes on centuries' worth of meaning and aesthetic significance. It is through the extraordinary power of poetry, the dead are revived by the poetic voice that sings their melancholic tune. Significantly, the exclamation at the end of *Zong!* alludes to the chant, the shout, the ululation, the howl, the shriek and the performance that is required to give concrete expression to the history and memories of this event. The punctuation marker and its signification elaborate upon the sonic components of the voice and the vibration of the flesh that confers personhood upon the traces of the murdered passengers. In the interview with Saunders, Philip asserts that she drew inspiration for the arrangement of her poems while attending a funeral in Ghana.[13] She comments that the traditional Ghanaian music comprised "beautiful haunting melodies" – a style that she transferred into her poetic expression.[14] The haunting leitmotif registers the unbounding flow of human experience that is expressed in the writing. A ritual is referentially most pronounced.

Similarly, in the undulating words of the section, "Sal," (which means salt), the reader is encouraged to hear rather than see meaning. The words modulate into infinite variations and their sounds vibrate through the wave-like gaps that lap across the page:

> her and me the song so la/ fa so la . . . /g long/ g long g long/ . . . spin a tale to be/ told not/ heard nor/ read not be/ un/ untold we/ were.[15]

The "g long g long" in the middle of the passage hints at the water slapping the hull of the ship. As a listening text, *Zong!* contains a cacophony of voices, human and non-human, enslaved and free. Members of the crew, for example, are seduced by a story that they cannot unhear: capitalism's siren song of incalculable riches. Yet, these are tales of riches that sacrifice human life. A listening framework proves especially important in silent spaces, for it is through listening that one notices what is changed, missing, forgotten and unattended.

Ian Baucom's *Spectres of the Atlantic* (2005) positions the Zong case as one that is "central not only to the Trans-Atlantic slave trade and the political and cultural archives of the black Atlantic but to the history of modern capital, ethics, and time consciousness".[16] Baucom's standpoint illuminates the vastness of the horrors of the slave trade, where one must consistently work in opposition to new forms of subjective exclusion and the modern grain of hegemonic history that continue to promote deracination and cycles of racial capitalism. By signalling towards the intertwining implications of chattel slavery, Baucom illuminates the covert forms of violence, which are constantly enacted upon various vulnerable people groups in the contemporary world. His work accommodates the unravelling of the myriad forms of inhumanities and indignities that span more than a century of imperialism. Here, the relational nature of history facilitates a spectral tracking of the remains of an empire which continue to endure and erupt as an unhealed wound in the contemporary world.

Apart from the spatialization and suturing of haunted memory, the poet draws on West African modes of spiritual practice to recoup and remedy a painful memory. Although there is no explicit statement in the collection that identifies Ifa divination rituals, there are several clues that connect with this spiritual practice. For example, at the end of Philip's acknowledgements, she makes the gesture to the spiritual reflection at work in her poems, "I thank my Ancestors for bestowing the responsibility of this work on me, Ase".[17] "Ase" is the Yoruban word for the power to make things happen or to change the present condition. It is used in Ifa divination to refer to the power of creation.[18] By adding "Ase" at the end of her verses, Philip affirms and incorporates an ancestral restorative energy and converts an oral tradition to a written one.

Transposing the matter of restorative interventions further, she gives epistemic shape to the untold traumatic experiences of sexual abuse and gendered violence aboard the slaving vessels. This is depicted in the section, "Sal", in which the main voice belongs to "someone who [is] white, male, and, European".[19] He is clearly identifiable as a person whose body is intact as he narrates and reflects upon his experiences on board the slaving vessel. He is protected from the violence and murder he describes. In this section of the text, he addresses a woman known as Ruth.[20] His broken narration conveys images of sexual assault which he has committed: "she/falls/fortunes over/board rub/and rob her/now I lose/count I am/lord",[21] "gin/ & rum of/ murder/ rimmed with sin/ her sex/ open all/ night rain/ a seam of sin &/ to market to market/ tin/ such/ to trap a fat pig/ a fat nig",[22] "cut/ her/ open her/ shape/ tie her/ ripe/ toes/ round/ and firm".[23] He speaks in extremely racist and violent terms and it seems that Philip recuperates his voice to probe the distinction

A CARIBBEAN POETICS OF SPIRIT

between the personhood that is accorded to him and the debased status of the enslaved woman who he rapes.

Superimposed onto this section are the Yoruba phrases that are used to disclose the deep psychic interiority and submerged narrative of the enslaved woman. For example, "ifá" which means divination, is placed adjacent to the English word "if" in many cases, thus prompting the possibility of "what if" the African perspective was recuperated? What if the captain did not justify murder for the lack of water? Philip's pairing of English and Yoruba lexical items widens what determines or provides another frame of meaning from the case. "If" is part of the logic for determining Philip's translation of the case and the repurposing of words that extend beyond British law. During this account of the enslaved woman's rape, the poet writes of the African king or "oba" who "sobs" inarticulately.[24] The weeping of the ancestral ruler intensifies an emotional or affective response to the cruelty of this betrayal and crossing. Ritual, through weeping, provides the necessary mourning and the possibility of re-interpreting or re-visioning murder as sacrifice, a sacrifice that may bring, as Philip states, "portents of a new life".[25]

Reparation is also afforded through a new media, which Philip uses to give form to the absent presences that halo the content of the poems. Demonstrably, the visual smudges illustrate printing overlays and draw attention to the production of the poem as part of its difficult reading experience. In the manuscript the margins perish, meaning is scattered and there are polyphonic, visual complexities which strain against organizational systems. The idea of multiplicity runs throughout the poems and the different approaches to reading the document challenge singular or fixed narratives. In the section "Ferrum", for example, the poet writes: "I see yo u to wri/te writ e a/ll ti /me me".[26] It reflects what Philip claims in the journal section as a "cacophonous representation" and a "fugal palimpsest".[27] To this degree, the contractual nature of the case is being challenged by the poet's authorial intention to evince an alternative record via a mode of reparative writing. Through the symbolic layering of words, she supplements rather than cancels new understandings of the historical experience. Spectral excess, which represents in part, the excessiveness

HAUNTED HISTORIES

and burden of grief in the diaspora, responds to the deficiency or gap in hegemonic representations and conceptions of the Middle Passage.

In a similar but unique sense, Jason de Caires Taylor's underwater museums, namely the figures in *Vicissitudes*,[28] illuminate this new dimensionality in art and offer an interpretive re-conceptualizing of the grievous sea journey. Here, the sea evokes both history and the archive. De Caires Taylor's sculptures, for all their otherworldliness, can be read as a space of ecological mysticism. The figures are part of an aquatic space that produce ideas of supernatural quality and incorporeality. Visitors to the various oceanic museums can sink themselves below the surface to encounter a sense of marine life more personal than a conventional white-walled museum. Unconstrained by gravity, their bodies are exposed to the feeling of weightlessness. While the sounds are muted, perceptibility is improved with the moving tide and natural conditions. In this solid monument of a ring of African children clasping hands together as the ocean takes them, de Caires Taylor's sculpture demonstrates an ambience of spectrality and mystery as the limbs are deformed by the altering colours of reeds, moss and crustaceans, which move with the changing filters of light that shine downward on them. The monument covered with armours of manacles and soft moss seems to occupy its own haunting space and temporality. The worlds that he invents and the narrative possibilities that he conjures encompass ideas of the spectral and of haunting.

Like the leap in form that Philip exercises, de Caires Taylor's underwater museum represents a new, contemporary frontier of artistic experimentation in other worlds, realms and media, the purpose of which is manifold, including the significant work of remediating a particular memory that has been written out of public record. *Vicissitudes*, not unlike the project of *Zong!*, interpretively takes figures which are associated with violent death and transforms them into a medium of new life. Both works of art function as a replica for a floating museum where the reader/ explorer must submerge themselves vicariously (or otherwise) into this intra-active world. It is an experience that demands new methodologies, practices and patterns of ethical thought. Moreover, these new processes

A CARIBBEAN POETICS OF SPIRIT

and frontiers of artistic expression are epistemic tools that contrast with Western beliefs about reality which are steeped in the idea of a single, pure or materialist universe.

The ocean is a liminal space of memory itself and is an apt symbol of the in-betweenness of death and life. The thematic concern with the depths of the ocean retains its significance in the section, "Ebora," which is Yoruba for spirits of the waters. Below the depths, there is a timelessness that creates its own haunting. To this end, the reader must persist with the effort of locating meaning and must work to unravel the submerged and cultural consciousnesses replicated in the confused syntax and phonemes on the pages. "Ebora" is structured around the spirit presences whose groans are lifted from the murky depths and plucked through a string of phonemes from the legal case. Philip's assemblage is symbolically surgical. Her pursuit of a representative patterning emulates the unthinkable reality of decapitation, dismemberment, rape and a host of other violations. To this extent, the artfulness of the book, especially in its use of sepia tones and vellum, reveals that even in its composition, the manuscript shares symbolic resonance with the experience of mental confusion aboard the British slave ship. These waves of experiences create a shared remembrance with other lives. Memory is, therefore, far more than a motif; it is a foundation for cathartic progression. It is also evidence of a manner of therapeutic intervention that may be derived from charting courageous excursions into the submerged regions of the past.

This creativity reaches an unchecked intensity at the end of the poems, where Philip zigzags across the page, which suggests a form of somnambulist writing. The act of being moved by a force outside of the self allows for the receiving and internalizing of knowledge that is dictated by energies from an immaterial world. In the section, "Ferrum," the poet articulates a symbolic epigraph: "There was a noise and behold, a shaking . . . and the bones came together; bone to his bone . . . the sinews and flesh came upon them . . . and the skin covered them above . . . and the breath came into them . . . and they lived, and stood upon their feet".[29] It is through an intensive and physical re-ordering of the archive that the names of the enslaved reappear from the depths. Unlike the poems in "Os", where the names of the many drowned are a series of footnotes, in "Ferrum", they are illustrated in an emboldened manner. It speaks to the return of historical presences as Philip satisfactorily performs her mourning rites. In other words, the dead have been ritualized into expression. Yet, while the text seeks to make meaning from this extreme loss and horrific event, black texts could never replace black bodies.

Philip unrelentingly aspires to build a form and space which undermines the rational mind and points to a structure of shared experiential realities as a basis of meaning construction. *Zong!* is thus a collective work of mourning executed with care and precision in the interest of 'ex-aquaing' repositories of black memory as a basis for more empowering cartographies of the self. As Hartman posits, the "past is neither inert nor given [and] the stories we tell about what happened then, the correspondences we discern between today and times past, and the ethical and political stakes of these stories rebound in the present".[30] Through the choreography of ritual and mourning, Philip crafts new expressions of forgiving but not forgetting. Her text functions as firewood to the literary imagination and stands as a potent framework that works against the material objectives of the slave trade by creating a more intuitive response which heralds the afterlife of the African passengers on board the *Zong*. The poems are therefore read as processes and arrangements that could hold clusters of events and meanings together. This writing style is echoed in other diasporic works of fiction in the modern world.

Through this method of wake-work, Grace Nichols, like NourbeSe Philip, moves with a discursive impulse to trace the role and functions of new cosmologies and knowledge-making in the African diaspora. In this vein, she is interested in those voices that may not have survived in the official historical records of slavery such as those of women. In positioning themselves as listeners to the wisdom of elders and other-than-human entities, Philip and Nichols use their poetry to share what listening for justice could sound like. In *I is a Long Memoried Woman*, Nichols employs the trope of memory to firmly situate the events of the Middle Passage in a temporal past and constrain its effects on the body of the surviving speaker in the New World plantation. Memory is not simply a matter of

A CARIBBEAN POETICS OF SPIRIT

tuning in to the past, but also of giving it space to reform itself as sensate and valuable in the present.

Traumatic memory, as represented in *I is a Long Memoried Woman*, is radioactive insofar that the haunting recollections of the oceanic journey and plantation servitude are passed on through generations. A reconstruction of this dynamic is encapsulated in the poet's creative use of dreams, the mythic imagination, spirituality, sorcery and telepathy. In the collection, the speaker becomes a shaman in trance who seeks out the cure to the generational pain of servitude that is resident in her body. Nichols, in a manner similar to Philip, aims to fill the holes or gaps in history with a narrativizing of unrecorded experiences. She dismantles the colonial grand narrative of Caribbean memory and affords new forms of historiography. In the context of the long-memoried woman, the colonial archive is not a legal transcript but is equally a death sentence. The transgenerational persona is continuously awakened by the ghost limbs of her ancestors who intrude into her body and present reality. The unsolicited surfacing of history into the present, according to Stuart Hall, is always grounded in the manner in which Caribbean peoples are positioned by and within the narratives of the past.[31] Taking a lead from Hall, this chapter argues that ancestral memory is so powerful in the psyche of Nichols's long-memoried woman that it begins to command its own attention and she is made to listen in to its eruptive power.

Significantly, both *I is a Long Memoried Woman* and *Zong!* begin with an invocation to "water". First, it may simply echo pathways to a new, transcendent realm, while in another sense, the ocean is positioned as an archive, a tomb and an underwater repository of bodies which transmute into mythologies. Moreover, both writers engage the register of water metaphorically to locate diverse and complex navigational ways to link its transcendent quality to a particular set of memories and associations. Water's persistence evokes the possibility of the spiritual to deduce shared connections, reckonings and collective power. By working through different temporalities Nichols and Philip bring the presences of history to bear in fresh ways. In Nichols's collection, however, the question is no longer how to represent water, but how to survive it. To this degree, the metaphor of the Middle Passage connects to the land as consistently engaged through a focus on cultural ruptures and forced separation. The book begins with the foci of the journey through the ocean while demonstrating its traumatic lingering effects within the moving lives of those on land.

The collection was motivated by a dream Nichols had of a girl swimming from Africa to the Caribbean with a garland of flowers. The poet asserts: "When I woke up I interpreted the dream to mean that she was trying to cleanse the ocean of the pain and suffering that she knew her ancestors had gone through".[32] The book is separated into five segments, with each chronicling a different stage in the journey of the unnamed persona whose life spans other women's ordeals in the diaspora. Her context reflects the uncanny link between those generations who are still searching for healing in the modern world. On this ground, it seems that the poet is concerned with the intersections between identity and the ways in which collective memory is possessed of agency and becomes vital in acts of resistance and healing.

The speaker is at once a spiritual and material presence and her body holds the fragments of past lives together in the diaspora. The images of return, the encrypted past, haunting recollections and plurality of perception buttress the nature of her transhistorical presence. This fluidity in consciousness repeatedly demands that it be confronted and addressed. At the start of *I Have Crossed An Ocean*, in which Nichols begins with an extract from *I Is a Long Memoried Woman*, the speaker describes her continuous brushes with death in her dreams: "Even in dreams I will submerge myself/ swimming like one possessed/ back and forth across that course/ strewing it with sweet-smelling flowers/ one for everyone who made the journey".[33] The lexical signifiers of "dream," "submerge," "swimming," and "possessed" capture the mutable role of the journey and are apt signifiers for locating the fluidity of her consciousness during this time. The challenge is to make or etch out an alternative language that would mediate this communal sensibility.

According to Gabriele Griffin, the dream in Nichols's poetry reflects "a nightmare of the disintegration of the self [that is] wedged between

A CARIBBEAN POETICS OF SPIRIT

the past and present".[34] Historical pain, with which the speaker is negotiating, is reinforced in the gaps, silences, ellipses and holes in the poetic layout.[35] The intrusive nightmare is inevitable and the impulse to avert it sends an invitation to realize the horror in the psychic domain. Nichols delicately probes beneath the exterior life of the long-memoried woman, an intelligence that will serve as a major catalyst in her agency. Through remembrance and historical recollections, she is propelled into a search for avenues through which she may endure and survive the perils of plantation servitude. Her subconscious swimming ritual can be viewed as cathartic as it heralds a mode of ritual return to Africa through space and time. This complex process of tracking a highly fragmented and submerged history is congruent with the theoretical debates of Edward Kamau Brathwaite. In *Roots*, Brathwaite observes:

> [Africa] is a permanent part of our heritage. It comes in a way, as an almost physical inheritance . . . where in nature, drought and lushness, the flower and the desert, lie side by side. It is a spiritual inheritance from slavery and the long story before that of the migrant African moving from the lower Nile across the desert to the Western ocean only to meet the Portuguese and a History that was to mean the middle passage, America, and a rootless sojourn in the New World.[36]

Transposing this historical psychic and physical uprooting with mutated passages of dispossession in the diaspora, Brathwaite reflects on the pattern of the indeterminate tide, which is difficult to record. In *Missile and Capsule*, he provides the principle of the tidalectic to craft a new narrative form, which dovetails with the processes of Caribbean becoming since the wave hits many points of origins in its travelling and gathering of materials from the seabed. The process of becoming is then cumulative, and meaning is constantly sought from various encounters outside of time and space.[37] The logic of Brathwaite's tidalectics acquires new significance when paired with the embodied rhythms and manifold 'crossings' of the long-memoried woman who moves between the Middle Passage and plantation life in the Caribbean.

Equally important is the initial image of the dark sea that recalls the female womb, and attaches symbolic reference to the sexual violation of enslaved women on the floating vessels. To remedy the pain that she feels, the speaker scatters flowers on the ocean's surface to speak for the nameless millions who will be mourned. She can be viewed as a type of pall-bearer, carrying the ship of death. The sexual violence repeats itself in the poem, "One Continent/to Another," where the speaker details the gruesome rape of her ancestor and the task of giving birth while mana-cled: "Child of the middle passage womb/push/daughter of a vengeful Chi/[. . .]/into the new world/birth aching her pain/from one continent/to another".[38] Nichols spares the witnesses of the birth nothing when she asserts that, "after fifty years/she hasn't forgotten/hasn't forgotten/how she had laid there/in her own blood/laid there in her own shit".[39] The repetition of "hasn't forgotten" indicates that the memory of suffering has ossified into a state in which the speaker attempts to shield herself. Unalienable from this experience are the violent looks in the eyes of the white, male captors who seed the children of the diaspora. The ships are represented as floating brothels where the crew members would expel their repressed sexual urges upon the bodies of shackled women and girls. The speaker's psychic excursions illustrate precisely how discreet experiences of brutality exist in a repetitive and uncanny relationship with other events: past, present and future. The poems advance the point that memory is a continuous process whereby it is wielded to mediate a collective experience of silent suffering as well as solidarity. She finally awakens to "piece the life together" that she would lead in the diaspora.[40]

To remember the Middle Passage is to consider the acts of resistance and defiance to be found amidst a life of torture. In light of this, Nichols makes creative use of limbo as a conceptual tool to represent the inventions procured to redeem the self. Limbo is a signifying tool that combines historical realities with ancestral cosmologies. The Akan shape-shifting legend of Anansi is summoned for his malleability. Apropos of this is Wilson Harris's postulation that "limbo was born . . . on the slave ships of the Middle Passage".[41] According to Harris, "There was so little space that the slaves contorted themselves into human spiders".[42] During this

A CARIBBEAN POETICS OF SPIRIT

crossing, Harris contends that the figure of Anansi underwent a sea change which not only altered his name but his function in the diaspora. This offers a special kind of synchrony between cultures where an interstitial space of survival is procured. The limbo is a prolonged procession or journey and an explicit resistance manoeuver. Serving as a point of entry between worlds, the limbo dance takes as its primary object a power line that connects the gods above with the dying below. The dance of negotiating the pole held at the lower abdomen without falling, invokes the many-limbed spider, Anansi. It designates the space of the in-between as a site of resistance through a fusion of the numinous and material life.

This finds textual evidence in the persona's embodiment of the trickster god, in which she reimagines herself as containing all the extreme experiences between archetypal victim and victor. It becomes explicit in her resistance manoeuvers of code-switching, masking, parodying and veiling. In "Waterpot," she relates the daily enterprises of tending to the cane fields where she is hurried along "like . . . cattle", while "in the evenings/[she] return[s] from the fields/[and] tried hard to walk/like a woman/she tried very hard/pulling herself erect/with every three or four/ steps/pulling herself like royal cane".[43] Acts of resistance are displayed in the deliberate performances of walking erect and striding with dignity even though the speaker is treated like an animal. Her identification with the sugar cane, suggests a deeply ingrained affinity with the land. The attempt to reclaim the self that has been debased is set firmly against the overseers' indignant gaze. To nourish this growing sense of defiance, the speaker connects with continental African traditions as depicted in the last lines of the poem: "O but look/there's a water pot growing/from her head".[44]

The carrying of the water pot is part of the customs in her homeland, as women in Africa, perform the task of carrying water from the rivers on their heads in large jars. The image connects deeply with the exercise of drawing power from African roots. The numerous instances of psychical return to Africa mark an effort to mend the rift of separation caused by coerced movement. The rift can only begin to heal when these forgotten connections are once more set in motion. Family life and ancestral connections are therefore embedded in a communal imaginary that is moulded by shared, historical and generational traditions. The images of psychic projection inflect the broader transfer that is available through individual remembrance.

In the poem, "Days That Fell," the themes of memory, mourning old loss and renewal are similarly foregrounded: "And yet . . . /And yet . . . / the cutlass in her hand/could cut through/the days that fell/like bramble/ and the destruction that threatened to choke within".[45] The metaphor of the "cutlass" effectively functions as an arena of memory that reflects old stories of suffering and loss. The inability of the cutlass to "cut through the days that fell/like bramble"[46] is an expression of the inadequacy of this labour tool to mirror all the pain experienced by the speaker or to heal it. It is a circumstance that speaks to the entombing of memory in a form that remains inert and amnesic. The anguish that she feels is a result of the holes in her memory. The only option in this instance is to search for new sites on which a commemorative relation to the past might be established. Thus, the process of remembering enables and requires a form of listening beyond dominant modalities. The imperative to search for healing appears when the speaker begins to lean "closer to/the earth/ seeking, some truth/unnamed against the noon."[47]

In this material-spiritual reality, the earth becomes a source of knowledge and remedy, which is exemplified in the woman's downward movement into the soil. As she strikes the cutlass into the land, a seed of hope is planted. It becomes part of the renewal process that inseminates mother earth to bear fruit once more. She then gestures her body to the midday sun to fertilize her newfound power and agency. At this point, the voice changes from the singular first-person point of view to a resonant communal, "we";[48] and the women declare: "We must hold fast to dreams/ We must be patient/from the crouching of those huts/from the sprouting of these fields/We can emerge".[49] This refrain captures the oneness and unity of faith in the process of regeneration. Again, the symbol of the earth serves as a source of fertility and regeneration; it is a field in which new shoots are preparing to sprout.

A CARIBBEAN POETICS OF SPIRIT

Matters of resistance and healing assume a different shape in the poem, "Ala" where Nichols deconstructs one of the pernicious stories about the enslaved – that is their passive acceptance of fate. The poem records the story of Uzo, who outmanoeuvers existing power structures by refusing her condition as a plantation breeder. The clearest statement of her refusal is demonstrated in her acts of infanticide. As explained by Bennett and Dickerson, "the black [enslaved] female body served as one of the prime technologies of reproduction and commodification".[50] Uzo is placed in the broader system of servitude where she is objectified and bodily deformed beyond all powers of recuperation. For her non-compliance as a human breeder, her body is publicly stretched out and her flesh is covered with the product of the sugar industry she slaves at.

What is delineated here, are the interconnectedness between the living and the dying, the persistent humiliation and frustration inherent in an unjust system, and the point that life is frequently mourned and death is often celebrated. Uzo is tied to the stakes, "arms and legs spread-eagle", covered with molasses, and left to "the slow and painful/ picking away of [her] flesh/by red and pitiless ants".[51] The onlookers call upon Ala, the African earth deity, to materialize and reclaim Uzo's soul. The poem certainly captures the spiritual strength of enslaved women. In the end, Uzo's body is pinned close to the earth and she returns to Ala's 'womb' where her spirit finds rest. This image suggests not only the process of dying to be reborn and of devouring and being devoured but engages an interlocking of the human body with the cosmos.

Uzo's fierce love for her child, even if it may be misread by those who cannot fathom what actions are done to counter the sadism of slavery, is an example of fierce resistance against a brutal empire. Counter-violence takes the shape of revolutionary praxis that is evidenced in the network of words, myths, images and symbols. In other words, the poet gives voice to the trauma inherent in articulating the dilemma of women who must decide whether to keep a child and raise it in unfavourable – sometimes unbelievably difficult – circumstances or to have an abortion. It is an issue that persists in contemporary debates. A frequently voiced assumption is that abortion is an easy way out of difficult situations, a position that may at times ignore the reality that for most women facing an unwanted pregnancy there is no good solution. The poem, "Ala" facilitates this reflection and is a reminder that a woman in such a situation has only two extremely difficult alternatives, and no matter what she decides, the effect is felt long after.

The trope of agency therefore takes on both mourning and instructive roles, and Nichols provides therapeutic recourse through ritual. While Philip reshapes the legal document of *Gregson vs. Gilbert* to tell a submerged narrative, Nichols cleverly engages a non-linear and broken narrative form, particularly in her references to African-Caribbean cosmologies. Demonstrably, both poets bring the past to bear in new ways through a highly experimental poetic craft. The space of agency opens through the intrusion of spirit presences that infiltrate the current milieu of the speaker. This is grounded in the poem, "I Coming Back", which is introduced via an incantatory, repetitive tone. The speaker recites:

> I coming back 'Massa'/ I coming back/ mistress of the underworld/ I coming back/ colour and shape/ of all that is evil/ I coming back/ ball-a-fire/ and skinless higue/ I coming back.[52]

Her pitch is elevated and prayer-like. This interlocks with her high level of ritual devotion. It is within this lure of song and incantation that she moves forward from a position of objectification and servitude to high priestess and female shaman. Spirit presences seep into the persona's consciousness where she imagines her vengeful ancestral mothers and sisters returning from the realm of the dead to exact revenge on their white masters.

The back-chat and protesting rhythm of the poem convey the combined power of speech and song. Moving away from an environment of disembodied voice that responds to projected pain, she wrests control from her torturer and fabricates a tongue of her own. In his essay, "Cross-Cultural Poetics," Édouard Glissant describes the power and significance of communal relations. He asks: "What is the Caribbean in fact? [It is] a multiple series of relationships ... we sense that the sea exists within us with its weight of now revealed

A CARIBBEAN POETICS OF SPIRIT

islands [. . .]. In the Caribbean each island embodies openness. The dialectic between inside and outside is reflected in . . . a [mythic] imagination [that] liberates us from being smothered."[53] For Glissant, the islands of the Caribbean operate with interlocking aspects of myth, creativity and collective consciousness. They bespeak contact with entangled psyches, and methods of transference as appropriate responses to traumatic historical events and repressive regimes. In keeping with the concept of transference, Nichols describes how her speaker in, "Night Is Her Robe," is enveloped in the auspicious moonshine as she emerges from a forest that breeds presences. The persona emerges from the woods as a quasi-goddess after she reconnects with an ancestral spiritual network to repossess the rights to her body and mind. She embodies a deep craft, its purpose dual – for good and evil – and her resistant acts extend beyond the material realm into the domain of sorcery, which is characteristic of Obeah and Voodoo practices in the Caribbean. According to Sarah Lawson, Caribbean syncretic magic as utilized by Nichols, "is an important cultural retention in the Caribbean. It needs to be seen as part of a complex matrix of women-centred cultural activities which range from herbalism at one end of the spectrum to a belief that it is possible to control the actions of others".[54] Embodied in the woman's gathering of "strange weeds/wild root/leaves with the property/both to harm and to heal",[55] is a process that honours the spiritualist and redemptive traditions of Afrodiasporic communities. Even when the body is disfigured and the mind is marred by extreme turmoil, Nichols asserts the overwhelming power of spirituality as a method of rescue, therapy and psychic ease.

In the poem, "Yemanji," African spirituality and mythology are similarly engaged as communicative enactments and agents of power. As the persona walks alongside a waterway, she imagines meeting Yemanji, "Mother of all beings sprawled/ upon the rivershore, her long/ breasts (insulted by her husband)/ oozing milk that lapped and flowed".[56] The tears of the speaker conjure a river through which Yemanji appears. The river is symbolically a site of purification and rebirth. Yemanji, Yoruba goddess of the ocean, exemplifies all women who have crossed the Atlantic and she empathizes with the speaker's humiliation and bondage. Yemanji's breasts are described as "long", exhausted and insulted by the sexual and maternal affronts she has endured.[57] Her battered body parts and swollen stomach speak of the generations of silent sufferers. However, the milk that they produce becomes one with the river's waters. The poet proposes that the black female body is not a site of commodification but a liberated, life-giving entity that can serve as a nurturing model for future generations. Furthermore, the speaker's encounter with the water deity facilitates an imaginative re-evaluation of continental African cosmology and history. By implication, the legends of the diaspora's original peoples are legitimized, and the persona entertains the possibility that these are the true nexuses of self-affirmation, power and healing. The effect lends to the comfort of belonging. The frame of simultaneous journeys, Middle Passages and crossings thus formulates a potentiating praxis in the quest for self-definition and agency.

To continue the process of liberation, the persona is thrust into the world of the gods in "Of Golden Gods" and "I Will Enter". Although she is physically bound to the plantation, she transcends her physicality via spiritual journeying through time and space. Such journeying allows her to associate with other spirit women (Meso-American), who suffer similar oppression at the hands of the Europeans. When she encounters the presence of the Taino woman she declares: "Memory is written/in each crumpled fold/you can still remember/how they pitted gun against/ arrow/steel against stillness/Stunned by their demands/for gold".[58] This cross-cultural connection permits a particular view of time and space that is never-ending, fluid, cyclic and mythic. These inter-group or cross-cultural relationships also demonstrate the link between bonds of maroonage. The long-memoried woman who utilizes knowledge from other ethnic groups performs a science of resistance in which she methodically and patiently collects every new knowledge that is available to her. In this detail, she embodies a simultaneity between worlds, realms, times and spaces and links plural consciousness and lives.

Ancestral and kindred spirits continue to assert themselves in meaningful and complex ways in accordance with the long memoried woman's diasporic circumstances. In "Of Golden Gods," her "chameleon spirit/

A CARIBBEAN POETICS OF SPIRIT

take[s] its exit"[59] and journeys into "Inca ruins . . . /Mexican plains/
. . . Aztec rites/ . . . [and] genocides".[60] These psychic travels explain
the ways in which she is a seeker of knowledge. As she taps out of the
plantation's deathly context, she begins to blaze a trail for herself and her
sanity. Nichols is certainly leveraging the temporal continuity between
individuals and their collective community. It stands as a poetic obser-
vance of intersectional identities. This evocation of ancestral networks is
spatialized in the deliberate use of run-on lines, broken time and surreal
conversations to negotiate psychic fractures and derive healing. Nichols's
fluid narrative technique abandons narrative linear advancement for the
pulsion of cross-currents. Her radical cross-cultural aesthetic certainly
makes the ghosts of history felt as they intervene in the modern world.

This ushering in of change via narrative and aesthetic invention is
cumulatively embodied in the enslaved woman who watches, sings, slaugh-
ters, escapes and telepathically joins other communities to participate
in a cross-cultural New World rebellion. Nichols says of the protagonist
in *I is a Long Memoried Woman*, "She breaks the slave stereotype of the
dumb victim of circumstance".[61] Thus, to discursively engage the ethos
of *I is a Long Memoried Woman*, is to deduce the ways in which the grip
of coloniality is consistently evaded and undermined. In principle, the
collection evinces the point that therapeutic interventions can be found in
the in-between moments of creative survival and resistant acts. Hope is
presented at the end of the collection in the simplicity of possibility alone.

In "Holding My Beads," the speaker stands with the "power to be
what [she is]/ a woman/ charting [her] own future/ a woman/ holding
[her] beads in [her] hand".[62] The string of beads that she holds interlocks
with the memory of the African beads worn around the pelvic region by
young and free Igbo girls. In the diaspora, the persona is piecing together
Old World memories in her contemporary life. Her re-stringing project,
which is reflective of cross-cultural designs is performed to produce a
new template that will lead to new routes. Identity is depicted as a process
that is both mutable and rooted and must be negotiated and collected
through various creative processes. The maternal voice symbolically bids
her children to step into a "wide future".[63] The circuit of histories – embed-

HAUNTED HISTORIES

ded in the string of beads – signposts Nichols's fashioning of profound connections formed through generations and the task of safeguarding the power of memory. These after-images are imaginatively pursued as generating spaces in which trauma can be alleviated.

In the creative work of both Philip and Nichols, the entrance of ancestors creates the sense of otherworldliness which is integral to daily life in the black diaspora. The preeminence of polyvocality, multiple journeying and the collapse of linear time generate defamiliarization which constrains closer scrutiny of the present. The sense of the spectral is also enhanced by locational choices which blur the divide between the living and the dead. Territories which seamlessly coexist suggest the need for greater attention to the nature of diasporic consciousness through which an unsilencing of the unspeakable provides immense liberatory praxis. Such is the ideological power of experimental writing. The articulation of such power, albeit in different contexts, resonates in the next chapter as revealed in the works of George Lamming and Erna Brodber. What emerges is a cluster of interrelated ideas that establishes a wide scope of possibilities that produces the flexible qualities for new ideologies through the frameworks of myth and ceremony.

CHAPTER 4

Re-Architecting Freedom

Myth, Ancestors and Ritual in George Lamming's *Season of Adventure* and Erna Brodber's *The Rainmaker's Mistake*

DEHUMANIZATION SPAWNED FROM COLONIAL IMPULSES CONTRIBUTED TO A fractured ontology in the Caribbean, the evidence of which includes psychological suffering and the constant questing for psychic wholeness. This is not to claim, however, that the Caribbean is a pathological site of woundedness. As suggested in the previous chapters, the selected texts rehearse representations of historic atrocities, while also signifying a compelling refusal to comply with Western, stereotypical worldviews that resist representations of Caribbean space and people as tenacious, creative and outliving the nightmares of their histories. Setting themselves within the range of narrative experimentation that Caribbean writers have deployed to explore the forces at work in early and contemporary Caribbean culture and society are George Lamming and Erna Brodber. In *Season of Adventure* (1960)[1] and *The Rainmaker's Mistake* (2007),[2] both Lamming and Brodber delineate and complicate how the newly emancipated Caribbean subject grapples with the unfamiliar concept of freedom during seasons of national formation.

This is accomplished through a profound engagement with the issues of memory and non-memory, the myth of origins, existential dislocation and the ways in which colonial practices have invented the descendants of enslaved communities as incapable of creativity and self-productivity. This inquiry frames the larger concerns within nationalist and post-nationalist discourses of freedom and the ideas can be engaged through several of Wilson Harris's and Gordon Rohlehr's conceptual frameworks, including the mythic imagination, possession and limbo. According to Harris, the utility of the creative imagination provides a new structure to envision Caribbean communities as thriving and resourceful in the wake of historical atrocity. In the essays, "Phenomenal Legacy,"[3] "History, Fable and Myth in the Caribbean and Guianas,"[4] "Profiles of Myth and the New World,"[5] and *Tradition, the Writer and Society*,[6] he conceives positive patterns of Caribbean ontology by expanding the measurement of human time to mythic time through which echoes, associations and kernels of knowledge are curated.

The folk aesthetics and myth that Harris envisions are also delineated by Gordon Rohlehr in his essays, "Folk Research: Fossil or Living Bone,"[7] "George Lamming and Kamau Brathwaite," "Dream Journeys,"[8] "Where is Here? What Jail is This? Who are We?,"[9] and "Possession as Metaphor".[10] Rohlehr advances an experimental form that will reactivate the presences of history, which, when sutured, lead to positive self-image and intuitive knowledge systems. According to Torres-Saillant, "[t] he work of Rohlehr has set up an aesthetic link between folk forms and literary artistic forms"[11] which breeds a useful connection with buried histories. It allows for a circulation of counter-discourses and methods that are essential to understanding the fullness of Caribbean ontologies and even of space.

However, it should be noted that while Rohlehr and Harris's discursive strategies for recuperating the submerged self indeed cross-pollinate, there are distinctions which this work acknowledges. Before articulating these differences, it is useful to reflect on the connections between both thinkers. Rohlehr's variegated Caribbean aesthetic continuum functions, in part, as a companioning dialectic with Harris's mythic imagination. Throughout his lifetime, Rohlehr has steadfastly fleshed out epistemological matrices, which arose from a quest for a form that emphasizes the shape of Antillean hurt including its silences, erasures, gaps and fissures. His scholarship, therefore, stands as a potent repository of the lived realities of Caribbean people and its mediation through literature.

A CARIBBEAN POETICS OF SPIRIT

His approach to asserting a distinct Caribbean form, enmeshed in the cultural and folk realities of the region's people to recuperate and heal the traumas of a materialist, post-independent society, echo concerns raised by Harris. Harris's specific notions of limbo, the cross-cultural imagination, the phantom limb and the mythic imagination conceive a reality beyond deterministic cycles of subjugation and disempowerment, and point to the existence of "inarticulate feeling and unrealized wells of emotion belonging to the whole Indies".[12] This is not unlike Rohlehr, whose quest for a form through an intersection of the past and present via an analysis of contemporary culture, becomes the bridge between material and mythic domains.[13]

However, where Harris's quantum-like formulations endow Caribbean subjects with vast potentialities for interconnections, Rohlehr's practical criticism is shaped by the intensity of (raw) cultural production itself, including visual art (LeRoy Clarke and others), theatre, Carnival, the gayelle, literature and other types of creative discourses readily located in Trinidad and Guyana. Such an approach is entrenched in the active imperatives of communities and rhetoric. It is in this manner, that Rohlehr's critical contribution diverges from Harris's; for while Harris unequivocally asserts approaches to the destabilization of Western literary traditions particularly through vast quantum philosophies, Rohlehr extends this critical position through a simple but profound blend of cultural archaeology and literary criticism that arise out of the immediate and ever-changing materials of people's lives and society. It is here that Rohlehr is most at home, sustaining and interrogating the manner in which literariness becomes the common artistry of daily practices. Both scholars, however, have crystallized new narrative forms for reading through the many fissures of history, which are creatively echoed in *Season* and *Rainmaker*.

Season of Adventure is a text that contests the epistemologies of colonialism, which have distorted visions of the self and the nation. San Cristobal is a young republic – a microcosm of the New World – whose people struggle for balance in the trail of empire. Power now lies with a ruling elite who are unresponsive to the needs of the peasantry. Lam-

RE-ARCHITECTING FREEDOM

ming looks for reconciliation of this divided society through the flowering consciousness of Fola and her partnership with the peasantry. Fola seeks out the power from the *tonelle* to circumvent the displacement and alienation that defines her disenfranchised experience. *Season* begins by establishing the link between archetypes, possession and myth, and the enterprise of redefining the newly independent Afro-Caribbean subject. Ideas of spirit are presented by Lamming as a major structural element (and metaphor) in the text, which therefore establishes a coherent modality that exorcizes oppressive legacies which disturb the contemporary self.

Lamming's engagement with a metaphysical universe towards an articulation of the submerged aspects of Caribbean consciousness is worthy of close attention and connects with Harris's concept of the Caribbean mythic imagination. In this work, myth is applied to experiences of a people who rely on folk-based beliefs to nourish their artistic vision. In her study of myth and history in the works of three Caribbean writers – Alejo Carpentier, Édouard Glissant, and Wilson Harris – Barbara J. Webb surmises that it is the aim of these writers to "transform the void of historical rupture and fragmentation into an open-ended vision of possibility"[14] via the conceptual use of myth. Myth is the sedimented aspects of culture that pertain to every ethnic group in the Caribbean and South America and which can be re-tooled in literature vis-à-vis settings or locations that contain psychic gateways, totems, spirit companions and a sense of time that is fluid. This is evident in Harris's works as his methods eschew the assumption that Caribbean space and history are one-dimensional. Harris also provides the concept of the Caribbean unconscious,[15] for example, as a resource from which writers can unearth the vestiges of culture and recover "epic stratagems" via a creative process to subvert stereotyped ways in which Caribbean peoples have been made to exist.[16] These epic strategies comprise the symbolic rhythms of Caribbean existence, including the oracular and vestigial presences that are imbricated in the universe.[17] In *Season of Adventure*, Lamming enacts this spatializing via his insertion of syncretic ritual spaces to illuminate the point that the project of understanding freedom requires a commitment to psychic passages.

89

Similarly, in *The Rainmaker's Mistake*, Brodber's mythic innovations are expressed in a vision of the cosmos in which the divine, the animal, the human and the vegetal interlock. The narrative moves into an expansive terrain of folk and sacred traditions, ancestral pools of reflections and use of spiritual portals to subvert the stigma and perceptions of abnormal psychology, soul sickness and cultural impotence. A sociologist turned creative writer and thinker, Brodber aligns herself with the mythic scope of Harris's work. Her allegory debunks the imperial stereotype of the enslaved population as brown yams through a signal to mythological initiation. If one looks at Brodber and Lamming's texts in this light, what is apparent is a concerted attempt to theorize the tapestry of mythologies and presences as part of the movement in the fabric of Caribbean experience. The politics of a Caribbean metaphysical universe is therefore not arbitrary, but becomes socially relevant to opposing old and new forms of conquest and oppression. These revisionary experiences propose that the Caribbean universe is made up of a series of parallel universes, secretive portals, cross-cultural myths and coexisting presences. Worthy of similar attention is Rohlehr's assertion that "myth" is a concrete tool or process of poetic divination, which a writer may structurally engage to remap excursions "into suppressed [and] censored memories of an otherwise inaccessible ancestral past".[18] Indeed, Rohlehr exhibits this pattern of myth-making through an enterprise of literary shamanism in his essay, "Possession as Metaphor: Lamming's *Season of Adventure*." For Rohlehr, the mythic imagination moves beyond its definition as a sacred repository of cultural memory and becomes a highly structured principle that opens pathways into other novelistic enterprises.

Paying homage to Lamming's reconciliation of Afro-Caribbean folk traditions with literary expression, Rohlehr elucidates the potential of possession, with particular emphasis on freedom. Possession, at its most basic definition, entails the collapse of boundaries between the material and spiritual realms, and is signalled by a heightened consciousness. In *Season of Adventure*, it is operationalized via the Ceremony of Souls, a Vodun ritual, to facilitate a conversation with the dead. The ritual is performed within the domain of the Forest Reserve to expose the deep-rooted and enduring self-hatred which are fundamental legacies of the colonial order.[19] Landscape and location become psychic and internal configurations. It should be noted that the paradigm of possession does not seek to stabilize realities or energies, but offers a steady process of rereading and reinterpreting history. One must also take into account the caution that Derek Walcott gives about any movement into the past, which he asserts contains a mixture of the acid and the sweet.[20] Indeed, Lamming and Brodber do not sentimentalize a return to ancestral spaces, but critically probe how the fissures of history have become a creative repository to reflect on one's current context.

For most of Lamming's novel, Fola is possessed.[21] What begins as a coerced visit to the *tonelle* by her history teacher evolves into a cultural adventure and spiritual exploration into the forces that have aesthetically denied Fola her "blackness".[22] When she first becomes aware of Liza's possession, she is catapulted into her own girlhood, and in particular she confronts her most terrifying fear of rats. Here, marks her descent into the unconscious and submerged parts of the self. In this counter-discourse to the colonizing forces that are still attendant in San Cristobal and the elite's symbolic ruling order, Lamming deems folk-based ritual necessary. The next catalyst to Fola's initiation into her symbolic, collective history is the libation she is made to drink by the houngan. At this point, she is heavily surveyed and made to feel unwelcome by members of the communal gathering since she is representative of the oppressive mulatto middle class.

She is tempted to run but is stopped by the spellbinding glance of Aunt Jane, an old "witch", and priestess, who is the spiritual mother of the *tonelle*. Rohlehr uses the term "witch" to describe a rebellious and highly individualistic woman, whose collaboration with divine powers provides concrete strategies wielded to destroy extremely violent and inequitable systems of control.[23] Aunt Jane, not unlike Miss Mathilde in *The Rainmaker's Mistake*, draws from African-derived cosmologies and divination to appropriate acts of resistance, cure and recuperation to Caribbean peoples in moments of crisis. Aunt Jane is an old Orisha priestess whose knowledge of herbs can restore fertility to Fola's step-

A CARIBBEAN POETICS OF SPIRIT

father, Piggot. She is variously regarded as a spiritual mother, Obeah woman, oracle and wise woman. Her secret potions can unlock what Western medicine cannot facilitate. What Fola subsequently experiences is a feeling of being drilled to the ground and in this sense she becomes a vessel of reawakened spirits who seek to bridge the ruptured line of connection between mother, father, and daughter.[24] In other words, she becomes a living gateway through which multiple temporalities manifest. Her subsequent excretion reads as both a condition of nervous collapse and a sign for the shedding of emotional barriers, stoical defences, and coping mechanisms for the deep wounds that she feels at this point.

In fact, one of the startling revelations in *Season* is Fola's systemic denial of ancestral memory. The cultural regulations of Maraval Hills, a space that thrives on greed, deceit and high fashion, tempt her to betray her ancestral heritage. Notably, Fola is the stepdaughter of the new police commissioner, a social position which further complicates her relationship with the peasantry. Piggot's character is an apt example of the deep split in sensibility of the group of colonized whose identity remains ambiguous in the newly independent island-states. His perception of the Forest Reserve folk is that they are heathens, existing in spiritual darkness and deserving of violent disciplining, which he effectively articulates to Aunt Jane.[25] His segregationist disposition reflects the racist attitudes of the master narrative instilled in him by the former agents of imperialism. Although he ironically hails from the Reserve, his political and cultural indoctrination has created a type of self-estranged personality. In one dimension, he has inherited the racial prejudices of the metropolitan whites and satirically depends on a self-definition that thrives on an appetite for imported things. This is evident in his preference for drinking the imported, tinned orange juice rather than the fresh oranges grown locally.

Consequently, at the end of her spiritual journey, Fola comes to recognize the insult she had learned, an insult which all her infancy had suckled like an udder. And the udder was Charlot's history: the essential history of all Charlot's world.[26] Apart from the isolating cultural habits of her hometown, colonial pedagogical indoctrination has similarly created a great distance between the Fola and her heritage. The impulse to erase things African – a bedrock of Caribbean being – finds demonstration in her initial displacement, rootlessness and inability to find a father in the Forest Reserves. This quest to undo her disinheritance climaxes in the Ceremony of Souls. The Ceremony is a spatial metaphor on several counts. It becomes the narrative's medium for purging the guilt, shame and remorse rooted deep within a people's consciousness. The interstitial space between the spirit and material world allows for a cracking open of the hard shell of Fola's past.

In principle, the hounfort (place of ancestral worship) is a zone where spirit is able to touch spirit in the quest for the power to retell an unspeakable history. Ancestral veneration is projected on the idea that spirits coexist with the living, and are influential in their daily lives. This relationship undermines any complacent image of the self in conventional reality. Within the sacred space of the *tonelle*, the houngan intuits the spectral voices that are being summoned from beyond the grave. Fola's experience climaxes when she sees through the mists of time her dead father's soul, "wailing for a daughter it had never seen".[27] The energy that is beckoned from a purgatory of water implicitly signifies a modality for negotiating other worlds that leads to a new kind of knowing. Orienting oneself through the meridians of space and time is a form of ancestral reclamation.

The wailing that is heard disrupts concrete environments and creates fissures that open passageways to dialogue. According to Carolyn Cooper, divine possession provides a validation and projection of memory that otherwise remains hidden or lost.[28] For Fola, this encounter creates a ceremonial attainment of self-assertion. Her journey comes full circle through the potentialities of the ceremony. For example, her encounter with the presence of her father, and the reconciliation with her mother, which the ritual affords, illuminates Lamming's allegorical use of the ritual as a journey which every Caribbean society needs to make in order to rediscover its grail of affirmation. After all, bodies are sentient and social, and the agency that is allowed has political ramifications.

Significantly, one of the first phases of Fola's journey begins after she returns home from the headiness of the *tonelle*, which manifests itself in ghost dreaming. The first memory that surfaces is that of her grandmother, described as that "old witch of a mother",[29] who frightens her with a dead rat. On the level of spirit, Fola has begun a process of self-healing – a psychosomatic therapy which involves the raising of dead ancestors trapped in the subconscious. The secret, healing aspect of the resurrected grandmother-witch is signalled by the fact that the hand which holds out the dead white rat to Fola is crippled. Rohlehr asserts that the grandmother is as much a Legba figure as the possessed woman in the *tonelle*, whose "crippled swoon" had catalysed Fola towards her own possession.[30] One can also creatively discern a connection between Fola's grandmother and Aunt Jane as they are presented as healers. If at the time of Fola's dreaming that her grandmother was an agent of malice, her function may also be defended as one that serves to strengthen Fola's resolve to sever ties with the psychic distortions of Charlot's Old World order and the hypocritical, social customs of Maraval Hills, both of which are the white rat's carcass.

The *tonelle* experience heralds a disconnection from the Old World of Charlot as well as the unformed 'new world' of her arriviste parents. The confrontation between Agnes and Fola at the State Ball is symbolically depicted in terms of the *tonelle* and possession metaphor. Attached to the mix of lure and giddy excitement at the ball is a burgeoning of Fola and other than Fola. The deliberate name-change signposts a clear redefinition and rebranding of the self and her mission. This is emphasized in her attitude of backchat aimed at Agnes, who is wearing one of her dresses. The rage at her mother is unconsciously the result of the sexual attention that the newly awakened daughter feels should be hers. Fola's rising current of anger and unconscious desire for equal acceptance is felt in the human and meteorological dimensions of the text as Lamming presents this scene against the backdrop of a rainstorm: "She would have liked the rain to free them from this solitude of threats and dead recriminations".[31] Since water is the medium used to release the spirits of the dead from their purgatory state, it seems fitting that the writer would pool together the otherworldly energies associated with the *tonelle*, in service of signposting the cleansing confession and admission of guilt that does not happen immediately between Fola and Agnes. Here, the novel is particularly focused on invoking energies to negotiate and cleanse the malignant effects of the larger imperialist and colonial project at hand.

The new phases of Fola's journey continue to be marked by active, self-propelled service to the peasantry. Her alter ego of "Fola and other than" is consistent with her quest for a space of revolution. It is a consequence of a deep encounter with spirit presences – an adventure she seems to enjoy and endure. At this point in the narrative, she emerges as a social worker with a sensitized mission to restore the facelessness of the women in the maternity ward who await their abortions. Her urge "to rescue each woman from the anonymity of her number – B532, A151, C36"[32] is not unlike Queenie's mission in *The Rainmaker's Mistake*, which is to undo the damage of a topsy-turvy postcolonial society through action and re-education. Fola's aim to "make her own history, give it life and motive which she herself might not understand"[33] sets the framework for positivity and well-being.

Her reformed disposition is also fulfilled in the implementation and planning of the drum revolt with Chiki, the rebel artist, and Gort, the steelpan drummer. It is a point that suggests another potential of her possession. When the government issues a prohibition on the playing of the steel drums, Gort rallies in overt protest with the steelband men from across the island to Freedom Square. The rallying rhythm of the drum is a blend of nascent steelband and *vodun* drum. It constitutes a fictional union of two deeply syncretized yet unique Caribbean musical forms. More specifically, Gort's steel drum is a syncretized archetype of the ancient, sacred congo drum, the music of which ruptures temporal and spatial boundaries. Paravisini-Gebert and Olmos expound on the derivations and sacred anatomy of the congo drum, which is used in Afro-Creole religious rituals and celebrations. The scholars elaborate on the manufacturing of the congo (drum) and mounting of the drum skin, which functions as a conduit of psychic energies. During ritual performances, the spirits would manifest themselves through the fabulous beats. Ritual music is harnessed as a type of performative intervention that confronts histories of racial violence. Congo magic was a method of feared divination and reliable enforcer of black resistance against European imperialism.[34] By this articulation, Gort is a shaman of sorts, whose music brings forth spirit beings who join the human community as collaborators in dismantling the status quo of San Cristobal and unleashing the creative potential of the folk underclass. The creative will of the people endures with the gospel of the drum when Gort keeps its future alive by teaching the rhythm-language to the children of San Cristobal. According to Lamming, the rhythm carries "the language which every nation needs if its promises and its *myths* are to become a fact".[35]

Soon, the government collapses and a Cambridge-educated Kofi James-Williams Baako, a native of San Cristobal, takes over as the new president until elections can be held. Lamming's political underpinnings cannot be missed, as the name of his fictional leader, James-Williams, would seem to indicate that the novelist believed in the promised leadership and socialist leanings of the Oxford-educated Eric Williams and C.L.R. James. The signifying governance that had been fuelled by hegemonic impulses is here being intentionally challenged and overturned. Although the novel ends in the ambiguity of purpose, partly due to the burning of the *tonelle*, Lamming affirms that justice and inward healing can be accessed via an awareness and willingness to journey beyond physical borders. Here then, an alternative episteme, rooted in a rich tradition of mythic creativity, becomes in effect the central character of the novel.

Lamming's poetic emphasis on spirit indeed presents a re-conceptualizing of the West Indian novel in epistemological and formal dimensions. Noting this aesthetic embrace, Rohlehr argues that since *Season* was published in "1960, year of *Palace of the Peacock*...Lamming was, via Fola, [echoing] Harris's aesthetic achievement. This could only mean that West Indian writing felt itself at the brink of new and strange explorations after the exciting realism of the fifties".[36] Brodber in *The Rainmaker's Mistake*, reflects an unbroken line of inquiry as she intensely evinces a unique style of literature on the multivalent functions of the Caribbean mythic imagination. In her allegory of colonialism and its violent traumatic outworkings, she explores such themes of social mayhem and the reconstruction of the shells of selves in the aftermath of empire.

These issues are explored through the specific narrative features of non-linear time; allegorical plot; the inclusion of a culturally hybrid community that abolishes authoritative representations of history; and a polyphonic perspective that blends different territories and voices (dead and alive), which collectively enable a recognition of her multicultural reach. Brodber also experiments with ideas of embodiment which combine temporalities, personalities, ancient philosophies, folk designs and occult arts to allow her cast of characters to excavate buried histories and multiple consciousnesses that are key factors in breathing life to their ontological chaos. She elaborates on this multi-purposed fictional principle:

> Logic would insist that a person or people who can access the heritage of their ancestors, who can integrate their ancestors' experience of reality into their lives to help them to interpret reality, [and can] attach the present to the memories of the past, would no longer be natally-alienated, no longer slave.[37]

In other words, Brodber moves towards a reparatory project to locate an alternative methodology that will procure a coherent and culturally relevant way of gathering data, while examining and applying it to the lived experience of African diasporic peoples. Her poetics signpost a re-engineering imperative to redraw portraits of the Caribbean self outside of the impeded images of historical and contemporary experiences.

The Rainmaker's Mistake spans the slavery and post-emancipation era and charts the struggles of the formerly enslaved to achieve physical and psychic restoration. The writer seems to ask, how can humans who are devalued as yams retrieve their ontological integrity as people of self-worth and shape their existence beyond the intention of the British architects of freedom? The text presents an interplay between Caribbean syncretic spiritual pathways and the uncomfortable, repressed history that the descendants of enslaved communities grapple with in seasons of imminent freedom. The quest for wholeness and meaning is at times arduous, frustrating and disturbing. Brodber is interrogating the process of re-invention for the subject who has long been deemed obtuse by the persistent strictures of racism and internalized self-hatred. Her text reads as a catalyst in the intergenerational transfer of ongoing inequities which condemn one to lifelong denigration. In the novel, she provides interventions in the creative imagination and subsequent strategies to assert an existence of one's own – one that is fully understood as human. Identity is depicted as an organic growth and appears as a physical, physiological, historical and relational process.

The yam motif is symbolic and is used to convey Mr Charlie's mercantilist view that reduces the enslaved African subject to a labour tool as well as excrement coming from his body. The protagonists and other members of the group are depicted as emotionally dead and are unable to make sense of what they recognize as the rhythm of plantation culture. The image of the dried-up and bruised coffee tree conveys this human deformity. Queenie notes:

> Coffee trees sometimes fade: they lose their leaves: they lose their gloss and glitter; they lose their dots of light green and red – sometimes yellow – of the berries decorating the glossy, glistening leaves. They become dried sticks, but as you encounter the dried sticks, images come to you of the once verdant coffee plant. You even smell its past of full beauty. Like the spirit of the coffee hangs round about its dried up self, it exists now for you in two dimensions: its actual self and its former self.[38]

Shalini Puri points out the inseparability of the natural, spiritual, mental and physiological violence in Brodber's oeuvre.[39] Puri contends that Brodber's concept of psychic bruising encapsulates the processes by which neo-imperial violence is violence to both spirit and body. This is embodied in Queenie's assertion that: "We began as yams. Mr. Charlie's seeds turned into yams, into us. [. . .]. There are several kinds of yam. They fall into two categories – soft yam and hard yam [. . .]. The inside of the soft yam tends to be white and hard, a variety of yellow, but all yams are dark-brown on the outside [. . .]. [O]ur necks were long and rubbery",[40] which dramatizes the psycho-social fragmentation that ensues.

The grotesque images used to convey the psychic bruising of the community evoke the nightmarish feel of Brodber's fictional plantation universe, which connects with contemporary realities of bonded labour, and other forms of defilement that inhibit organic human growth and development. These social issues weave in and out of this project. The yam's performance discloses qualitative profiles of modern Caribbean society and the world at large. It responds to the different ranges and profiles of social death. The crises of social injustice and inequities become pertinent since Mr Charlie's totalitarian regime has wiped away the group's spirit and their understanding of self. It is here that Brodber returns to ideas of the numinous to provide recourses to healing via syncretic pathways.

Marie Sairsingh, in her dissertation, *Africana Philosophy and the Metaphysics of the "After-Man": Examining Selected Texts by Erna Brodber*[41] explores how a study of Brodber's works might enable new ways for engaging Africana philosophy in broadening Caribbean literary representations of spirit. Sairsingh engages discursive traditions on race, Pan-Africanism and other strands of black radicalism towards a re-envisioning of black ontology. According to Sairsingh, Africana criticism is much more than a deconstructive reaction to white supremacy and racial enslavement. She emphasizes the importance of expanding alternative paradigms with the intent of addressing historical exploitation, reorienting the legitimacy of ancestral traditions and its role in peace movements. While fruitful in its broad cultural framework of Africana philosophy, the limitation with Sairsingh's project is that anti-colonial paradigms are recovered and framed within continental African – particularly Bantu and Yoruba – praxis. Sairsingh's analysis of Brodber's works is also largely framed within Wynter's concepts of the post-human or the after-man to construe understandings of black ontology.[42]

This is where my analysis differs. For while Sairsingh recognizes the potential for the application of Africana thought to existential explorations of Caribbean literature, she does not necessarily make a case for the similarity in "affect" or influence between the shape of *spirit narratives* and the tapestry of Caribbean histories from which they emerge. The islands themselves, as Rohlehr contends, "with its landscape, geography, history and folklife, is as much an ancestor as is [our] flesh and blood mother".[43] As such, my analysis is aligned with the critical insights of several *Caribbean* intellectuals for exploring the mutations and many inflections of spirit

A CARIBBEAN POETICS OF SPIRIT

as manifested through the landscape, social systems, customs, ruptures of community, nation, family and sexuality. In this way, the shape of the hurt of New World history is far more than a backward glance at the ancestral past. The task is to make Afro-continental traditions mingle with New World ideas for reading spirit, which evinces the processes for Caribbean transformation, not in the stasis of a comparative reference, but in the dynamic of the whole.

In the context of the group with natal alienation in the novel, Brodber alludes to Orlando Patterson's postulations on the correlation between historical and social trauma spawned from chattel slavery, which inspire her use of the yam motif. Patterson notes:

> The slave was a dominated thing, an animated instrument, a body with natural movements, but without its own reason, an existence entirely absorbed in another. The proprietor of this thing, the mover of this instrument, the soul and reason of this body, the source of this life, was the master. The master was everything for him, his father and his god . . . his authority and his duty.[44]

Mr Charlie is like Columbus, who, in his desperate quest for labour, introduced a forced industry of labour, bodily mutilation and murderous wastage of human life in the New World. He is progenitor and authoritarian, whose population responds with invariable obsession to his commands. He is also founder, civilizer, self-appointed diviner and manic imprisoner. The group's narrative becomes a species of submerged knowledge that only begins to de-mystify when he announces, "It is 1838 . . . you are free".[45]

What immediately follows is the wonder of Woodville's sinister laugh, which conjures a tornado that brooms out Mr Charlie and his house into the sky. One may posit that the tornado exposes the interior realities of Mr Charlie's plantation by blowing away the walls that concealed the group's existence. The tornado is a catalyst that resurrects the group's repressed memories in order to establish connections that will bring change. Brodber conveys the idea of a dynamic relationship between the corporeal and the incorporeal worlds by interweaving the natural elements with the community's spiritual awakening. This connection reveals a complex relationship between Caribbean people and their environment – one that cannot be reduced to a binary opposition. By imagining a shift in the community's reality through the eye of the storm, Brodber invokes the chief of the sky gods who is associated with thunder and rain.[46] By way of implication, the writer is pointing to the spiritual and cultural interpretations of natural phenomena that are ancestrally shuttled into the New World. The storm may also symbolize nature's campaign against the human violence and cultural alienation that were rampant on Mr Charlie's plantation. A bizarre time-lapse occurs and the plantation is broken into three continents.

Scholars such as Curdella Forbes,[47] Kelly Baker-Josephs[48] and Annie Paul[49] have observed that this is Brodber's innovative strategy of reassembling the African diaspora via the mysterious seaways. The separation is a literal tearing of the lithosphere that continues to diverge until it eventually breaks away from the continent, forming new seas and new islands. A transformation occurs:

> The water from the river overflowed the man-made banks and spilled over into the area where we stood, and so heavily did it spill, and so constantly did it flow that it made small rivers separating us – Woodville on one side, I-Sis and Sallywater on the other, and the rest of us in between. Three separate continents. Three sides of each washed by water, the fourth connected to our past.[50]

Adrift in time and space, Queenie and company are on the brink of a pre-empted future. Queenie, as self-imposed leader, seeks to gather information on the group's history. Meanwhile, Essex describes the group's rapid physical alterations as in the ways that the women begin to experience a menstrual flow. What unfolds is Brodber's epistemological undoing of the group's neutering and lobotomy surgical procedures that altered their minds and bodies, and which made them function as mechanical labour units.

The process of unravelling the community's newfound freedom also finds demonstration in Queenie's attempts to decode the myth regarding

A CARIBBEAN POETICS OF SPIRIT

how the plantation people came into existence. This is concretized in her journey across the seas. Her crossing can be read as a myth-making enterprise, with its fabulous connections between the mortal and immortal worlds based on parallels and analogies. Queenie is a female shaman or conjure woman who is fated to cross Legba's gateway, and whose actions fill the gaps that pertain to her kin's identity. Her piecing together and gathering of hidden narratives to weave a tapestry of collective experience, her empathy to alternate forms of knowing and charismatic leadership plausibly affirm her as a root-worker. Her departure from Cabarita in search of the scattered regions and lands embodies a need to connect the broken lines between the diaspora, and the awareness of a shared history.

Symbolically, she is traversing a violently inseminated womb in the sense that the Atlantic is the navel of capitalism, since Europe conceived the project of mercantilism by inseminating the Caribbean womb with the seed of Africa. She must navigate through the intense seas, mooring between spectacular currents, aquatic ecosystems and atmospheric circulations. That she is poised between sky and water further concretizes her liminal disposition between the world of the known and the unknown. The marvellous feel of this voyage is epitomized when her craft arrives on I-Sis's land, and she confesses, "I came through the largest gap into the semi-circle: that gap was a *gateway*".[51]

The period of discovery in the diaspora is one of intense socio-cultural and economic change. Not only does Queenie learn about I-Sis's and Sallywater's forced concubinage to Mr Charlie, which reveals a history of miscegenation, but she discovers and sends word to the others in Cabarita about the vast technological advancements on the other lands. In this sense, she is not a passive bystander to her own destiny – no longer written to be Mr Charlie's abject prisoner to prepositions – but is alive in her comprehension of global realities. The point is not to erase history but rather, to assert belonging and approximate realities through fiction. Interestingly, Queenie's axial journey is not unlike Fola's re-entry into the womb of her hidden past in the *tonelle*. The journeying motif leads to still points of self-recognition, affirmation and the claiming of a space within a meaningful sense of community. Brodber is, in this way, invested in locating possibilities that are to be found in the nebulous links across communities. Harris describes her mythic ways of reading reality and asserts, "My impression is that Erna Brodber brings into play an unusual myth-making talent in her . . . novels at a time when myth is denigrated or undervalued in favour of a realism divorced from the intuitive imagination".[52]

Her jigsaw narrative style in accessing layers of a resourceful past is further spatialized in Queenie's extracting of information from the sea corpse, Woodville. Queenie's intention "to know everything that he [Woodville] knew and to somehow know why he came back . . . why he felt he should find us"[53] reflects the continuous need to excavate folk memories. While Woodville may be read as an allegorical representation of an earlier ancestor, he can be perceived as a dark shaman controlling the game of his narrative. Woodville had placed his hopes on a "gentleman's agreement",[54] trusting that he and his brothers would live a prosperous life in the New World. Centuries passed and any hope of prosperity was betrayed. His collusion in Mr Charlie's plantation narrative complicates his role in the yam myth and his involvement in the community's psychic bruising. The title of the novel is revelatory as it unravels the rainmaker's misjudgement, which allowed him to be charmed into the vices of the colonial enterprise. His half-drowned corpse, with white waves swishing against his body, stands as a potent symbol and repository of a corrupted past, which he attempts to share cryptically.

Woodville as sea corpse is a significant trope to be considered. It seems that as his body becomes submerged into the sea following the uncanny storm, he becomes one with the formless flux of life and with the history of past lives imagined to have sunken into the Antillean seabed. His immersion into the ocean of spirits and of memory, and the threnody of water which accompanies his half-death is a testimony of a desperate quest of some kind, to tell the "half that has not been told".[55] The theme of submerged history is interwoven throughout this project. Woodville's frenzied drifting through a placid gulf may be understood as a quest for collective redress and reckoning. He is no longer the frustrated plantation womanizer, but a detached, vulnerable intelligentsia and shell of a man. It is no surprise that Queenie gropes towards unravelling his coded responses in her quest to recompose the community's fragmented history. While he cryptically discloses the truth surrounding the nicks on the children's necks, which account for their asexual existence, Queenie must continue to "work out" the other submerged aspects of their history.

In lieu of Woodville's disability, Queenie must recover knowledge from a coven of old spirit guides. The knowledge of London, who is the ancestral Abdul, is worthy of close attention. London's submerged persona can be read as a wraith-like presence. Like Woodville, he is sealed into silence even when cruelly violated. However, this psychic repression shatters after Queenie eases him into mental relaxation. Queenie is thus a diviner whose desperation for truth and competence in hypnotherapy touches London deep in the underwaters of himself and reveals to him his true spiritual situation. He is subsequently induced into a trance that catapults him into a distant realm and pool of ancestral memories. The nakedness and horror narrated by his incarnated self are truths that Queenie and the rest of the group urgently need to piece together the fragments of their lives. Through his extraterrestrial consciousness, Abdul narrates the tale of two brothers' innocent trust in their eldest brother, Tayeb (Woodville), who heard that "there was a new world a-coming".[56] Guided by the promise of prosperity, they took along their sister, I-Sis, and the curious company of the wise woman, Miss Mathilde. Abdul recounts Tayeb's matricide in his failed attempt to recover a matrilineal heritage by invoking an ancestral weather-modifying ritual of rainmaking. However, the bitter recognition of the loss of ancestral memory is compounded by their "mother's body [which] is swept away by the tide of Tayeb's rain".[57] The story provides a scenario where the characters, after enduring the hardships of crossing the Atlantic and undergoing the process of seasoning, suffer amnesia. As a result of his brave decision to tell his submerged truth, Abdul begins to assert his own authority, both as author of his own consciousness and as restorer of the group's history.

This transformation of historical rupture into an open-ended vision of possibility is also realized in the ancestral character of Miss Mathilde, who is a potion-maker, witch and herbalist – as evident in her store of ritual ink, feathers and quills. Her medicinal concoctions are useful in lengthening Woodville's lifespan. She is comparable to Aunt Jane in *Season of Adventure*, whose healing wisdom and divination practices are presented as life-giving. The items that surround the community in Cabarita, such as yard chickens, bones, feathers, dried coffee branches and shells, animate the scene with strong undertones of Afro-Caribbean spiritual and divination practices located in Santeria and Vodun.[58] By suffusing the space with Afro-Caribbean syncretic iconography, Brodber intimates that resistance to colonialism is intricately associated with ancestral cultural practices of the Caribbean.

In this sense, there is a relationship between the older members of Cabarita who are human hosts identified by their ancestral names, and those who are living in the present-day generation. Neil ten Kortenaar fittingly asserts that:

> [T]he link between spirit and host is mutually beneficial: the spirits gain bodies through which they can act in the present, and the living acquire memories that extend back centuries [. . .]. There is, however, nothing of ownership or [tyrannical] control in the ancestral spirit communion described by Brodber. Such communion constitutes not a [repressive] takeover of the self but rather an enhancement of the self.[59]

Through the technique of embodiment, Brodber enables her characters to find a register or phantom tongue to transmit the atrocity of their subservient existence and the ensuing healing mechanisms that follow. Name-changing becomes a sign of the shifting identities or mutations that occur throughout the text, as London is the ancestral Abdul, Woodville is Tayeb and Luke is Kofi. Interestingly, the dual process of naming and unnaming, whereby myth and history intersect, is also established in *Season of Adventure*, as in the case of Fola and "other than Fola". In both texts, multiple voices coalesce and serve as commentator and guide through the spiral labyrinth of the stories' fragments. In *The Rainmaker's Mistake*, the experiment with polyphony and the first-person plural works against a Western tradition that isolated the subject from the community. The multiplicity of voices participates as a speculative presence in each of the stories, which reflects a desire to formulate a coherent account of experiences previously erased in one way or another.

It is also important to recognize that there are other regions of knowledge-making in the text, as demonstrated in Luke's solitary, mythic tale of the Family Lace. Luke experiences severe withdrawal symptoms from the group following Mr Charlie's and Woodville's exodus. His narrative of the Lace People is a reflection of his concealed confusion, which materializes as social withdrawal and indifference from the impending horrors that surround him. His isolation is an effect of the demands of the cultural universe competing for prominence in his head and heart. He, like Fola, is caught up in the throes of self-definition during an era of imminent acquired nationhood. Filling in the gaps of what he does not know with desire, he creates his own myth of the islands and of existence. The inclusion of Luke's myth reflects Brodber's cross-cultural experiment that assembles a range of cultures, which are in dialogue with each other on the mutual ground that each has been a victim of the onslaught of colonialism, the aftermath of which is a groping towards self-authorization. That the narrative of the Lacettes interpolates sacred components of a pre-Columbian culture whose groups derived power from their connection with the cosmos signposts Brodber's profound engagement with New World mythologies.

The narrative of Papa Lace and Mama Lace, whose Lacettes danced around the moon and stars, heralds Brodber's cross-cultural and spiritual vision that assembles a range of different cultures. The allegory dovetails with the historical reality of some Central and South American cultures, for whom the myth of creation was an inherent outcome of spiritual activities within the elements. Among Orinoco and Amazon natives, creation began with the birth of the sun and the marriage of the primal sea to the primal sky. Scholars such as Brazilian anthropologist Eduardo Viveiros de Castro (*The Relative Native: Essays on Indigenous Conceptual Worlds*),[60] Alan Kolata ("In the Realm of the Four Quarters")[61] and John Bierhorst (*The Mythology of South America*),[62] give critical insights into the agential potentials of these Indigenous cultural systems. This syncretization of cultural myth for Brodber is arguably the very crux of communal cohesiveness, which is reflected most convincingly in the polyvocality and multiple authorship of Queenie's and the group's history.

Luke's invention of the uncannily tall, industrious people whose ability to live amongst the cosmos endows them with elemental powers is a species of those Cabarita inhabitants who engage with the world of work while awaiting Mr Charlie's return. While Luke's alternative story is an indication of an unhealthy coping mechanism to deflect the truth of one's origins, as Mr Charlie did before, it provides a creative entrance into Brodber's poetic excursions into Caribbean native mythology. This experimentation reflects her cross-cultural impulse to affirm native folk traditions as power sources to reprise stories of injustices. Just as bards, with their enigmatic arcs of fantastic beasts, explain the mysteries of life, novelists may evaluate the epiphanies of literature and the cultures from which they emerge, to disclose truths about survival, mortality, strength and perseverance. In choosing to synthesize a world that is foregrounded in existing Caribbean cosmologies, Brodber is signalling to the unforetold potentialities that can be realized in these indeterminate spaces.

The polyphonic nature of the text involves not only layers of plural voices, but cross-cultural dimensions and existences across time. The convergence of corporeal and spiritual realms encapsulates Harris's definition of the phantom limb that describes how the limb, which is severed from its body (Africa), finds redemption through psychic re-assemblage with ancient cosmologies.[63] Like Lamming in *Season of Adventure*, Brodber suggests that the psychic retrieval of one's history must involve both a deep descent into the shattered space of memory and a re-narrativization of the historical struggles of a people that remain buried in anonymity. It is an exercise that calls attention to Brodber's own textual procedures that encompass an inclusion of orality in her storytelling process. That Queenie and the others must ultimately arrive at regions of truth without a stable muse, divine guide or creator is a clear indication of Brodber's affirmation in the power and role of education.

Education, through the mechanical inventions of Essex and Luke, is presented as a potent weapon in the exorcism of social death and the shaping of individuality and consciousness. Queenie's continuous attempt to "work out" the questions of her community's history arguably exceeds that of Fola's in *Season* who, after she has functioned as the vessel of spirit, and inspired the seminal confrontation between the classes, now wonders what her mission will be in the mundane, non-festive, non-insurrectionary world of daily living. She considers becoming a teacher, but the novel ends in ambiguity before this can happen. Queenie, on the other hand, is anthropologist, historian and social worker, dedicated to the community and concerned about the socio-political and cultural redemption of her people, even before Abdul's hypnotic revelations reveal to her the true depths of the work she has undertaken. At the end of her mission, she resolves to lead a life of motherhood and commitment "to search and to reproduce and to cultivate, [a life] in the free".[64] Her assertion of freedom rejects any fixed definition; rather, she invokes a sense of liberation that is as perpetual as it is promising. The revisioning of the past affects a refashioning of the future, like a healer's hand. It is a style that is rooted in acts of flight and diligent spadework.

In *The Rainmaker's Mistake*, negotiation of the self, history and community takes the form of an almost literal reclaiming, renaming and re-assembling of one's lineage. In *Season of Adventure*, Lamming recognizes the mutual validity of ancestral modes of perception, spirituality, divination and healing. The myriad assemblage processes in both texts are exemplary of the inventions curated to counteract the ideological wars waged against a people who have been systemically depersonalized. These nebulous links illuminate a latent but potent dimension of a people that are relied upon to safeguard families and communities, and to signpost a viable modality that contests the impact of erasure and amnesia. The combined work of Lamming and Brodber suggests both the potential to imagine the unspoken 'text' of spirit presences and to underscore the gift of second sight. Both *Season of Adventure* and *The Rainmaker's Mistake* shine a light on how carefully and diligently one needs to proceed with the phases of nationhood and independence. Together, they provide a prophetic outline of the later contours of spirit that writers and cultural architects would attempt to expand and explain.

CHAPTER 5

Writing the Absent Presence
Locating Discourses of the Unspeakable

THE DEVASTATING IMPACT OF EMPIRE AND EUROPEAN CONQUEST on Indigenous populations, the African bodies exported to the New World, and the ravaged
environment of the Caribbean islands, as previously explored, have left
the region with "open veins".[1] This historical invasion continues to be
processed in the minds and lives of people in the contemporary world.
The burden to locate literary pathways to undo restrictive conceptual
structures, and oppressive constructions of value and non-value, has
steadily occupied the imagination of creative and cultural architects. In
a selection of stories from *The Haunted Tropics: Caribbean Ghost Stories*[2]
including, Maryse Condé's, "The Obeah Man, Obeahed",[3] Shani Mootoo's,
"The Bonnaire Silk Cotton Tree",[4] Gisèle Pineau's, "The Voyage of the
Centipede",[5] and Patricia Powell's novel, *The Fullness of Everything*,[6] the
resurgence of old traumatic wounds in the modern world reflects the
complex issue of threatened ontology. In these contemporary writings,
ghosts allude to the presence of that which has been unduly expelled or
dismissed. Although themselves immaterial, they gesture towards the
materiality of colonized and especially, abject bodies.

The task is to unearth the ways in which particular people groups
who bear the burden of standing in the shadows, existing as wraiths and
ghosts[7] in the peripheries of culture and society are framed, and respond
to the structural assault of neo-capitalist orders. They are partly borne out
of the deleterious consequences of being culturally tabooed, 'divergent'

A CARIBBEAN POETICS OF SPIRIT

and 'bastardized' in the absence of societal approval and recognition. From this position, these groups are discursively positioned to stake out their claim. They operate on a representational level as a stand-in for the abject. The concept of abjection is associated with the scholarship of Julia Kristeva. Working from an ideological orientation of redress to social woundedness, Kristeva defines the abject as "what disturbs identity, systems, order. [It is] what does not respect borders, positions, rules. The in-between, the ambiguous, the composite".[8] She argues that the process also involves ridding communities of the unwanted, and of re-making the nation with "clean and proper bodies".[9] This is a relevant perspective for understanding the ontological and social stature of the characters in the selected works. An evocative case in point is Shani Mootoo's short story, "The Bonnaire Silk Cotton Tree", where the author frames the Trinidadian wilderness as a space inhabited by marginalized and unwanted beings who do not properly dwell within the desirable boundaries inscribed by capitalist ideals. Mootoo's narrative identifies the concept of the abject with grotesqueness, as illustrated in the disruptive orders of jumbies, ghouls and zombies, who express their peripheral status as racialized other via the transgressive nature of their embodiment.

I would like to contend that the emphasis on the abject works to disturb rather than define identity. The very definition of the term invites alternative modes of symbolism and, therefore, leaves to the reader a task to uncover efforts at self-refashioning. This theoretical unknotting of Caribbean ontologies also calls upon the philosophies of Édouard Glissant, namely his "poetics of relation" (a paradigm that challenges totalitarian systems of meaning-making), and his demand for a "rhizome identity", which is a proliferation of poetic and cultural processes that combine to divulge cultural, social, political and ontological sovereignty.[10] As David Scott argues in, "The Re-Enchantment of Humanism: An Interview with Sylvia Wynter", the task to re-engineer the complexity of Caribbean ontology requires an epistemology "completely outside our present conception of what it is to be human . . . and therefore outside the ground of the orthodox body of knowledge which institutes and reproduces such conception".[11] Several interpenetrating meanings thus abound in the selected narratives. It is apt to note that while the framework of the abject is overtly evident in Mootoo's story, this chapter is largely concerned with the language and narrativization of domestic violence as well as histories of rape that freeze human agency in the modern world. Thus, the primary materials stage knowledge about what is unstable or what takes varying forms of concealment in myriad geographic and historical locations.

The complex nature of Caribbean being and identity also correlates with the processes of "reparative reading", as proposed by Eve Sedgwick. Sedgwick provides the method of reparative reading that is critical to debunking hegemonic ideological structures and which opens up scholarly inquiry to material that has long been concealed in oppressive and "paranoid" reading strategies.[12] From this perspective, the call to assert epistemological tools derived from a world of in-betweenity and flux includes the coalitions of alliances, domains and beings that are formed between the spaces of the material and immaterial worlds. This strategy imbibes liminality as a conceptual framework. In other words, life forms are imagined not in stable articulations of being, but rather in entanglements of differentiation, complications and dispersions. This idea of an eclectic sense of self situates life not in monolithic sameness or homogeneity, but in a dynamic change of diversity and difference. Reparative strategies articulate a grammar of futurity: not simply a world that does not exist, but one that could be constructed through attempts to repair historical harm and trauma. Addressing contemporary genocidal forms of warfare thus demands an ontological shift.

Pivotal to the argument are the notions of subalternism, oppression and exclusion, as advanced by Homi Bhabha, whose discursive decolonial agenda is negotiated vis-à-vis the concept of the interstice. Through the third space or interstice, Bhabha actively seeks to reconstruct a hybrid definition of identity that is devoid of polarities and binaries.[13] Reflecting confluences with Bhabha's postulations, is Gayatri Spivak who works through subaltern schemes of representation, by bringing to light diverse patterns of circulation, transition, movement, exile and displacement.[14] Yet, one wishes that these broad postcolonial concepts gave saliency to ideas of the spectral, through which another dimension of decolonial thought might ensue. In other words, that which haunts the peripheries is not always subject to conscious memory and processes, but erupts within the new mutations of empire.

The narratives of Shani Mootoo, Gisèle Pineau, Maryse Condé and Patricia Powell are sensitive to the legitimizing forces implicit in subtle acts of ontological retrieval that are mediated through fiction. Texts give saliency to processes of social remembering and may provide a repertoire of conceptual frameworks to enable more precision about those interstices and intervals where remembering happens. These narratives of encounters conceive a conceptual thinking that is equated with a language that recuperates marginalized areas of experience. In other words, the haunted texts evince a form – via a wounded language – that no longer takes comfort from Eurocentric traditions, but from the expanse of interior histories which move beyond the sameness of human cruelty. This movement is read as an image of the self without borders, and thus, each writer's purpose is aimed towards a social outcome that is different and new.

It must be acknowledged that the selected short stories from Munro's edited collection are situated within the linguistic heterogeneity of the Caribbean. While this work recognizes the historical, socio-political and cultural distinctions between the Anglophone and Francophone Caribbean, the close reading of the selected stories is positioned within an intra-Caribbean consciousness, which I adopt specifically for this chapter.[15] Moreover, while a comparative approach is subsequently deployed, an attentiveness to the particular historical developments in Caribbean migration during the 1950s and 1960s is necessary for a clearer understanding of Condé's and Pineau's politics of representation. In *Postcolonialism: An Historical Introduction*, Robert Young notes that during the 1950s and 1960s, London and Paris were important meeting points for researchers, journalists and artists from various parts of the French and British colonial empires.[16]

France had a significant influence on the imagination of Maryse Condé. It was a space where the seeds of political and intellectual activism germinated in her writing.[17] After spending nearly thirty-six years in the metropole, she returned to Guadeloupe in 1986. The circularity of crossing thresholds, boundaries and journeying trickles into her narrative. In spite of moving between geographical and literary traditions, Condé's evocations of more general human concerns circumvent the binary models of colonial thinking. In the short story "The Obeahman, Obeahed", for example, the representations of human isolation, cruelty and abuse that are attendant to Caribbean realities are scalable to societies worldwide. By examining the extent to which these thematic tropes have travelled across and beyond the Caribbean, and by exercising an undervalued comparative process, this chapter discloses the potentialities of trans-Caribbean connections. An interdisciplinary dialogue therefore leads to more nuanced and productive inquiries.

Gisèle Pineau is similarly influenced by France but is sure to emphasize her Guadeloupean roots.[18] Her own understanding and experience of living in self-imposed exile has influenced her thematic preoccupations with memory and displacement. In "The Voyage of the Centipede", the familiar themes of cultural uprooting, amnesia and the repression of childhood memories are reinforced. Not unlike Condé, there is a focus on the circularity of aggression against female characters and the recuperation of supernatural encounters to mobilize healing and change. The combination of fact and fiction within the Caribbean ghost genre allows both writers to interpolate collective memory with personal journeys towards the intent of recovering silenced stories and to disturb hegemonic discourse that ignores the plurality of the Caribbean universe.

Within the structure of the ghost narrative, characters are porous and settings are permeable. In some cases, absent presences are resident in human bodies. In positioning the concept of the 'absent present' as a point of focus for poetic praxis, this chapter argues that the writers indeed challenge prominent realist traditions through a critical engagement with the metaphors of zombification, death, corpses and necrophilia. The notion of the disembodied presence is used as an entry point to interrogate social categories, personal choice, unconventional modes of representation and eclectic identity. It also provides a social commentary

A CARIBBEAN POETICS OF SPIRIT

on the value of difference in the 'other' and their threatened ontology due to lack of justice and attention.

The short story, "The Bonnaire Silk Cotton Tree", problematizes the ideas of abandoned justice and cold murder cases. Mootoo spotlights the under-documentation of marginal lives from prominent discourse. Her thematic preoccupation with hybridity cannot be missed. This becomes apparent when restless duppy spirits thrust their rhizomes into the world of the living in an effort to assert a clarion call for community action and attention. Nandita, the protagonist, is seeking representations of herself as a valued member of a larger social project and recourse to artistic fame. In her comfortable coexistence with the jumbie and duppies in the wilderness, she is able to locate her social difference and feel at ease in her own skin. The forest becomes a space of freedom to express her personal, professional and social rejection without censure or recrimination. Mootoo focuses on the complexity of the solitary self by emphasizing her protagonist's journey into the northern hinterlands. However, the Beelzebub creature tricks Nandita into a deal with him; in exchange for her services, he will grant her artistic prosperity.

Significantly, Mootoo utilizes the thick woods and the arc of the imposing silk cotton as symbolic portals that exist between the spirit and material world to render the Caribbean as a hybrid space populated by otherworldly beings who search for avenues of redress and representation. The Port-of-Spain forest, which swirls with phantoms, is perceived as a character in its own right, as Nandita affectively connects with the shadows, darkness, impenetrability and eerie feel of the place. She finds parity with the phantoms, since, like the souls trapped in the landscape, she also needs to remake her ill-fated artistic reputation. The kinship of liminality affords an enabling environment to fashion creative acts that dispel each subject's social and cultural erasure. Here, the abject is depicted as the elusive presences who take on varying forms of camouflage.

Many types of interactions occur, such as the pouring of libation to gesture towards the jumbie. Evidently, the slippery slope of language is paramount to Mootoo's enterprise, and is like a second skin for Nandita, who needs to quickly adapt herself in the presence of her uncanny company. The tone of the jumbie is dark and he is a cunning fellow, skilled in the use of jest and double dialogue. Symbolically, Nandita's chameleon-like and witty dodging of his clever proposals invokes the notion of *douendom* in Caribbean mythology, here aligning her to the *bolom* or the unborn figure in Walcott's *Ti Jean and His Brothers*.[19] They slip into the darkness as they await rebirthing to constantly new and changing situations. The metaphor of the *douen,* as deduced in the subtext of Mootoo's narrative, illuminates a capacity for self-healing and metamorphosis through an encounter with incorporeal forces. Eventually, Nandita learns that the communities of spirits hidden at the arc of the tree are the uneasy souls of those persons who once had thriving, successful lives in the mortal world. For most of the narrative they maintain their invisibility and only materialize as muffled utterances. They are eventually revealed to be the victims of the most heinous unsolved crimes. Their elision from mainstream justice has turned them into fearsome monsters in Nandita's first gaze. She learns that they represent those deaths which have been mishandled, perverted and botched, and their disembodied states are signs of torture, oppression and domination.

Their incarnated forms resonate with specific Caribbean histories and mythologies about beings who shed their skin, which had been beaten by slave masters and had substances such as garlic and pepper applied to their open wounds in acts of torture. This colonial memory is, indeed, reframed in Mootoo's storyline where one recognizes the implicit historical constructions of racial crimes and the negligible representations of such cases. This is revealed when the jumbie makes known that the spirits comprise:

> every person who get killed on this island since the beginning of the first injustice all the way to the present-day wanton-ness – from native people in the days of the early Spaniards, to the slaves of the British, to the present-day victims of robberies[,] drug-related, greed-related and . . . power-related crimes . . . all of us on whom justice turn its back.[20]

In this detail, the author acknowledges the types of ghosts who return as instructive guides to Nandita. Moreover, and as the excerpt reveals,

A CARIBBEAN POETICS OF SPIRIT

discourse is a way to attempt to lay to rest the victims of historical atrocities, or if not properly 'bury', then discursively confront the terror that haunts the modern landscape. The competing nature for the quest for justice is complicated by the ways that race and class intersect. Emphasis is given to the importance of being valued enough to be documented and remembered with intentional praxis that places merit on intracommunal relationships. Unless due redress is provided, the spectres continue to loom in various transmutations. The plot provides the stimulus that violence is not only a cultural malady but is, in effect, a callous disregard for human life.

The recourse to social action and intervention finds expression in the form of Nandita's photography, as she complies with an invitation to use her photographs to capture and subsequently exhume these submerged traumatic narratives. The ghosts' desire for corporeality signposts an effort to move past their restless state. Thus, the jumbie makes clear his point that visibility of their wounds is essential to the task at hand. Nandita's images will thus function as a type of pall-bearing that carries the images of the injured bodies. Through a wide-ranging exhibition, the photographs become an interlocutor for the deceased, stopping – as a pallbearer would – to make reparations and accept atonement from debtors. For this reason, fiction fosters critical reflection on extant human realities from different angles. Such an inquiry not only responds to the social and political breakdown in the world, but returns scholarly attention to those who have been outlawed, dumped, disregarded and closeted. In Mootoo's story, the jumbies and duppies continuously remake themselves through the creative imagination and rituals of remembrance, therefore intending a radically different future that thrives on the demand for attention, action, recognition and reparation.

The duppies' plan of action also encompasses an effort to materialize themselves amidst the crowd of masqueraders on J'ouvert morning.[21] It is an example of the form of agency that extends beyond the limitations that duppies are presumed to have. Nandita's photos would ultimately throw light on this small gathering of presences who are seemingly immobilized by the trauma of their deaths. Her haunted pictures, manoeuvering in the wind through Port-of-Spain, carry the idea that atonement must be made. The images are of those whose "head bash in, eye poke out, neck break, vagina rip apart, heart blown out, brains hanging out, hand chop off, blood dripping, dripping fuh so".[22] It is congruous to cite Jeannie Thomas's perspective on the function of the ghost narrative which she observes, "help[s] us look more closely and analytically at [history], culture and the environment".[23] The small and large stories that Mootoo interrogates certainly reach into the national historical ruptures of Indigenous genocide and chattel slavery. Accordingly, when the meanings of the past and present comingle, the ability to forge a viable approach to living in the present emerges. Nandita's resolve to use her photographs to return justice to the elided presences suggests as much. The re-insertion of absent experiences into mainstream discourse thus confers upon the artist/writer manifold responsibilities: historian, social worker and editor, as she discursively makes space for the inclusion of these temporally displaced experiences. It reflects an attempt to fill the space left by critical inattention to multi-national crimes and violence.[24]

The thematic concerns of concealed violence, forced submission and the abuse of power are likewise delineated in Maryse Condé's "The Obeahman, Obeahed". A reading of this story engages the modalities of Caribbean spectralities and magical rites to offset the silencing of bodily injury and abuse. The narrative chronicles the enterprises of a necromancer, Carmélien, who occupies a permanently liminal position between the spirit and material worlds. He is a rejected lover who kidnaps the corpse of his love interest, Bella, and conspires to keep her as his slave. Like Western capitalist enterprises and the barbaric, colonial project in the Indies, Carmélien can hardly resist the temptation of Bella's mulatto body. This operation of coerced bodily transaction is approximate to what Christina Sharpe refers to as "monstrous intimacies", where violence and forced submissions are perceived as affection.[25] Through necromantic rites, the black female body is cast as a commodity that is fetishized through sexual objectification. What Condé's ghost story alludes to is the unrestrained obsession that the wizard feels for the young maiden. His spying on her through the everglades while she washes her garments on the rocks of

A CARIBBEAN POETICS OF SPIRIT

the river is a useful instantiation. His prowling beneath the golden apple trees to observe her evening tea rituals interlocks with Saidiya Hartman's formulations in *Scenes of Subjection*, in which she describes the complex effects and differences between looking and being looked at, and the deep violation and nightmare of having the body turned into a spectacle of secret pleasure and enjoyment.[26]

Under Carmélien's spell, Bella is caught in a permanent trance. She never speaks or makes eye contact, but only wanders around Carmélien's house of spooks. What is at stake here is the material integrity of the human that is resurrected to cook her incarcerator's favourite dishes of pork and green plantains, while keeping house and playing his mistress. The writer draws attention to stereotypical forms of coerced, domesticated and feminized living to spotlight the often-ignored value and worth of womenfolk in almost every community. The omniscient narrator recounts that:

> [B]y day, [Carmélien] could never get enough of her cooking [. . .]. At night, he could never get enough of her in person [. . .]. [S]he would lie down docilely, take off her clothes and let herself be taken whenever he felt the urge. The only thing he didn't manage to do was get her to keep her eyes open while they made love. She would squeeze her eyelids tight as soon as he came close [. . .]. [S]he did not utter a sound, [and] he had the feeling he was penetrating a corpse.[27]

Bella's closed eyes during intercourse – and the necromancer's inability to get her to keep them open – are especially significant as it speaks to the power of female interiority and the inability of the male incarcerator to control it even by supernatural means. There is also the chilling sense that Bella functions as a sex machine who exists only to please her captor. Condé is here presenting a complex intermingling of life and nonlife, which submits the point that one's nightmare (Bella's) can be another's fetish (Carmélien's). Bella's incarceration also plays out in the contemporary realities of sequestered wives or women who endure spousal abuse or arranged marriages.

Within this besieged existence, the imprisoned subject haunts the

WRITING THE ABSENT PRESENCE

domestic space. Such liminal statuses impose a state of unspeakability and a torpid temporality, which, according to Joan Dayan, resonate with ideas of "the phantasm or the zombie [who is] a soulless husk deprived of freedom; [in this manner, he/she] is the ultimate sign of loss and dispossession".[28] Bella's zombie disposition invites an interpretive dialectic with the criminal enterprise of human trafficking and modern-day sex markets set aside as flesh factories. This is supported by Bella's corpse-like disposition; she lumbers about with blank eyes and obeys the commands of the necromancer who sexually invades her on a whim. By undergirding her narrative within the larger structures of disempowerment, Condé exposes specific operations that have kept women zombified and closeted in almost every vernacular community.

The heightened imagery and vivid setting equally intensify the girl's subjugated state. This is emphasized in the images of confined/closed spaces, in particular, Carmélien's one-bedroom house, covered in thick cobwebs and crowded with potion cabinets. However, beyond the reach of the necromancer is the monitoring activities of Agénor Achillius, Bella's former love interest, who is aware that her body has been unceremoniously removed from its tomb. He convinces Ali Samba, a famous shaman, to investigate the unfolding mystery. Samba is versed in helping his clients circumvent personal obstacles via a number of highly specialized potions, for which he charges a high premium. It seems that Condé is highlighting the effectual reliance and appropriation of syncretized Caribbean science traditions to remedy social maladies, both in local and global cultural landscapes. This relationship between mystics and the community exemplifies the sometimes convoluted ways in which spiritual arts function in the Caribbean.[29] The mythos of the science worker as irrelevant is belied by the continuities that ritual and magic have accommodated, allowing African-Caribbean spiritual practices like Obeah and Vodun to align with modernity and be transformed as new technologies that are available in this era.

Samba's mysticism is well-positioned to offer enhanced power over Carmélien's sinister magic. Aided by the use of his counter-necromantic formulas, he adapts ceremonial resources as a part of the process to exorcise Carmélien's spell over Bella's soul and body. Her life will be remembered for the milepost when her spirit was finally set free on Ali Samba's day from the notorious enterprises of the Obeah man. In the end, her soul is able to journey and join her ancestors in the afterlife. The hope invested in ceremonial ritual is instructive and the belief in counter-spells seems to be a requisite for returning social and cosmic order. In this simple but evocative tale, Condé creates a frame for the urgent discussion on the myriad ways in which violence and foul play are negotiated in ghostly fictions. Her narrative throws light on how the suppressed female body might be explored through expressions of decay, death and necrophilia. The image of Bella's re-animated corpse certainly troubles the waters of culturally legalized systems such as child marriages, domestic servitude and debt labour, whose subjects live a half-life on the edges of life and death and whose identities are perpetually erased and bodies consistently abused.

This pervasiveness of bodily oppression in Caribbean communities is also resonant in Gisèle Pineau's narrative of mental illness and family hell. In "The Voyage of the Centipede", women's and children's stories of rape are quickly concealed in the interest of saving a dead patriarch's reputation. It is a revelation that is gradually revealed to the reader. The issues of incest and child rape are arguably some of the major pits of Caribbean communities, which can be read as a *kumbla*[30] space that stifles and cripples those from within. Indeed, these huge family secrets thwart spiritual and psychological maturation and consequently become an expression of subtle violence and festering wounds that are well concealed. While there is a demand for spiritual healing in Condé's and Mootoo's stories, mental disease brings a premature close to human life in Pineau's tale. The story draws from the protagonist's memories of child abuse and, subsequently, the present and past are mutually influential. Rather than confronting the horror of her continual rape by her father, Jessie opts for secluded living in France.

Jessie's fear of men and the islands of the Caribbean is pacified by fantastic and supernatural encounters in France. For this reason, the narrative traces the consequences of repressed violence as the writer charts the linkages between childhood maltreatment and a sense of continued victimization during adulthood. This pans out in the broad themes of self-delusion, physical unattractiveness, avoidance behaviour and acute nervous conditions. Hector's strong-arming telephone call to his sister (Jessie) to inform her of their father's death, and his self-aggrandizing bombast that seeks to cajole her into returning to the island for his funeral, catapult her into distant memories of molestation. Pineau is here pointing to a range of shame reactions, including shyness, withdrawal and debasement in its most extreme form. Moreover, the theme of sibling bullying, particularly the limitations placed upon Jessie by societal and domestic spaces, is an obvious source of her disengagement from the world.

Memory is used as a tunnel to show how the submerged past intrudes unwillingly, like a ghost, into the present. This is indicated by movements into streams of consciousness and interior monologue. As a consequence, the text is riddled with as much uncertainty as the representation itself. Rather than directly describe the horror which she feels at the thought of returning to Guadeloupe, Jessie drifts into breathlessness and unexplainable encounters with spectral beings. The evidence is to be found in her vacant expressions as she becomes enraptured

> by a somber series of fascinating and chilling thoughts [. . .]. This notorious domestic tyrant, this country crackpot, with a thick dick and skull [. . .]. She would very much have liked to know what he was thinking as he left this world [. . .]. Had he passed away without suffering, flickering out like a dying candle?[31]

The open-ended, fractured narrative style superimposes with her wraith-like existence, which is mediated by an intersection of temporal and spatial vectors. Notably, her telepathic abilities are feared by her siblings. In the family lore, "she was capable of seeing things invisible to ordinary mortals".[32] Pineau's story is subsequently arranged to construct a vision of a woman at odds with prescribed social roles. She is one who deviates from the 'natural order' and thus, her story becomes deformed and distorted, and her character is condemned as monstrous and strange. The

A CARIBBEAN POETICS OF SPIRIT

concept of the scapegoat may be asserted, which suggests the vilification of certain groups or people who are deemed as outcasts because of their deviant or awkward characteristics that deflect meaningful attention. Scapegoating reflects the stigmatizing of those with limited power and who are made to bear disproportionate responsibilities for social ills and anxieties.

Jessie stands as her own island, sealed off not by water, but by an invisible wound of unresolved sibling bullying and forms of societal ostracism. It comes as little surprise that for her, self-imposed exile is necessary and moving away from the place she knows as home seems appropriate. Her desire to avoid returning to Guadeloupe for her father's funeral may be due to the difficulty in developing healthy interventions to confront the root of her trauma and the crises that surround her secluded living. After her uneasy telephone conversation with Hector, she silently moves through her apartment and recalls a dream she had the night before, which begins with an invocation of the dark phases of her early childhood. In her nightmare she was:

> Walking without knowing where she was going, climbing over giant [dead tree] trunks with enormous branches. [She recalls that] years ago, [the] land was no doubt green with an impenetrable forest. Proud species and regal fauna. And while she wandered in her dream, she instinctively realized that her surroundings represented her life: a chaos, a dying world and a life of solitude. Then she stumbled and clung to the branches. She had to sit down on a dismembered, fallen tree whose half-burned trunk seemed to have survived a fire. She began stroking it, mechanically, brushing the dry, pockmarked bark with her fingertips. It looked like the emaciated torso of a tall black man with black polished nipples like lead marbles. A very old dead black man. Her father, Auguste, dead. She had already found herself in this position. She was about twelve. He had called her. She had answered, "Yes, Papa!" He was lying down on his bed. Naked. Quite naked. With eyes closed he asked her to come closer and sit on the edge of the bed. He told her to place her hand. There.[33]

Here, she recalls encounters with a hypersexualized, seductive parent who has done irreparable damage to his daughters. Rather than use the perversely erotic image of Jessie lying naked in bed with her father, Pineau confronts the reader with ulcerated, penile images and depictions of dismemberment as evident in the "half-burned" and "pockmarked" tree trunk.[34] With the help of this parallelism, the allusion to the green landscape echoes Jessie's longing for an innocent childhood. The dismemberment images and devastation of virgin territory characterize the cringing reality of child rape that is operational in the story. The painful memories intrude unwelcomingly into Jessie's present reality. Recognized through its fleeting presence, the patriarch's spectre emerges in his daughter's dreams and leaves a horrifying impression, not only within the actual setting of the narrative, but within her body and mind, as evident in her degenerating mental health.

Since, for Jessie, explicit expression of her pain is avoided, language is moulded through implication and euphemism to communicate power struggles and secret abuse. The violence is subtly coated in ordinary language and the nightmare reveals how emotional terror is tied to the embodiment of subjectivity. As a result, strange places collide, time periods intersect, and images of silent suffering in the material world converge. Jessie's marginal existence in the modern world illuminates the point that a repressed history of adolescent abuse does not culminate in a healthy sense of womanhood, but rather in a nervous meltdown. Language communicates her threatened ontology and the conditions that are responsible for her erratic outbursts. A multiplicity of realms, domains and perspectives pervade the narrative and is necessary to piece together the fragments of Jessie's consciousness. Indeed, she suffers from severe difficulty in lucidly narrating past events, as evident in the numerous gaps and splices that disrupt the narrative cohesion and the reader's ability to follow her line of thought. It demonstrates the ways in which Pineau's work functions to unsettle time by straying away from linear descriptions of maturation. This fluid narrative style is also revealed in the lack of punctuation markers to pin down the source of reporting, which reflects an impulse to quell Jessie's disturbed social and psychological landscape, where she is trapped in a world of shadowy figures that underpin her demented demeanour. The absence of consistent grammatical control

A CARIBBEAN POETICS OF SPIRIT

draws attention to what is textually present (that is, the appearance of disembodied beings), but also to what is not: Jessie's agency and empowerment to cope with and heal from a traumatic past.

Her visions of dead people reflect her nervous breakdown. This is illustrated in the appearance of Annette, whose frequent intrusion into the narrative adds to its fluid spatio-temporality. In the family's history, she was the youngest of the siblings. When their mother, Ginette, dies, Annette takes to a life of drugs and poverty. Described as a "meek soul",[35] Annette endured sixteen years of teenage horror, as divulged in the subtext of sexual abuse. In Jessie's imagination, her sister had returned to Paris to "forge ahead and start off again on the right track", after wrestling with addiction and starvation.[36] However, the young girl is but a figment of Jessie's imagination. She is deceased, and is but a spectral presence, as hinted by the drop in temperature in the apartment. In fact, there is the revelatory point that she died fifteen years prior to Hector's telephone call, which opens the narrative. Her disembodied state is disclosed in the following passage:

> Once in Paris, Annette still needed to rest. She did as little as possible. She had come back from the brink. She had gone through worse than darkness. She spent three months *hanging* around the apartment, more often lying on the sofa watching television rather than helping Jessie in the kitchen. And then she began to pay visits to Hector in his far-off suburb. She returned from her trips full of stories that she *whispered* to Jessie in the evening [. . .]. They [would have] dinner as usual in the kitchen face to face [. . .]. Annette would leave her plate *untouched*. [. . .]. Later on evenings, Jessie would slip between the sheets; she felt her sister's *presence*. [. . .]. Little Annette was *shivering*. The bed was *ice cold*. Jessie curled up and wrapped herself around Annette's body.[37]

Like the infectious fog and the creeping coldness that pervade her apartment, so, too, does Jessie sink into a dangerously fragile and deeply isolated state. There is the overwhelming sense of looming harm and threat to life from vivid memories of loss and shame, which cause revulsion.

Spectres that materialize in the imagination are a way of underscoring a most painful memory trapped within the psyche, struggling to be heard. One may perceive Annette as both an actual (deceased) sister and a symbol of Jessie's abused inner child in need of reparenting. It is in this sense that Jessie's embrace of her sister's ghost constitutes the mimetic dynamics of repressed traumas. One's denial or non-disclosure of abuse deters healthy recovery. Annette's spectre also stands as an obvious dimension of Jessie's incapacity to come to terms with the young girl's death. It signals the protagonist's inability to perceive the memory of her sister as a vestigial residue of a terrible past. In effect, Pineau's use of multiple consciousness and domains demonstrate the ways in which repressed pain erupts and intrudes into everyday life. The final gesture of institutionalization shatters the promise of futurity and healthy recovery, which leaves Jessie as a perpetually muted and disempowered character.

Everything is blotted out when she is drugged and nudged along by her siblings onto an aircraft bound for Guadeloupe. Like salt added to a gaping wound, Jessie is bullied by her brothers and sisters, who seek to supplant the darkness of their debased sister to save the family from shame. This moment sheds light on the anxieties that breed oppressive relationships in the framework of the family. Much to her horror, Jessie awakens to the overjoyed faces of women with madras head-ties, zouk dancers and happy Creole girls. The contempt that she feels during these festive gatherings reveals a subtext of marginalization, ostracism and public humiliation. She begins to experience feelings of embarrassment as it is a reality she is far removed from. The situation constructs a threatening pantomime of taking one hostage against one's will.

At the funeral ceremony, she becomes enthralled by a centipede and its hundred legs dancing between the folds of the mauve satin sheets that cradled the corpse of her father. The significance of the story's title cannot be missed as the symbol of the centipede, with its many legs, illustrates what Jessie is unable to recognize in her own complex identity and unarticulated pain. The metaphor of the venomous insect is relevant as it gives form to the weight of Jessie's being, and grim reality that she is stuck within her own skin because of unarticulated hurt and shame. The narrative demonstrates a simultaneous imperative to flee home and an incapacity to leave it behind. There is thus a creeping violence at the

A CARIBBEAN POETICS OF SPIRIT

heart of this tale, as the self becomes a hostage to unarticulated pain, and not unlike the anatomy of the centipede, is detained or held by the presences of many other forces that amplify each other. The funeral is subsequently a peripheral focus of the narrative as it looms in Jessie's thoughts right from the start to the end of the story. Not long after, she is interred in an asylum on the island in a final note of self-defeat.

While a self-destructive silence lingers in the end, which forecloses possibilities of mobility and healing, Pineau offers a commentary on the lethal consequences of unexpressed griefs and generational hurt, which hang like a millstone around the protagonist's neck and draws from her any possibility of freedom and justice. Jessie ultimately appears as a mere shadow and a psychological prop chased by the ignored spectres of her past. Pineau's creative project commits to quarrying the contours of the human psyche. It is a narrative innovation that destabilizes normative or homogenous assumptions about violence, abuse and trauma.

A grounded, experiential humanism is proposed as a methodology to dismantle conventional binaries of race, gender and class, which recurrently impede alternative ways of reading human life and social maladies. What begins to resonate is a multiplicity of perceptions of peoples and groups affected by the myriad of violence in Caribbean societies, the diaspora, and the world at large. The three stories decode a sphere of humanity that continues to wrestle for ontological validation and healing, and point to the urgent need to unravel alternative therapeutic pathways to cope with the dehumanizing effects of exploitations, private griefs and cruelties. As Karla Holloway avers, this is the substance of fiction; for it is through the text that the reader is encouraged to pass into new understandings.[38]

Patricia Powell's novel, *The Fullness of Everything*, is another compelling narrative of familial misunderstandings, ritualized modes of masculinity, the fear of social uselessness, unacceptance, child abuse and paedophilia. At the heart of these issues are two brothers, Winston and Septimus, and their philandering father, Samuel Rowe. Not unlike Carmélien's proclivities in Condé's short story, Rowe views women as objects of sexual plunder. During one night of carnal pleasure, he rapes eleven-year-old Beverly, which results in the birth of his love-child, Rosa. This becomes explicit through memories and recollections since the novel opens with him disabled and silenced by a stroke. The plot develops into a moving tale of emotional impasses where generations build layers of defences against each other. This seepage is the real cause of the breakdown in human relationships. Yet, little critical attention is given to the novel's representations of the characters' psychic pain and the spiritual traditions employed as healing remedies, which yield new insights into survival and atonement.

The protagonist and eldest son of Rowe and Nora is Winston, who suppresses traumatic memories of childhood abuse, which manifests itself in masqueraded codes of masculinity and curtailment of self. Consequently, he slips into a shadowy mode of existence in the American metropole. The novel concentrates on numerous escape strategies to which the characters resort in their attempts to ignore their personal hurts and to lead ordinary lives. The first section of the text examines the ways in which childhood rejection filters into adult, existential damage. Powell seems to revise the surging shifts in Caribbean literary writing, specifically in the Jamaican cultural imaginations of masculinity and the body of growing literature that concerns itself with issues of alterity and homophobia.[39] Instead of being the revered firstborn of Mr Rowe, Winston was abhorred for his unholy, "sissy walk" and girlish screams as a teenager.[40] He was often beaten by his father for his gawky body and non-normative tendencies, which suggests that it was a matter of deep dishonour to display subtle homosexual tendencies.[41] Like the other fictions examined in this chapter, Powell sheds light on the complex ways in which human identity is curtailed.

In this text, the imposition of corporal punishment engages shame as a tactic to discipline deviant sexual expression. Winston is made aware of the cultural and personal imperatives to define himself along the lines of masculinity, but grapples with an unwillingness to surrender to the codes of heteronormativity at this stage in his life. Powell's narrative recalls the leveraging of cultural hegemonic traditions over that which is deemed deviant. Furthermore, the story echoes a history of colonial,

A CARIBBEAN POETICS OF SPIRIT

state-supported expectations of hyper-masculinity in men in the former Caribbean colonies. This inheritance is, however, challenged by Powell through her explorations of homoerotic discourses.[42] In one dimension, the curbing of Winston's brush with homoerotic desires by his father reintroduces British colonial taboos that reinforce polarities of race, gender and sexual orientation. Ritualized modes of masculinity are therefore read as a type of re-colonizing and regulation of male adolescent adventurism. It is also plausible that Rowe's trifling lifestyle leaves his first-born son starving for a father's love, which is pivotal to creating a solid, inner self that craves love, attention and acceptance.

The opportunity to be himself is provided in the unmonitored space of the American metropole, where Winston flees to pursue a career in academia. He does not return to the island for twenty-five years. However, the unaddressed hurts of the past inhibit his ability to negotiate and cultivate intimacy, as revealed in his struggle to form intimate relationships. We are told: "he had been no good at love, and had no idea how to hold on to a woman"[43] and, "at the centre, everything was a frozen sea".[44] Winston's crisis draws the reader into a social connection with him; we see this character as he is – contradictory and complicated, and deeply tied to a most painful history. Bachelorhood is presented as a quasi-closet space, since it provides him with a façade of accepted standards of social norms that veil his sordid family. In this sense, the novel addresses the opacity of identity, which is regulated around histories of secret matters of the heart.

Immigration is presented as a self-saving act in the wake of a patriarchal and heterosexist island order. The choice to spatially distance one's self in an attempt to cope with the larger issues of unacceptance and discrimination is illuminated. It is an articulation of the ideological liberalism of northern metropolitan cities in allowing greater ontological freedom. Yet, transnational journeys that accommodate reinventions of identity remain in a strained state of relation, as those living in self-imposed exile return to the islands for atonement and even comfort in seasons of distress. It is interesting that Powell's narrative opens with Winston's recurring dream of his father's corpse, which is bloated and floating in the "emerald current on the May Pen towards him".[45] The dream world prompts an interior dialogue with the suppressed ghosts of his childhood and, in one sense, portends what is to occur in the coming days. The nightmare precipitates his receipt of an urgent, sealed telegram from Kingston that carries the message of his father's impending death. Subsequently, he resolves to return to Jamaica.

The journey from Kingston's airport to his childhood home in Septimus's black hearse is symbolic of Winston's turbulent trajectories, including his search for ontological wholeness in universal cosmologies and deities, which have helped him to heal, in part, from a childhood of rejection and adult insecurity. Upon returning home, he is reacquainted with all the reasons as to why he had first left and never looked back: the ultra-masculinity of men and the violence against women passing as power, which he had so abhorred. Powell also gives focus to the deep turmoil of the other male characters who struggle with sexual deviance. This is evident in Septimus's addiction to prostitution and preoccupation with the dead. He is the younger of the two brothers and Rowe's favourite son. However, he is haunted by his family's sinister history which sickens him to the point of becoming a mortician. He attends mortuary school in Jamaica and finds fulfilment in comforting the grieving. His occupation suits him, as he is described as an emotionless character and resembles the corpses to which he attends. The narrator notes, "perhaps he had become like them, deadened [. . .]. He doesn't know how to nourish himself . . . and the dead cannot nourish him".[46] The world of the dead becomes a symbolic space to scrutinize and dissect the self that is severed from any meaningful and recognizable emotional register.

Septimus is equally haunted by hallucinations of his wife's affair with Robbie Chen. As a result, he channels his pent-up carnal urges and anger in his sexual plunder of women. But his risky, unchecked appetite for intercourse results in his deteriorating health as he wrestles with gonorrhoea. At the root of his wounded spirit is a deep desire for meaningful companionship. In one aspect, he is an abandoned sibling, whose brother deserts him on the island to pursue a life of social freedom elsewhere. There is also the absence of his twin sister, Althea, who died

A CARIBBEAN POETICS OF SPIRIT

in a gruesome car accident, and who visits him in dreams. We are told: "Since Winston's departure, he [Septimus] had been falling apart".[47] His bereavement is complicated by factors of alienation, undisclosed family secrets, sexual outbursts and the secrets that entomb him. Eventually, sex loses its nectar and he is left with the task of articulating the deep issues that haunt him. This is illuminated when we are told that, "he [Septimus] does not have words to describe anything. He is up to his chin now with anguish. Soon the damn thing will drown him".[48] His half-life becomes discernible in his strained relationship with his son, Hanif.

One way of understanding this character's buried hurts is to consider the concept of the cryptophore, as delineated by Nicolas Abraham and Maria Torok. The cryptophore is a subject who displays "apathy, insensitivity and unresponsiveness" and ultimately "absence from one's own life".[49] This dynamic of encryption and secrecy is useful in unpacking the idea of incomplete mourning. The crypt is one who cannot express their best guarded secrets, thus becoming a 'living' tomb. By censuring one's pain, one's psyche is numbed or anaesthetized. Since the grief is sealed off, a parasitic relationship between these secrets and the temptation to avoid their acknowledgement ensues. The weight of this denial is likened to a presence that haunts and unhinges the mind of the living. Septimus's secrets erupt ontologically. Powell encrypts this character with layers of ruination and hurt: there is the secret of Samuel Rowe's infidelity and Rosa's birth, the cryptic dream that Septimus experiences concerning his wife's infidelity, and the secrets surrounding his brother's sexuality and love life. Indeed, the patterns emphasize a psychoanalytic turn in the literature. Freud likened the psyche to Rome, with its layers of ruins, and there is a similarly buried modality in Powell's text at the level of context and characterization. Septimus's crumbling ontology is overtaken by the forces of familial pain and betrayal. He is surrounded by the ruins of his father, the premature death of his twin sister, and Winston's abandonment – all of which are signified in his resolve to become a mortician and live as a ghost in the shadows. Nevertheless, buried and forgotten hurts still leave referents that mark their occurrence. Powell's encryption plays out in Septimus's burial of his hurts, and, as Torok and Abraham assert, in the need to psychically swallow the loss. What Septimus swallows is the sinister secrets that lurk within his lineage. The reason he resorts to tending to the dead – a quite literal crypt – is to conceal his unresponsiveness to a life of profound pain and insecurity that he also bears within himself. By building in these layers of contingencies, Powell is demonstrating a unique mode of cryptophoric studies. It comes as no surprise that the characters grapple with what they feel to be mysterious and malevolent forces. Torok and Abraham observe that the possibility of healing may be derived through expressive therapy and hypnosis. When this occurs, the haunted past loses its hold and is no longer phantasmal, but enables reconciliation and peace. In *Fullness*, Powell affords transformative interventions through the small but significant moments of confession and human touch.

For Septimus, relief comes in the simple act of acknowledging his fatherly responsibilities. This is illumined when he allows himself to be soothed by his son's laughter during a game of football: "The boy falls first, and he falls in a tumble over the boy, the pile of limbs struggling still for the ball, the laughter, his face washed with sweat, his heart hammering, gasping for air".[50] Powell is here illuminating the miraculous function of sound/the sonic (Hanif's laughter), which distracts Septimus from his tormenting sensations. In a peaceful setting beneath the mauve blossoms, Septimus feels the tears burst into his eyes and he confesses, "I'm not as fit,"[51] while running his fingers through his son's wiry hair. The unbridled love which he displays to his son was all that "the boy ha[d] waited and waited his whole life for".[52] Septimus's statement stands as a loaded assertion, with innuendoes of his past failures as a parent. Here, his parental guilt seems to slowly melt away in the possibilities of atonement and meaningful dialogue. The scope of confession provides the purgative release of pent-up emotions. It is a moment that facilitates processes of healing and renewal between father and son.

Restoration is also sustained through the ritualistic pathways of the supernatural. The spiritual world, with its alternative cures, dovetails with the potentialities of confessionary moments. This is presented in the actions of Marie-Jose, whose character is shrouded in magic and mystery.

A CARIBBEAN POETICS OF SPIRIT

Her methods of coning bring relief to Winston in his most anguished states. While on their visit to Jamaica, she would administer ointments to his body. Her craft has deep resonances with Wiccan spirituality and also recalls the nurturing ways of ancestral magic and cure in Caribbean communities. She explains to him that, "the coning was basically prayer [. . .] between you, your higher self, and an entire council of beings, guardians [and] angels. When the council arrived, [he felt] a sensation like heat chiselling away his icy heart and filling his limbs slowly as he started to sob".[53] This physical encounter emphasizes the importance of unconventional attempts and approaches to healing opportunities, through which Winston is able to release suppressed contempt (towards his family) and rage. Powell is here affirming an association between the sensual and the divine.

A return to the body as a primary site for healing psychic traumatic wounds is one of the first steps in a series of ritual movements. On this point, touch is used to refer to the closeness or co-mingling with the sacred and the carnal. Laura Marks's formulation of the haptic as a smooth space that must be moved through by constant and compassionate contact is useful in thinking through the affective spaces that Marie-Jose invents via her magical rituals.[54] Additionally, sexual intercourse is presented as an act of divine healing for Winston. During a night of serenity, Winston attempts to modify his introverted tendencies by making uncommon love to Marie-Jose.[55] In this detail, the body is presented as a sacred vessel, and as skin touches skin, a sustained psychosomatic healing occurs. In those moments of ecstasy, he hums songs which "he's forgotten: 'What a Mighty Fortress is Our Lord'; 'What a Friend We Have in Jesus'; 'All Things Bright and Beautiful'".[56] Music, church hymns and childhood choir melodies are cultural tools that assist in Winston's quest for and return to psychic and spiritual wholeness.

An exploration of the reach of the divine through the sensual indicates the power of merging realms and universes in Powell's evocative fiction. The story demonstrates that spirituality is at once a fully human affair as it is a mystical one. During this night of heightened pleasure, he is visited by the spirit of his recently deceased father in a dream. Not unlike

WRITING THE ABSENT PRESENCE

Pineau's narrative, the force of the dead patriarch exerts influence on the living. However, Powell's novel concludes with a sense of upliftment as Rowe's ghostly presence returns to seek Winston's forgiveness. Several ideas emerge at this point, one of which evokes the sense that the visit from the dead patriarch reflects anxieties about unfinished business and the cultural value of forgiveness. Furthermore, it highlights the functionality of Marie-Jose's magic, which restores a personal equilibrium, as revealed in the brief father-son exchange.

Borrowing from the Caribbean folkways of caring and nurturing, Marie-Jose's tantric healing methods also work through the spirit presence of Althea, Winston's sister. She is one of the spirit beings that appear through Marie-Jose's incantatory rituals, and communes daily with Winston upon his return to Jamaica. Althea, like the trickster spider myth, Anansi, is a slider between realms and a timeless witness to the family's hurts and grievances. She is perhaps the only witness to the molestation of Beverly Charles by Rowe. Her spirit hovers over the family's house and offers oracular wisdom to Winston, which brings him much comfort in moments of anguish. To this extent, boundaries between the incorporeal and physical worlds are relaxed throughout the narrative. It is a point that considers how the characters exist in matter, energy and simultaneous environments.

The characters also achieve healing through creativity. This is disclosed in the figure of Miss Nora, the matriarch, who suffers silent abuse and maltreatment from an unfaithful husband. While her sons take to confession and methods of sacred intimacy to heal their secret hurts, she uses the creative process of dress-making as a means to manage her pain. On one occasion, "[w]hen her intense emotions flung her into depression, she hurled herself into the sewing room at the back of the house and did not emerge again until the white, lace-wedding frock that had two yards of train running behind it was complete".[57] The manipulation of fabric to make quaint garments allows her to release her suppressed pains and resentment. The power to invent and embroider enables her to become a person of authority, autonomy and productivity. Regardless of her husband's cruelties, she channels her energies into fabricating

133

A CARIBBEAN POETICS OF SPIRIT

beautiful tapestries. Powell suggests that creative work may carry the touch of the divine, as it bears the potential to soothe the ravaged and grieved psyche. Art, in this sense, appeases and satisfies both carnal and spiritual voids. Powell is thus insisting on the imperative of minor subjectivities (wives, children, the sick and mentally distressed) and how the deeper structures of power seep into individual lives.

While Mootoo, Condé, Pineau and Powell have illuminated the ways in which the body has been misused and abused,each writer has uniquely and comparatively presented in-between spaces of healing and empowerment where human beings may collaborate with manifestations of the divine and the spirit world, to unsilence shame and curate restorative pathways to healing. The inclusion of the incorporeal realm in these texts demonstrates the need to create a culture of care where polar opposites (carnal/divine, material/immaterial) are brought into balance. It constitutes a dimension through which the transcending of troublesome societal, cultural, familial and human differences is achieved.

Regarding the need for innovative pedagogies and conceptual directions, bell hooks observes, "Keeping an open mind is an essential requirement of critical thinking. I often talk about radical openness because it becomes clear to me, after years in academic settings, that it was far too easy to become attached to and protective of one's viewpoint, and to rule out the other perspectives".[58] By engaging the concept of the absent presence, one is able to let go of attachments to stable categories and reach out towards new possibilities. As these four stories have demonstrated, this may be achieved through a reliance on theories of intersections and hybridity. Indeed, these concerns can be broadened to current cultural anomalies, where hierarchies are still very much alive, growing in strength and manifesting with covert pride. This is witnessed, for example, through governments' attempt to control women's reproductive rights, or in the number of trans or coloured people who are disproportionately murdered each year. To this extent, a narrative about spectral presences provides the space to exteriorize internal woundedness and envision redemptive potentials found in moments of ecstasy and compassion.

The writers have clearly demonstrated that characters may unburden themselves in moments of confession and acts of spiritual practices, which can be fruitfully mined as signposts for exorcizing the ghosts of the past that intrude into the present, unannounced. Breaking the silence becomes a powerful but under-utilized strategy that permits psychic restoration. Accordingly, healing strategies may be found in a simple shift of perspective. The narratives have included most importantly, an awareness of the other, and the subsequent ability to learn through the vastness of human experience. They, therefore, leave the reader with the question: What are the seismic shifts in the Caribbean imagination that facilitate other alternative modes of seeing? To this question, Walcott's *Omeros* and Harris's "Arawak Horizon" examined in the subsequent chapter, provide some responses.

CHAPTER 6

Tracking Signposts to a Caribbean Poetics of Spirit in Wilson Harris's "Arawak Horizon" and Derek Walcott's *Omeros*

THIS CHAPTER EXAMINES THE CREATIVE RELATIONSHIP BETWEEN Wilson Harris and Derek Walcott, whose fictions reflect a submerged reality which transmits itself to the artist. More specifically, the texts illustrate that the aesthetic markers of liminality, the deeply felt ideology that the land is a physical and psychic sanctuary, and a nexus of ancestral power relations provide an alternative approach to envision new ways to be human, amidst accelerating forms of neo-capitalism and dispossession in modern times. Both Walcott and Harris have suggested that a seismic shift in the Caribbean imagination is necessary for conceiving alternative modes of being that are vigorous enough to withstand the impacts of new hegemonies that seek to pauperize and undermine developing nations and its people. In both "Arawak Horizon" and *Omeros,* a coordination between humanity/ personalities and spirit is achieved. In this way, humanity takes unto itself divinity.

I begin with an interrogation of the deep impact that the Guyanese topography had on Harris's psyche, which has its roots in his early vocation as a government land surveyor in the 1940s and 1950s. Harris turns to the landscape as a concentrated conduit of memory, which is so powerful that it compels one to listen in to its eruptive power. Inspired by the faces that he perceived in the ravines, rapids of rivers, tides, waterfalls and rocks, Harris developed a literary methodology that distinguishes itself from linear Eurocentric structures. In one aspect, he becomes aware of a reality that cannot be measured except through the intuitive imagination. In "Impressions After Seven Years", he expounds on "the need for an exploratory tradition that will seek to relate disparate bodies [and domains], not only in a particular society such as this [Guyana], but throughout a world civilization that is fast being conditioned by rigid emplacements and tragic confrontation."[1] He is thus positing a turn to an experimental narrative space that may engage a cross-cultural view of Caribbean cosmologies. It is also significant that Walcott, in several of his works – including *Another Life, The Prodigal,* "The Spoiler's Return", "The Season of Phantasmal Peace", "The Schooner Flight",[2] and *Omeros* – has equally relied on a cosmo-spiritual sensibility to probe questions of cultural politics and Caribbean identity. Through these narrative explorations, each writer embarks on a task to generate an aesthetic and theoretical value system, which acts as a counterbalancing force to the logic and seduction of Western materialism.

The grievous effects of colonial history are spatialized in "Arawak Horizon" and *Omeros* via the appearance of haunted bodies and ravaged, uncanny environments, which are repurposed as vessels of old energy. In the narratives, both writers perform backward glances at the Caribbean's originary violations, but have equally alluded to the urgent concerns of the modern world and new regimes that destroy the hopes of ethnic communities. In "Arawak Horizon", for example, Harris laments the neglect of root culture and soil heritage[3] by creative architects. The unnamed protagonist who is a cultural orphan bemoans the sterility of artistic forms, which stifle the potentialities of cultural memory. There is an awareness of the timeless march of humankind in an empty landscape of ancient structures but which contain the possibility of new life lurking behind material planes. Throughout the sequence of events in "Arawak Horizon," the concern is with the act of crafting a unique symbology that unveils or raises ghostly voices concretely to the surface, where they become audible. Similarly, in *Omeros*, Walcott, through his manipulation of the epic, unearths contexts of a therapeutic and divine sensibility in the wake of a culture nearing spiritual impotence. In both

A CARIBBEAN POETICS OF SPIRIT

texts, each writer reflects on colonial and postcolonial expropriation and disillusionment.

The act of retooling an unseen but palpitating and instructive universe becomes linked with graphic representations and dream-journeying in Harris's short story. His style of narrative hybridity (as delineated in the pursuit of material and immaterial realms, the melting pot of human and non-human knowledges, and the comingling of past and present time scales) foregrounds creative insights that yield provisional modalities of freedom. The narrative commences with the journey of the unnamed narrator into an inchoate universe which has suffered total destruction. That he is unnamed and cryptically labelled as both "he" and "I" symbolize the creation of a narrative from the ashes of history. He becomes one who diffuses preconceived biases and activates the ghosts of other selves. His story is one of incremental psychic and physical journeying, which is undertaken to retrieve those fragments of history that have imploded and been erased by violent European models. The story can, therefore, be read as an allegory for the historical genocide of the Caribbean's First Peoples, in particular, the Arawak tribe. The narrator explains:

> I dreamt I crossed the Arawak horizon at a point on the arch of space known as the mind of the skeleton where a giant sculpture rose out of ruined magma into skyscraper day and night. Once upon a time it had been a total fire that could not be domesticated or swung away into the heavens like a great door or sun in space and it locked all men out (tyranny or insulation) or in (as factor of extinction). Yet the key to that door fell into my hands long afterwards and I began to re-trace the undreamt-of steps of the prisoner of life through the Arawak sun.[4]

The dream becomes a symbolic map that supplies the basic plot and guide to the narrator's phantasmagorical journey. Language is a medium that operates fluidly to accrue meaning between objects, territories and subjectivities.

Raja Patteti aptly asserts that "Harris takes the help of dream[s] to trace the subterranean tradition that grew out of the gulf between peoples and culture".[5] This gulf, with its painful memories, points us to the state of

ARAWAK HORIZON AND OMEROS

waiting. The subterranean or buried tradition can be associated with the despoiled tribe which will surface again. Harris is invested with hope, as signposted in the motif of the dream from which new shapes will be released and a new language will be reborn. As Patteti explains, Harris's dream universe carries the idea of patient regeneration incurred through a meeting of realms, races and cultures. This idea is sustained in the opening image of the arc in the story, which represents a capacity to uncover connections that reside in deep layers of what appears to be lost areas. As the plot progresses, the narrator shores up on the ruins of a dormant volcano that contains sacred inscriptions. The natural world is presented as a talismanic entity and the protagonist's contact with primaeval nature leaves a decisive mark on his sensibility. Harris, it seems, is building new discourses about communal renewal rituals aimed at facilitating an awareness and validation of alternative knowledge-systems that were transfixed by imperial powers as primitive. He is also looking beyond the monolithic, linear categories of time and space:

> The landscape is alive, it is a text in itself, it is a living text [. . .]. There is a dialogue . . . between one's internal being, one's psyche, and the nature of place [. . .]. There has to be some sort of connection, some sort of bridge, which allows one to sense all sorts of relationships which one tends to eclipse, which one tends not to see at all.[6]

The focus here is on the pockets of caves, streams and mountains, which are intuited as credible, actual spots of the mind and spirit. Harris's creative and critical works, in fact, frequently oscillate between these two realms. Thus, "Arawak Horizon" plausibly reads as a journey into an incorporeal, spirit realm as well as into the interior landscape and powers of the mind. The reader, like the unnamed narrator, is lured and gently led into an imaginative tunnel through which one hears and sees a pre-colonial civilization. The impact is the re-engineering of a usable past that enables the discovery of new possibilities.

The magma-like cave is an archetypal womb of presences, as evidenced in the narrator's early observation: "[t]o inscribe these with a pin of light [is] comparable to a child's X-ray in the womb [. . .]. The first prisoner to

139

A CARIBBEAN POETICS OF SPIRIT

creep through the walls of fire was inscribed by the child as O".[7] The womb-like quality becomes a stunningly creative and metaphysical premise, since it functions as a hole through which the imagination plunges headlong into a hinterland of imperishable possibilities. This notion of the hole or gap recalls Harris's writing on the nineteenth-century novel of persuasion and its consolidation of character in *Tradition, the Writer and Society*. Harris speaks to a refusal of fixed identity and opts for a conception of form that transforms the abysses in memory left by traumatic events such as genocide. In "Arawak Horizon", the symbol of the hole operates as a gateway to psychic structures that lead to transcendental states. This attention to psychic intercourse is spatialized in the image of the "O" in the narrative.[8] The orgasmic references embedded in the "O", or womb, suggest penetration and stimulation of the senses. During the protagonist's underground journey, he bewails the islands' materialistic impulses, which lead to passages of spiritual darkness. Harris does not conceal the tormenting element in the creative process, and the challenges of penetrating a seemingly mundane womb that has been over-exposed to imperial forces.

It is through the creative imagination, however, that the narrator is able to perceive traces of life in the apparent sterility of things. The ideas of void and resonance find instantiation in Harris's formal use of graphs. For example, as the narrator retraces the "hollowness of the landscape",[9] he comes upon runes, which operate as Indigenous matrixes and receptacles of knowledge. These runes are concealed beneath the surface of imposed structures of modernity. But as he patiently continues on his journey and garners knowledge, he hears spectral groanings emanating from the caverns and hollows of the mountain. By discerning the life and whisperings lodged within the fissures of the earth, his awareness begins to expand. This encounter symbolizes a re-sensitization to a presumably barren, exterior universe that has been assaulted by Europe's civilizing projects. In principle, his spiritual consciousness surveys anew the fate of his native sensibility, which has had to endure annihilation at the hands of the colonizer.

In *Fossil and Psyche*, Harris explains that material rocks, stones, shells

ARAWAK HORIZON AND OMEROS

and bones do, in fact, retain vibrations from their original lives, through which the creative imagination is able to retrieve and enter a fruitful dialogue with the past.[10] This alternative re-telling is a core characteristic of postcolonial discourse which is significant in projects that challenge representations of Caribbean space as singular – a trend that Harris deems to be deeply unsustainable. This urgency to recover resources from runes is conveyed throughout the stories in *The Age of the Rainmakers*. Harris is evincing the potentialities of partnering with alternative systems of knowing as a precondition for the emergence into a new state of consciousness. The narrator's task is to locate these lost presences and re-assemble their voices in the wake of a culturally castrated generation. As he follows the presences that "creep through the walls of fire",[11] he decodes a formula that is essential to restoring the health of his community.

However, the traversal of this primordial cave is not an easy task. What begins to appear before him is a chain of numbers, which unfold from zero to nine. The empty zero graphically typifies a wound and incompleteness. This is not an endorsement of despair, but a recognition that recovery from historical catastrophes requires a series of repeated choices. This is sustained in the journey of the protagonist, who continually seeks to recover ceremonial knowledge. He articulates and communicates the ongoing nature of this recovery as a cyclical process. Eventually, he comes to understand that each number when turned or rotated in different directions gives birth to new images. This is a demonstration of Harris's rich, metaphoric network in this experimental tale. For example, the number zero or "O" turns into a key – "Q" – when a stem is added to its base.[12] It becomes an instrument, which the protagonist uses to unlock further doors into a wider cosmic realm. Embedded in the metaphor of the zero is the point that negation and death have its limitations. However, it is but only a point or state in which it curves again into another plane or horizon and potential life. This is arguably the central crux of Harris's artistic efforts. By close observation of the submerged clues lodged within the Caribbean environment, Harris offers insight into the cultural practices that are grounded in Indigenous praxes for survival. To maximize the potential of the dead is to achieve eternal life.

A CARIBBEAN POETICS OF SPIRIT

The protagonist soon learns that the shapes are portals through which ghostly forces emanate. They now find a release in the inscriptions, which he traverses with care. This understanding provides a clear expression of Harris's conviction regarding language's immaterial connotations. For him, language carries the ability to stir fresh meanings and disperse unbounded possibilities.[13] Words and shapes commingle to create a very personal and cosmic re-interpretation of Caribbean Indigenous mythology and its relationship with the contemporary self who stands in retrospect of this vast history. This exemplifies Harris's general theory of Caribbean art as an attempt to defy fixed polarities. The graphic writing causes a shock similar to the fall of a stone in a pool. The energy fans outward and then inward again when it has rebounded from the edges. The ripples in the water are animated by a current, which causes them to react to each other and to be transformed by different collisions. In this context, words are liberated from fixed or overdetermined meanings as they are continuously re-purposed. The aim is, in part, to create a variety of social connections on the symbolic level by drawing inspiration from a rich legacy of folk-based practices. This finds textual evidence in the protagonist's chiselling of shapes in the darkness.

The invisible energies are brought into sight as he begins to bodily mutate into numbers. He confesses, "I began to fold [my] limns in the cosmos [and the] inscription . . . looked like the kneeling figure of a . . . 2."[14] In one dimension, he is enacting the pain and trauma of the Indigenous holocaust and the image of conceding or bowing to the enemy. What Harris is proposing is a delicate balance between the reworking of those silent histories and an embodiment of the full sweep of human emotion and the horrors of torture within a particular historical reality. The sacred numerals become a concretization of energy, breath and vibrations. Through this innovative and dynamic play with font and symbol, Harris is, in effect, assembling a new choreography of Caribbean writing. He is instituting a metaphoric gateway into ideas of the numinous as the narrator humbly becomes tempered in a spiritual consciousness.

His painful experience of twisting and turning into unnatural shapes is not merely a physical performance of memory, but a deep internalizing of the burden of a particular historical experience of conquest. At the level of allegory, he becomes a vulnerable subject, in which the price demanded by the spiritual guardians is a nakedness and exposure of the soul. It is a process that involves absolute self-effacement in a manner that leaves him physically and psychically broken, yet simultaneously inspired by an inward energy that empowers him to see and listen in ways he never thought possible. This is more than a Caribbean or New World condition, but is arguably true of those societies that have emerged out of multiple, recurrent catastrophes that resist easy articulation and apprehension. His swivelling illustrates the idea that dismemberment can be redeemed, however painful the reassembling might be. Through Harris's artistic metaphor of shaping and processes like rehearsal, ritual and liminality, the protagonist may be perceived as an artist of sorts, whose gesture of unfolding the palimpsest of numbers and hieroglyphic fonts serves to read him in this manner. Here, the boundaries between the character, the artist, the shaman, the writer and the painter are deliberately blurred so that readers find it difficult to track the lines of rhetorical framing in Harris's experimental work.

As the plot progresses, our protagonist kneels to pray to his ancestors in a sacred room within the cave called the zemi room. Embedded in the concept of the zemi is the idea of parallel worlds, since traditionally, in Arawakan culture, the zemi were treasured and protected objects, including stones or shells that possessed supernatural power.[15] Within this temple space, he transcends the stasis of time and space. He bends his knees and his silhouette looks like the number "5".[16] As he peers into a pool of memories, he feels a grievous and tormented history on the level of bone and body. In effect, he experiences the re-entry of the ancient gods into his consciousness and they resume their mythic identities. This is suggested when he claims, "As I closed my eyes I began to embody an ancient . . . naïve Arawak . . . figure".[17] Harris, in a round table conversation with Gordon Rohlehr, comments on his use of spirit possession in his creative works: "[T]here is a psychical possibility that those Indigenous groups can inform, instruct and change each [individual] by *trials of the imagination*. It . . . is a sign, an omen of change that takes place . . . At times, a character may become aware of holes in his neck into which this new [energy] or head is planted."[18]

In "The Novelist as Shaman", Gregory Shaw tells us that these juxtapositions of mortal and deity in Harris's work reflect a universe that is in the process of becoming.[19] The coalescing of spirit and man in one consciousness facilitates a pattern of rebirth. As the narrator sheds layer after layer of his former self, he gradually experiences a new vision and makes room for unsuspected possibilities of life. From the tendrils of his broken joints, he begins to grow new limbs. At this point, the spiritual nature of the quest comes increasingly to the fore, which sets in motion avenues for self and communal fashioning. In this concentrated spiritual setting, he is able to metamorphose into a communal self and assumes the duty of shaman, where he becomes a type of hero whose journey into another realm restores the missing, psychic and cultural link between generations. However, he must rely on the guidance of spirit beings to illuminate the way. This is achieved when he effectively reorients himself through cognitive processes via which they emerge and distil meaning. One way of discerning this interface between humankind and spirit in Harris's fiction is to observe the manner in which the enthralling past leaps over into the present through his use of superimposition, in that one image (or memory) is placed over the other, giving a sense of simultaneous happening. This is the critical time of the in-between.

For Harris, fresh meaning is not only accrued through metamorphosis, but through exploring the creative space of the in-between. The interstitial or liminal space, according to J. Michael Dash, constitutes a conceptual dimension that is related to a critic's or writer's belief in a space of wonder, awe, enchantment and other universes/domains that seamlessly coexist with the material world. Dash contends that the liminal is a "mythic world, outside of time, whose values [are] antithetical to the modern world".[20] Expressions of liminality may be perceived in threshold or transitional spaces. It may materialize in "images of light fading in the room, veiled longings and the encroachment of the formless darkness [. . .]. [I]t evokes states of consciousness that nervously shift between the boundaries of self

ARAWAK HORIZON AND OMEROS

and the world, inside and outside".[21] Dash's lexical signifiers of "forces," "thresholds" and "infolding"[22] connote the idea of portals which, when traversed, activates new modes of perception. The medium of the interstice itself, where everything is interconnected, prompts one to 'unfocus', to shed old concepts and paradigms and to refocus on fresh insights/visions. In "Arawak Horizon," Harris's critical use of "doors", "arches" and "thresholds"[23] raises questions about the ways in which language becomes molten. A critical part of Indigenous self-determination is the right to know: the right to return and the right to form a non-imperial grammar that is heard as scattered cries and truth claims about stolen and eradicated shared worlds.

In this narrative space, words shift their boundaries and flow into other words. The narrator claims, "I embodied a . . . dying race [. . .]. I stood at the door or window of the sun on the very edge of the precipice [and] . . . I was conscious of . . . something [that moved in] the wind".[24] Thus, at the precipice of consciousness, he has found himself at an interstitial zone, a crossroad of new possibility, where he is enthralled by the affirmative energy of a supernatural universe seething with presences. Harris provides a way to exist in a distant past, while continuing to operate in the present and plotting new futures. It is here, that the cultural orphan finds a measure of peace. It is the fullest evocation of making peace with rupturous spaces. The idea also applies to a reading of narrative space that can be continuously refashioned through movements into mythic time. The power of the writer is concentrated on exploding the rigid binary between structures, characters, realms and Western concepts of time and space, which are perceived as static and tyrannical. The narrative, therefore, progresses in depth with its emphasis on ritual intelligence, rather than surface reality. The imagination that leaps and plays among the sacred inscriptions is liberated from the limits of a materialistic world and discovers the self-revelation of the interstice. Under pressure, the natural world begins to prophesy; to evoke legend and dread omen out of the materials of everyday horror. In re-sensing the primordial energies, the narrator's consciousness breaks free from the restrictions of worldly control. This breakthrough in form is reminiscent of the persona's

A CARIBBEAN POETICS OF SPIRIT

disposition in Martin Carter's poem, "Listening to the Land", whose ear is pressed into the earth in a reverential gesture of unconscious prayer.[25] In other words, the Caribbean natural world is never just a vision, but is part of a larger kaleidoscope of intention, sensation and relationships. This is also conceived in "Arawak Horizon" where the land becomes a conduit for the voices of the undead. Notably, Harris's universe of apparitions is not argued for, but is simply affirmed in the faith of the protagonist and symbolic inscriptions that he perceives in the landscape.

Runes are portals through which spectral presences are actualized. Their materializing is witnessed when the narrator affirms, "As I opened my eyes I was struck this time by the faceless bowl . . . like a bone in which some creature . . . had gnawed a hole in the room of the Arawak sun".[26] The bone is converted into a presence or an organ of memory. This presence writes itself into expression and becomes a talismanic tool. It is an enactment of a native intelligence through which the illusions of Western modernity are challenged. Thus, Indigenous folk-based traditions testify to the force of latent perspectives and its enabling of fulfilment, which may be acquired through a surrender of predetermined ways of being and knowing. This reach into ancestral cosmologies is central to Harris's intuitive aesthetic. It is a sensibility that aims to remediate and re-purpose the region's catastrophic histories into new and instructive fictions, and which debunks generalizing statements such as V.S. Naipaul's myopic assertion that "history is built around achievement and creation, and nothing was created in the West Indies".[27]

Harris's appointment of Caribbean space as a critical vessel of memory and ancestral nexus of relations eschews and replaces Naipaul's charge with alternative understandings of the lifeways of the region's ethnic communities, whose value systems are life-giving and instructive. Harris thus plausibly enables a vision of life's continuity that appears to have vanished due to forces of empire. This is suggested when the protagonist in "Arawak Horizon" claims, "I felt now I was half-assembling, half-groping towards or into something related to an immense witness of . . . spirit".[28] The narrative is therefore a private expression of the lingering trauma of the Indigenous holocaust in the psyche of the modern-day generation.

ARAWAK HORIZON AND OMEROS

More urgently, it signposts the need to situate the architecture of this pain as a unique New World sensibility that is still in the process of being formed. Silvio Torres's argument comes to mind in which he asserts that Harris's style "represents an utter refashioning of the conceptual and interpretive models bequeathed to the islands by the colonial transaction".[29] The difficulty in deciphering Harris's cryptic messages, Torres continues, "reminds us of the hurdles and stress involved in the pursuit of authenticity", and the gargantuan task of fashioning a form that will echo the plasticity of the archive.[30] Harris is activating a symbology, which becomes a model to point the way out of colonial fragmentation and new states of unknowingness. The aesthetic effort aspires to a drastically different philosophy of Caribbean reality and history that is enacted by way of a cosmically attuned imagination.

In terms of fictional methodologies, Harris also makes creative use of shamanic rites to address historical and environmental wounds. For example, the protagonist in "Horizon" employs water divination as he peers into a crystal bowl and witnesses a "barren newfound stretch of wilderness".[31] The wilderness is a portent of the sterile, modern Caribbean. This is perhaps Harris's eco-critical commentary on hunting, pollution, the illegal poaching of species and other exploitative enterprises that endanger wildlife. As the narrator rubs "dry bones together",[32] he commences a ritual that induces visions of the leaping spirits of wildlife, which stride into space and whose movements induce bountiful rainfall. By following the spirit of a deer, the protagonist encounters the goddess of fertility, who imparts the knowledge that the quest to healing and restoration involves a surrender to all humanly "intents and purposes".[33] Implicit in her admonition is the surrendering of materialist attachments in favour of a re-sensitized and altruistic engagement with community. Such a deep and interior form of thinking is at the basis of Harris's ideas. In this, he is close to the mystics, alchemists and diviners. Yet, it is important to note that Harris cannot be associated with any particular faith: his concern is not so much with finding divinity, as with discovering the kernel of creation beyond the obstacles of despotic systems. His focus is on the role of the creative writer and the fresh work they create. It is an

A CARIBBEAN POETICS OF SPIRIT

example of the intellectual service necessary for deconstructing the barriers between materiality and immateriality, between genres, fiction and philosophy – all of which can meet in one single revolutionary medium.

Harris affirms in an interview with Peterson and Rutherford that his quest is "obviously . . . to find a different vocabulary . . . to break through . . . one-track sensibilities".[34] He notes that a sensitive reader to Caribbean imaginative fiction is able to ascertain this reality through tracing the "ruined sacred fabric of (ghost towns) . . . spiraling flute mirrors . . . the ascension of the spirit of the living and the dead".[35] The extended framework of spirit is fundamental to an alternative awakening and re-calibrating of the roles, functions and rhythms of Caribbean identity and being. New interpretations of cosmologies and ancestral faiths have given rise to the discernment of mechanized violence and perils that persist in contemporary times. Indeed, the survival of "spirit" is threatened by humankind's technological hubris. Through this line of inquiry, Harris proposes ritual remembering that delivers a powerful inventory of how people groups make meaning of their lives and historic catastrophes, which can be mined for contemporary (and future) applications.

At the end of the narrator's journey in "Horizon", he witnesses the coming together of the sun (fire), sky (air) and water (wind) and claims: "I was involved in the curious reversal of the stasis of immortality [as I moved through the] winds of fortune . . . The sun [had] turned round and round [in] whose arch of fire was the wealth of divinity I inherited from space, tail of my Arawak cosmos q signposting the spine of the wind in the stars – treasury of The Rainmaker".[36] In this vista of elemental forces, he is also able to experience passages of renewal and rebirth. The horizon is an unlimited space in which the ground of his being unfolds. This is poetically induced in the writer's creative deployment of numerals, which conveys a mathematical rightness and precision about this numinous encounter.

It should be observed that the Arawak horizon of souls is not to be perceived as an idealized or dream-like vista. Instead, it is a solemn sight and domain that heralds the commencement of a praise-song for a people's existence. It reads as a metaphor for a vision that is simultaneously compassionate and detached. Although these Indigenous spirit presences are deeply involved in humanity's fate, their histories are coloured with tragedy. Notwithstanding, the horizon is a limitless morning for the Caribbean subject. This is embodied in the image of "the Arawak sun"[37] that burns through the mist and enables the protagonist to see the host of ancestors before him. It heralds the point of a new beginning and deep feeling of re-bonding between old and new communities. To this degree, the conceptual framework of the phantom limb can be invoked as it facilitates a re-assembling of dismembered man and god. This ritual theatre of spectres becomes a potent metaphor, which enacts as well as describes transformations of cultures. The protagonist discerns the presence of his ancestors with a clarity that begins to slice into the soul of things. Within this extra-terrestrial space, he simultaneously recognizes his own complicity in forgetting. A recourse to accommodating vestiges of cultures into new understandings of Caribbean identity is afforded.

Moreover, Harris's decolonial reading of time recognizes the violence of linear chronologies and globalizes a Sankofa-like gesture of continually reaching into multiple pasts in order to orient, narrate and organize the future. Like Harris, Walcott grapples with new forms of genocide which, in *Omeros,* is spatialized in the deep loss of spiritual connection in the human world. The fate of the fishermen is such that they are in danger of prostituting themselves and their island for the material gain of tourism. The icy hand of imperialism persists, with its mission to process the life out of everything that it visits. A consequence of this is the dearth of ancestral traditions and homage to the spiritual pulse of the island, which are required to cope with the effects of globalization and mutated forms of capitalism. Through an alternative perspective of a universe that seethes with the ghosts of history, Walcott, like Harris, envisions a blueprint for healing. It is through a process of experimentation with the epic narrative form that the St Lucian poet combines old and fresh archetypes with an Indigenous, nature-based language.

Perhaps there is something about the geography of the Caribbean, some peculiar energy that is buried in the islands, which Walcott is intent on illuminating. One may posit that he is plumbing the fragmentary nature of the Caribbean landmass, which mimics the shattered proto-language and cultures of its peoples. Therefore, Walcott attempts to represent the concept of Caribbean in-betweenity as a framework, through which he gives shape to the wounded psyche and fragmentation of the modern Caribbean subject in the wake of accelerating violence. In *Omeros*, he gives voice to the Caribbean subject, which is not simply the primal scream raised in revolt against the three hundred plus years of oppression, but encompasses the dynamic shape of people groups that comprise the cosmopolitan Caribbean, including the African, Indian, Chinese, Indigenous and European subjects. In other words, the Caribbean epic is rendered in a kaleidoscope of its own cross-cultural, mythic language. The narrative form includes aspects of intra-colonial and inter-colonial conflicts, which provides a mythic recovery, not just for one lost cultural worldview or group, but for as many as possible. The invention of a suitable narrative form gives rise to adaptations which lead to a style of writing that is fluid enough to renew itself. This is delineated in the cascade of images, shapes, sounds and visual aesthetics throughout the poem.

Walcott begins with the invocation of the muse: "O open this day with conch's moan, Omeros"[38] and "O was the conch-shell's invocation, mer was / both mother and the sea in our Antillean patois, / os, a grey bone and the white surf as it crashes".[39] The echo of lost lives, the memory of buried ancestors, the depleted resources of the Caribbean Sea, and the coral reefs which calcified into grey bones are exteriorized through particular shapes and images. "Mer" is also symbolic of the sea as a primordial mother. She is an uncanny, timeless energy to which the modern-day fishermen subconsciously return. The poet may also be emphasizing – through the image of the coral – the manner in which ancestral lives have dried up and turned into encrusted rocks, perforated with holes where there was once organic life. It is a compelling way of illuminating the concept of dying presences in the memory of the islanders. However, within the image of the conch shell which moans, there is something that lives and burns. An added posthumous dimension to this reading of "os", which is the Latin root for bone, fuses human fragments with the ocean.

The depth of meaning inherent in such shapes conveys an imperative

ARAWAK HORIZON AND OMEROS

to re-create something new from the debris of history. The use of a quasi-hieroglyphic style of writing locates the narrative within a dynamic visual and sonic realm. Walcott is deploying an orthography that subsists on symbols, crisscrosses and breaks in the poem which constitutes a ritual re-membering or re-assembling of the fragments of New World history. He is divine creator as he attempts to change the image from one of death to life and from sight to sound (as in the moan of the conch shell). This re-engagement with repressed energies awakens a latent consciousness that is activated through language. This artistic intervention, through the process of naming the space of loss, becomes a catalyst and architectural response for the restoration and manifestation of what was once buried. Walcott articulates this process of remaking mythic memory through "conjugating" the worlds of the dead and the undead.[40] He suggests that, "Deprived of their original language, the captured and indentured tribes create their own, accreting and secreting fragments of an old, epic vocabulary . . . to an ancestral, ecstatic rhythm . . . [where] nouns are renamed".[41] Walcott's anatomizing and play with words, syllables, phonemes and symbols crystallize in his poetic use of myths, tales, legends and great stories, which originate from an elemental existence.

This is even more evident in the motif of the bone, in which the corresponding themes of memory, pain and suffering are embedded, and the subsequent questions of where it came from and to whose body it once belonged to are probed. The image of the bone ("os") mutates throughout the poem, as depicted for instance in the "coral sores"[42] beneath the Antillean sea, and is grafted to plot new meridian lines on the atlas of Caribbean and even world literature. The poet's use of "os" elegantly resonates with NourbeSe Philip's poetic representation of the *Zong* Massacre and the fragmented language she uses to contemplate the deathly sea voyage. Ghostly echoes circulate throughout these discourses. Historical memory, in this sense, requires constant re-orientation and appraisal.

Furthermore, in a metrical sense, Walcott is following the rhythms of island life – both physically and psychically, as elicited in the lines' imitation of the surf crashing upon the shore at the opening of *Omeros*. This is further advanced in the roaring noise of the surf and the tempo of island life. The repeated "O" sound is also a symbol of the hole or wound in Helen's heart (she is caught up in an intoxicating love triangle with Hector and Achille). It is a signifier of the larger circular, personal, cultural and geographical wounds that are operational in the poem, and the diversity of characters who seek healing and belonging. Moreover, the poet's experiment with language and shapes vacillates between human, non-human and emotional sensibilities. For example, the use of circles gives voice to the inarticulate colonial and postcolonial circumstances that Caribbean peoples have faced. This is embedded in the orbit of the "O", which plausibly generates cultural connections among Caribbean people and expresses a need for communal healing. Many characters experience woundedness and their hurts are in need of proper suturing.

The sulphur spring volcano of La Soufrière also signifies the psychic damages of history, which still haunt the island. In another dimension, Walcott, the narrator, shares a wound with Philoctete, as evoked in their search for roots, while Plunkett has an old head wound and loses his wife, Maud, who suffers homesickness (another kind of psychical wounding) and death from cancer. Achille endures the heel-prick of love lost, while Hector suffers from intense jealousy. The "O", as described by Jean Antoine-Dunne, is thus a recurring signifier that is deployed to spatialize the diverse shapes of each character's hurt.[43]

In this regard, words reach toward specific sensibilities and are mediated through the senses as well as the creative imagination. More telling is that words, which appear the same, communicate different stories and tensions. They are deployed as vehicles of culture and carriers of vestiges, feelings and repressed anxieties. Language also works towards healing the wounds of empire, which the writer himself wishes to work through. Walcott's commitment to writing the previously unwritten shapes and conflicts of his island into visibility is most potently suggested throughout the poem. Notably, the writing filters the poet's specific cultural experiences, including his colonial education, his Creole heritage, the legacy of slavery and his grapple with mimicry and originality.

On the level of spirit, language serves the purpose of bridging the divide between the human and non-human realms. Within this creative space, the imagination calls up beings and presences which, according to Antoine-Dunne, demonstrates a "continuing circuit of relations that constantly re-members the past and reappraises and reinvents the future".[44] The pull of spirit and use of folk arts indeed signposts a scaffolding, in which hybridized and cross-cultural sensibilities can be fruitfully explored. The creative processing of a mythic past and unseen dimension conjures near-forgotten ephemeral presences, which are perceivable in new metaphors and richly layered words. The evidence is to be found in the landscape, which is alive and exerts anthropomorphic qualities.

This is illustrated in the "blackbirds [that] quarrel at breakfast",[45] the "eels [that] sign their names"[46] – a spatialization; "the crabs [that] lifted [the] pincer with its pen like the sea-dipping swift"[47] – a spatial metaphor; the "wind [that] hummed in the case of a girl's throat: *Omeros*", the "cicadas [that] chatter[ed] like [Maud's] sewing-machine",[48] "the yam leaves, [which] recoiled in a cold sweat",[49] the "lizard on the sea-wall [that] dart[ed] its question at the waking sea"[50] – a hieroglyph, and the "sea-mosses / [that] shook their beards angrily, like submarine cedars, / while [Achille] trod[ded] the dark water".[51] Here, Walcott constructs a bridge between the human and natural language as he imaginatively graphs a text of the inanimate world. It also harks to the ways that images accrue incremental meanings as the poem progresses.

The co-option of life from the proximal, natural surroundings into his narrative space is a central element in Walcott's artistry. This is perhaps where his and Harris's narratives diverge; for while in the particular context of "Arawak Horizon" Harris focuses mainly on ancient runes, relics and ceremonies from the First Peoples to express the power of antiquity and old magic, Walcott, in *Omeros* turns attention to the immediate, fresh and natural symbols to penetrate and ascertain new meanings, while also memorializing the Arawak presence as smoke and spectres that encircle the plot. This is a different kind of writing as it reinforces the point that spectral presences may also spring up from the contemporary, immediate and natural environment –and not only from the ancient past. Fresh and common sounds from the surf, wind, birds, trees and hurricane intermingle with spectral tongues and human voices to

A CARIBBEAN POETICS OF SPIRIT

demonstrate the equitability between organisms and realms. Walcott is allowing the natural voices of St Lucia to participate in his intellectual and creative enterprise.

Ideas of liminality are also discernible in *Omeros,* which further elaborates on the poet's turn towards ideas of the numinous. The concept of the in-between space is one which has been threaded throughout this book and has proven to be a theme around which matters of the supernatural emerge. To expand on its definition, liminality, as theorized by Homi Bhabha, connects with a history of colonial discourse that has been abusive to 'mixed breeds' and subaltern groups.[52] To invert this inequity and colonial antagonism, Bhabha's conception of the unhomely or third space that signifies creativity and contestation is asserted. The interstice or space between centre and periphery has been viewed in contemporary discourses as an alluring, almost seductive site of inventive resistance to hegemonic colonial narratives. Bhabha's postulation that liminality is a cutting-edge zone of negotiation, shifting boundaries, malleability and continuous metamorphosis, dovetails with expressions of spirits who are in-between entities straddling the worlds of the dead and the undead as if to constantly destabilize realities, conventions, laws, customs and even time.

The threshold space may also be outlined as a passageway across a boundary or an opening, which allows movement from one space to another. According to Iain Chambers, any definition of liminality, interstitial or threshold zones introduces what may be termed as a "border discourse" that is "consistently haunted and interpellated by the invisible; by what [struggles] to enter the arena of representation; by what is veiled or falls out of the field of vision of a predictable consensus".[53] Drawing from Édouard Glissant's concepts of root identity and relation,[54] Chambers suggests that the significance of liminal discourses lies in a quasi-rhizomatic dynamic of national identity. This introduces the potential of metamorphosis, the merging of consciousness and identities through the image of the proliferated root or rhizome.

In *Omeros,* not unlike Harris's "Arawak Horizon", liminality is spatialized through the supporting symbols of the landscape, ceremonies,

ARAWAK HORIZON AND OMEROS

rituals, archways, thresholds and objects such as mirrors and vessels. This circularity of realms, times, spaces and consciousness revitalizes new acts of perception in order to make space for non-Western, alternative sets of cultural modalities. One of the first and evidentiary signs of Walcott's preoccupation with liminal spaces is the image of light or sunrise that rings open the poem. Philoctete remarks, "'This is how, one sunrise, we cut down them canoes.' / . . . [the] leaves start shaking/the minute the axe of sunlight hit the cedars".[55] The sunrise, which is neither night nor day, light nor darkness, is evocative of Walcott's attempt to deconstruct Eurocentric patterns and is a move to concern himself with a hybridized cultural dawn. For Walcott, the metaphor of dawn is imagined also in the art of writing. This dim and dark image of twilight is deployed by the poet to challenge Caribbean artists to develop their identity in the twilight in which they live, that is, between their Indigenous, African, European, Asian and other ancestries. In his seminal essay, "What the Twilight Says",[56] Walcott depicts this dusky and mysterious space as generative, since in actuality the night gives way to the beginning of something new with the dawn. While critics like Patricia Ismond situate Walcott's use of the metaphor among nationalist movements, and Jahan Ramazani, in "The Wound of History: Walcott's *Omeros* and the Postcolonial Poetics of Affliction",[57] offers the inter-ethnic connections in the Caribbean through the metaphor of the amber, my analysis offers the standpoint that the notion of sunrise (the time of day between daylight and darkness) loops together corporeal and incorporeal entities, mortal and immortal worlds. Throughout *Omeros*, the recurrent metaphor indicates something that is not only sensed with the eye, but with all the other senses. The half-light or twilight not only makes the ghosts in the narrative more visible tenants of the real world, but the transition of semi-darkness possesses a distinct potency and mystery similar to the sensation of entering or crossing many different thresholds and arriving at moments of clarity.

Twilight represents the struggle to develop a unique artistic validity that is true to West Indian culture and effectively designed to eschew the monodic sensibility of the classic epic. Mikhail Bakhtin, for instance,

155

makes a valuable observation on the malleability of the epic and avers that "[w]e speak of the epic as a genre that has come down to us already well defined and real. We come upon it when it is almost completely finished, a congealed and half moribund genre. Its completeness, its consistency and its absolute lack of artistic naiveté bespeak its old age as a genre and its lengthy past".[58] In the context of the Caribbean, however, the epic has undergone a sea change.[59] As posited by Harris, the root of the epic seeped so deeply into the soil of the New World that it embraced and intercepted the many cultural deposits of every migrant group in the region, thus serving as a mythical and creative intermediary.[60]

While there are convergences with Walcott's deployment of the lofty epic genre, that is, with his thematic focus on history, identity and concepts of the nation, *Omeros* is culturally removed from the traditional Greek structure. According to Bakhtin, the epic relied on linear chronology to document a hero's rise to power. The classic epic, thus, concerns itself with national heroes and fathers who founded ideas of the nation.[61] The power of the classic epic was established by following the life of the hero, the single narrative voice and linear trajectories. In *Omeros*, however, Walcott offers a meeting of the syncretic remnants of the classic epic and Indigenous folk pathways. In other words, he tacitly engages the multiple psychical journeying of characters and the potency of plural universes, as opposed to one-dimensional or individual storylines. In this sense, both Harris and Walcott delimit the classic epic form and devise decolonial structures that give epistemic saliency to the small histories of Caribbean societies and, thus, accentuate articulations on the syncretic composition of Caribbean space.

This experimentation is invoked in the image of the sunrise – a meridian between day and night; it is an entity that is deeply inscribed in folk mythology as a locus of magic. It is a space in which certainties become less certain, and the "natural" appears to be unnatural. The image is suggestive of a rim of consciousness, where words waver with meaning and desire. Interestingly, Philoctete's tale possesses a haunting and unearthly quality, evidenced in the image of the fishermen who are set against the threshold of the dawn. What follows is their descent into the forest to begin their task of separating trees from their natural habitat. The narration is phantasmic, as it is predicated on an erosion of the clearly defined boundaries that separate material objects from the vapours of fog and mist apparent at the break of day. The fishermen's exhalations produce "feathers like the mist" and Philoctete's eyes are filled with "dew" as he contemplates the task before him.[62] The gods' fates are sealed as the fishermen prepare to harvest the trees for canoes.

The trees in this regard are passing through an intermediary stage between their former lives as gods and into new lives as canoes or vessels. Their mutation comes quickly and they are no longer physically trees but "pirogues crouched on the sand".[63] Their sacredness is magnified by the priest who blesses their entry into the ocean with a bell and the swift's sign. Walcott's critique of capitalism is clear as the economic realities of the fishermen have forced them to desecrate the forest, which they associate with divinity, as in the priest's blessing. It also correlates with the decimation of the Aruac people who originally inhabited St Lucia. On the level of metaphor, the trees transform from their formerly land-rooted existence, bound to a single place, into a new identity of water-based transport – a sea vessel – which the fishermen will use to navigate the Antillean ocean.

Achille's canoe, which bears the slogan, "In God We Troust", makes evident an early encounter with the process of naming and the divine power which the canoes symbolize.[64] These pirogues have been fashioned like words and verses, as implied in the acts of cutting, splicing, shaping and hollowing. It connotes the idea that writing involves an attentive representation of New World epistemic violence. The swing of Achille's axe is doubly symbolic:

> He swayed back the blade, / and hacked the limbs from the dead god, knot after knot, / wrenching the severed limbs from the trunk as he prayed . . . / The bearded elders endured the decimation/of their tribe without uttering a syllable / of that language they had uttered as a nation.[65]

The trees then nod in agreement "with the waves to forget their [former] lives".[66] It is a significant image that reflects the intersections between

A CARIBBEAN POETICS OF SPIRIT

continuity and discontinuity, and the recognition that the gods in their new form will function as guide and omen for the fishermen at sea.

The plethora of symbols denotes the recovery and continuance of an ancestral, sacred tradition within Caribbean communities and societies amid the vectors of change and rupture. It comes as no surprise that Achille, while aboard his spirit-imbued vessel, experiences a trance and follows a sea-swift, which leads his dream-like voyage to Africa in his search for tribal reconnection. In the bird's capacity to connect the spirit and material world, one can also perceive it as an omen of imminent dying and its presence marks Achille's fleshly death. The bird flying into the sunset is portentous and symbolizes a quasi-funeral procession. Its role can be posited as a sentinel of death in one life (St Lucia) and awakener in another (Achille's return to Africa).

The swift carries multiple levels of meaning and symbolism. In her swooping and crisscrossing flights, in which she stitches together Africa and the Caribbean, Walcott embeds the idea of syncretism, both in a ritualistic and literary manner. Moreover, in her fluid movements, the poet recovers lost images, cultural symbols, deities and icons, which he wields to piece together the psychic continuity of African animism with a materialistic Caribbean society. Here, the bird functions as a mind-messenger, both to Achille and the poet. This is evidenced when the seer, Omeros, informs Walcott (a phantom-like presence in the narrative) that his poetic craft, like the motion of the swift across the skies, is meant to stitch together hemispheres, stories, cultures and identities. The seer explains to the poet that this is "why the sea-swift was sent to you: / to circle yourself and your island with this art".[67] Not only is she the seer's familiar, but her flight seams together two disparate parts, two different worlds, two aspects of Caribbean identity – just as the artist attempts to bridge orality and writing, human and nature, and the dead with the undead.

Moreover, the hyphen, which the poet uses as a potent symbol to connect worlds, including the material and spiritual, stands as a shared sign between the sea-swift and the writer himself, to mirror their overlapping

ARAWAK HORIZON AND OMEROS

realms that they wish to merge. This becomes even more prominent when the poet notes:

> I followed a sea-swift to both sides of this text; / her hyphen stitched its seam, like the interlocking / basins of a globe in which one half fits the next into an equator, both shores neatly clicking / into a globe; except that its meridian was not North and South but East and West [. . .]. Her wing-beat carries these islands to Africa / she sewed the Atlantic rift with a needle's line, / the rift in the soul.[68]

Walcott is imploding form and deconstructing the classics in his quest to locate a style that harmonizes with his psychic and literary rift-like experience of belonging to two traditions. He merges Greek and Caribbean mythologies, where the gods are Aruac or African instead of Olympian, and his epic catalogues are not of warriors' names, but St Lucian fishermen. His innovation in form is also embedded in the transitory movement of the swift, who brings a much-needed catharsis, whereby he purges himself of blind devotion to classical allusions and illusions in an effort to see clearly the island for what it truly is. This belonging to a range of traditions is at the heart of Walcott's poetic oeuvre, as he recalls the dilemma of "how [to] choose / Between this Africa and the English tongue I love?"[69] In Achille's meeting with ancestral presences, Walcott interrogates these understandings of 'home' and 'belonging' through language.

The poem is, therefore, equally about the characters' descent into the concealed layers of the self and their discovery of meaning in the landscape. In this sense, Walcott's experiment with language is similar to Kamau Brathwaite's expressions of 'nation language', which Brathwaite defines as the alternative tongues that Caribbean people speak across the diaspora. In *History of the Voice*, Brathwaite provides a theoretical framework of the voice of the Afro-Caribbean that has been derived not only from linguistic patterns and dialect, but from music, song, guttural tones, the beat of ritual drums, speech, the influence of the land and natural forces such as the hurricane and noise.[70] Although Walcott's vision of a new language is arguably broader than Brathwaite's national/regional scope,

A CARIBBEAN POETICS OF SPIRIT

the expression of 'nation language' and the urgency towards crafting a 'new' aesthetic serves similar purposes.[71]

The breaks and continuities with worlds are given further symbolism in Achille's return to Africa. While following the semi-circular turn of the swift, which only he can see, he falls into a deep trance. Achille finds himself in a community in which he is completely unprepared to reside. Here, Walcott emphasizes the disastrous loss of familial names and the martyrdom that lay at the foundation of the New World. A spectral presence lets Achille know that he is home and that he has been led there by a divine messenger in the form of the sea-swift. However, he must depend on his own intuition and powers of perception to make sense of his circumstance, which he quickly does by identifying Afolabe as his father by the way he walked.[72]

An expectant hush falls over the settlement as the two men begin to communicate and Achille confesses that the ancestral African names have been lost in the diaspora. Walcott is illuminating the process of seasoning during the Middle Passage and the point that many enslaved Africans lost their ancestral names. Others were also given titles to enhance their perceived worth as human cargo to buyers, such as the strong name of "Achilles" from Greek mythology, which would be devoid of personal meaning for the enslaved subject since the name is converted to "Achille" without the 's'. In oral cultures, such as those from which many Africans were taken, names held significant import. Afolabe indicates that the name of a man is like his shadow; it is something of intrinsic and spiritual value. Since Achille's name had no meaning as evidenced in his confession, "We yearn for a sound that is missing",[73] he must intuit power from his father who reconnects him to his ancestry. Furthermore, Achille's lack of a sound reveals the profound linguistic challenges and displacement many Caribbean inhabitants faced when they were uprooted from their ancestral home. Interestingly, Afolabe informs Achille, "If the sound of one's name means nothing, then you would be nothing".[74] In this context, a name without meaning equates with a word or identity without substance. However, Walcott re-tools this gap between name and being as a space of creative possibility through which one is bequeathed

ARAWAK HORIZON AND OMEROS

knowledge via the process of fiction. Achille's choice to initially separate himself from his African ancestors offers Walcott a site to develop St Lucian/Caribbean culture in his writing.

Significantly, the conversation between Achille and Afolabe is scripted uniquely in *Omeros*. Their names, "ACHILLE" and "AFOLABE", are centred in all capitals, like a script for a play. It adds to the importance of the oral influence in this section and accentuates the point that the characters address each other ritualistically. Of especial significance is that the conversation is set in ancient Africa between a presumably uneducated fisherman and his majestic, ghostly father. It seems that Walcott is evoking the politics of language domination, loss and discontinuity. Afolabe is creatively positioned to restore the lost signifiers of Achille's world. However, Achille's descent into these deep, ancestral regions of the heart and history does not lead to absolute answers, but to the generation of more questions. This search for identity and the need to belong is at the heart of *Omeros* and Walcott's poetic experimentation, given that he sees it as consistent with the Caribbean experience. In this meeting with circular images, Achille experiences further displacement from his ancestral home, by witnessing Africans bartering fellow Africans into slavery. He notes that he cannot turn back time through the temptation of revenge. Consequently, he experiences deep, internal affliction and begins to drift into another terrain of memory as he walks across the seabed and crosses time and space yet again. Symbolically, the ocean functions as an ideally suited metaphor for navigating the meridians of culture, self, place and the quest for creating a self-determining history.

Different times and spaces are fused in this dream-like reality, which also illuminates Achille's desire for hermetic isolation amidst Helen's love affair with Hector. Nightmare is superimposed upon nightmare and the dream journey becomes Achille's own Middle Passage. Yet, his watery descent separates him from his world even as it confers on him the capacity to see history and his present reality in a new light, depth and dimension. His seamless movements between spaces are crucial to his survival and hence creative renewal. He recognizes that his mission, via this backward glance, is to reconnect and illuminate the dead souls, even the souls of those who died in the crossing from West Africa to the Caribbean. His encounter with the host of spectres beneath the sea, as embodied in the "huge cemeteries / of bone and the huge crossbows of the rusted anchors,"[75] functions as a spiritual rebirth.

The sea is positioned as another liminal space and medium of consciousness. Moreover, it is an entity that symbolizes the possibility of origins, an uncanny and original home; hence Walcott's play on the letters, "mer", which signifies a return to a primordial mother as a super-organism. In the bodily or corporeal sense, Achille is thought to have drowned. Yet, his immersion in the water and this psychic trance is the beginning of a process of recovery from cultural ethnocide. Of equal importance is the way in which this section of the narrative is written, which emphasizes how the magic of the sunlight enters the dark waters to inspire and conjure an Anansi-web of voices and marine dialect that only Achille can hear. The seabed is thus a window or corridor into a primordial territory and its traversal requires Achille to find original ways of making connections with the past. These connections are made within the intuitive roots of language.

Upon awakening from his deep trance, he returns to St Lucia and is able to adjust his current affairs in the context of ancestral cadences. It would seem that rather than plunging himself into a malaise of recrimination and despair, his encounter with spirit beings has the opposite effect of providing him with some measure of spiritual peace. The very shape of *Omeros* is plausibly forged from images of return, rituals, journeys and meridian crossings that combine with the poet's theoretical approaches to art.[76] It focuses on acts of self-discovery. Here, Walcott draws close to Harris, for they both take up the magic of the Caribbean land and sea, and wield it towards circuits of meanings and action. This responsibility is to inscribe, or as Antoine-Dunne puts it, "leap to a new state" of meaning which carries the promise of "cosmic harmony".[77] As artists, both Harris and Walcott attempt to generate fresh energies that are released through the conflict of colonial history and New World fragmentation.

This cascade of experiences, including the movements between realms and attention to the detail of the St Lucian landscape, is further tex-

ARAWAK HORIZON AND OMEROS

tualized in Maud's stitch-work, which is another central metaphor for Walcott's animistic and spectral poetics. Maud's quilt of "all the horned island birds"[78] is magical in the sense that she relies on memory to weave together a complex design of diverse spaces, realms, cultures and peoples. At one level of meaning, the Homeric resonance is with Penelope, the wife of Odysseus, who is patient and awaits her husband's return while she weaves a shroud for her father. Maud's quilt, however, comes to mean much more in the St Lucian context, as it is symbolic of the medley of wildlife that materializes on the island, including the birds from the Aruac rainforests and the totem of the iguana, whose tail is creatively imagined in the colourful, hanging tassels of her fabric. Maud's movement of spinning the needle in and through the cloth to reconstruct a vista of events, experiences and realms concurs with Walcott's poetic and writing processes and the rich array of meaning he constructs throughout the poem. Sewing for Maud is almost sacred and therapeutic as she suffers from deep homesickness (she longs for the coolness of Ireland). This is similar to the insistence on dressmaking and tailoring for Miss Nora that Patricia Powell describes in *The Fullness of Everything* (examined in chapter five), and the pursuit for healing through stitchwork.

The act of embroidering also becomes a seat of remedy, power, authority and comfort, as is the task of writing for Walcott. This is imagined in the birds perched atop Maud's quilt, who are poised to fly away at any moment. However, it is a bleak contrast with the imprisonment of Maud's emotions. More importantly is that her creative enterprise may be read as a shamanistic practice. This becomes discernible when her tapestry assumes a life of its own, as the birds come alive and peck at her fingers. The scene is almost fantasy-like as exhibited in the lines:

> Needlepoint constellations / on a clear night had prompted this intricate thing, / this immense quilt, which, with her typical patience, / she'd started years ago, making its blind birds sing, / beaks parted like nibs from their brown branch and cover [. . .]. They flew from their region, / their bright spurs braceleted with Greek or Latin tags, / to pin themselves to the silk, and crying their names, / pecked at her fingers. They fluttered like little flags/from the branched island, budding in accurate flames. / The Major

pinched his eyes and turned from the blotter – / green as a felt field in Ireland [. . .]. / The hours drowsed like centuries / [. . .]he pinched his eye sockets. Cannons flashed from his eyes.[79]

It seems that Maud's needle, when jabbed into the fabric, activates the spirit inside the moving images that she crafts. Her husband watches with awe, the manner in which "her hands in the half-dark out of the lamplit ring / in the deep floral divan, div[ed] like a swift / to the drum's hoop".[80] The act of flossing the embroidery pin through the fabric is almost hypnotic to Dennis. The shroud becomes a transcendental vessel. As he focuses on the bits of the creatures' wings, the hues of bright blue feathers and the brownish stems and veins of the designs that she weaves, he falls into a deep trance and the vision that he experiences is a reflection of what he yearns for the most – to be a young, valiant soldier. However, the heat and exhaustion of the island have consumed his dreams. The art of quilt-making bears the power of hypnosis and is like a magic mirror, which, when peered into, projects the most concealed parts of the self. This is arguably the effect of both Walcott's and Harris's works and the particular reactions they produce in their readers.

Maud's weaving shares certain qualities with Walcott's narrative process of tenderly bringing together fragments, seaming words and concepts to make a whole, and embellishing the material with creative thread-work. Images, cultures, lives and civilizations appear in colourful, new ways, as reflected in his use of animism and a spirit-infused universe. His innovations show up in the patches of Caribbean Creole, ancestral voices, spectral whisperings, marine dialect and syncretic imageries in the text's embroidered shape. Walcott explicitly likens his craft to the power of Maud's artistry when he asserts:

> My craft required the same / crouching care, the same crabbed, natural devotion / of the hand that stencilled a flowered window-frame / or planed an elegant canoe; its time was gone / with the spirit in the wood . . . I'd created / the fiction of her life . . . through this page's scrim, / and the ghost I will make of you with my scratching pen, / like a needle piercing the ring's embroidery / with a swift's beak, or where, like a nib from the rim / of an inkwell, a martin flickers a wing dry.[81]

Walcott is expressly exploring the shared territory between writing and sewing in the text. The effect is something like an enchanting parchment or palimpsest, where traces of the past surface in a unique form. It is an aesthetic that reflects an ambition to textually consubstantiate human and non-human elements. By employing multiple accents and cadences throughout the rhetoric of his poem, Walcott is creating an open-ended vision of identity and indeed of the nation. It is a technique that emphasizes symbiotic relationships between multiple voices, worlds and spaces, and which allots equal value to many perspectives, as opposed to a single, authoritative voice.

The ideas of stitching and sewing are also sustained in Ma Kilman's healing magic and cure, which she dispenses to Philoctete's gangrenous, fevered wound. Symbolically, his scar is a manifold reminder of the psychic burden of the Afro-Caribbean community's ancestral history, the violent uprooting of peoples and the rupture of bloodlines that remain unhealed. His sore and bleeding shin is spiritual in nature as it implies the pain that lingers in the wake of those whose burials remain mismanaged and unrecognized. Significantly, Philoctete, "believed [that] the swelling came from the chained ankles / of his grandfathers".[82] Like a torn web, his shin embodies the lingering horror of slavery. Moreover, he externalizes the ongoing pain, which his community experiences as a result of the economic and social imbalances instigated by colonialism, and continued by structures such as tourism that perpetuate racialized power dynamics, marginality and prejudices. The symbolism, politics and metaphysics are united in the bubbling and inflamed scar, which can only be cured by the demi-god in the village, in the form of Ma Kilman.

The agency of an incorporeal, divine and supernatural universe gains stature in the character of the village sibyl. Ma Kilman may be read as an archetype, in whose consciousness is inscribed a community's protection, healing and redemption. In principle, Walcott creates a character who can move flexibly through space and time, merging with and distancing herself at will from the voices she recalls from the abyss of memory. She also echoes in the mountain called La Soufrière. With her precise

A CARIBBEAN POETICS OF SPIRIT

gauge of Philoctete's illness, she concludes that alternative medicine and ancestral sorcery are needed to facilitate his healing. In fact, much of the exchange value between the landscape and Ma is based on a series of metaphoric codes, and the ability to perceive these traces in unusual spaces and territories.

As she goes to Mass and prays, she mentally recalls all the healing herbs and recipes she knows. Several ideas emerge here, one of which is Walcott's illustration of the power of syncretism and collective magic. The poet may be underscoring the pretensions of groups that consider themselves superior because of their racial, economic and privileged heritage. By situating Ma Kilman between the settings of the Catholic Church and the mystical goat path in which she brews her potions, Walcott is fuelling an ambivalent, creative newness of art that is associated with syncretism and cultural resistance. As a result of this fusion, the poet affords a formal method for envisioning a new people and a new art in the Caribbean.

As she keeps on exercising her memory, Ma climbs through the landscape to locate the source of the stench. She stumbles upon a line of ants on the ground that makes strange designs in her mind and swiftly understands that she must reciprocate these patterns in quantity and careful measurement in order to concoct Philoctete's healing:

[S]he climbed a goat-path up from the village [. . .]. / Then she staggered back / from the line of ants at her feet. She saw the course / they had kept behind her, following her from church, / signaling a language she could not recognize. A swift had carried the strong seed in its stomach / centuries ago from its antipodal shore, / skimming the sea-troughs, outdarting ospreys [. . .]. / She aimed to carry the cure / that precedes every wound; the reversible Blight / of Benin was her bow, her target the ringed haze / of a circling horizon [. . .]. / She nestled in dry seaweed [. . .]. / All of that motion / a pile of fragile ash from the fire of her will, / but the vine grew its own wings, out of the ocean / it climbed like the ants, the ancestors of Achille / the women carrying coals after the dark door / slid over the hold. As the weed grew in odour / so did its strength at the damp root of the cedar, / where the flower was anchored at the mottled root / as a lizard crawled upwards, foot by sallow foot.[83]

Walcott's use of the ants as sentient figures, which lead to revelation, develops the contingency of the divine. Moreover, the pilgrim of the ants, crawling and making pathways through the woods, is equated with a sensation of water trickling across the skin. In one dimension, the ants are divine messengers traversing through Ma Kilman's being and imparting to her sacred knowledge. In another sense, they suggest a resourcefulness associated with diasporan female lives, the power of networking and communal creativity that has characterized Caribbean womanhood.

Moreover, Ma Kilman discovers the secret plant through the divine assistance of the swift (her familiar) which brings it from Africa to St Lucia. The sibyl calls upon ancient African deities, including Erzulie, Shango and Ogun, who have gathered together within the healing serum of the flower: "all their power, / their roots, and their rituals were concentrated / in the whorled corolla of that stinking flower. / They were there. She called them".[84] The flower serves as a receptor in the magical transfer of the wound. Of equal significance is that Ma relies on the powers of Obeah to decipher the animist language through a trance. Like a shaman of the forest, her expertise emerges from her ability to control the spiritual realm through incantation, ritual and a vernacular of healing properties, which are latent in the landscape. Her intuitive connection to ancestral powers, the magic of the landscape and her tribal roots enable her to find a cure for both Philoctete's wounded shin and spirit.

Symbolically, she bathes him in a cauldron from the old sugar mill, which is a womb-like space filled to its rim with the magical potion made from the secret plant and the help of the gods. He screams and the "O: [was] the scream / of centuries",[85] and Ma scolds him like a mother during this ritual as he shrieks with the pain of centuries. By enacting a reversal of the agonized "O", he feels his "shin / drain in the seethe like sucked marrow, he felt it drag / the slime from his shame".[86] Walcott is here wielding the power of the metaphysical world, which is brought to bear on both the psychic and physical body. This is materialized in the careful sterilization of both Philoctete's fevered shin and his soul by the sorceress's bubbling brew and litany. It is important to note that fluid

A CARIBBEAN POETICS OF SPIRIT

and supernatural forces congregate with the natural and human world in unison to unburden Philoctete and the past that he represents. The revelation that there is much more to the seemingly latent landscape of the island, which was vibrating with imperceptible forces, gods and divine messengers, stimulates reconfigured notions of the self and community. The narrator notes for example that, "Under the thick leaves of the forest, there's a life / more intricate than ours."[87] The appearance of a divine landscape is an intrinsic component of Walcott's poetics of spirit. In alignment with a network of relations – the native plants, the medicines, the microbes, all of the island thrumming with life – is the practice of freedom and world-making.

After the ritual is completed, Philoctete rises from the ringed mouth of the cauldron, "like a boy in his bath with the first clay's / innocent prick".[88] He emerges as Adam in a new Eden as Ma Kilman returns something of a spirit of warriorhood to him. His healing indicates a more widespread potential for positive change through ancestral ritual and natural engagement. From the many traumas of slavery, a new meaning system steadfastly emerges. Walcott has certainly created a narrative capable of accommodating a character who functions as a powerful repository of ancestral energies. Ma Kilman is not just a wise woman, but she herself is a source of prophetic and poetic utterance as she unravels the layers of time and history through her magical gifts. Seeing through her eyes, the poet portrays St Lucia in a process of strange and wondrous alchemical transformation from woundedness to healing.

Since spirits, magic, ceremony and supernatural worlds have been struck through several notes in the text, these metaphors can be seen as part of Walcott's overall design. It is a movement that allows the issuing forth of new meaning and the creative potential of art itself. In both "Arawak Horizon" and *Omeros*, the continuous movement in and out of worlds and dimensions functions as a portal through which incorporeal beings emerge and impart healing remedies to individuals and communities. These presences are not illusions. Rather, they are the potent subjects of creative works that release the poet and the reader into new routes of meaning and into reservoirs of the small histories of those who

168

have been kept silent because of their difference. Art bears the power of a guide; its function is to bring the individual closer to the repressed parts of the self and of history. Walcott's negotiation of submerged pain (on a personal level) is revealed in his own imagined death, as he journeys into the underworld with the guide, Omeros. It is a journey of terror and psychic tremor as the poet sees other writers who are damned for their failure to develop purposeful, poetic methods that would bring clarity to the mire of people's lives.

The character, Seven Seas, is of interest as he is physically blind, but is a spiritual visionary. Embodied in his consciousness is the tradition of the griot; he is a travelling storyteller, preserver and custodian of sacred myths and wisdom. Worldly blindness allows Seven Seas to distil life's deeper meanings. It is his rich interiority that admits him into a world of acute perceptions and prophecies. As Walcott begins to fall into one of the pits of Hell, he is saved by the seer. The narrow escape forces him to reflect on the nature of his own practice. At this point, the histories of the Caribbean peoples and communities spur a new awareness as evinced in his words, "My light was clear".[89] The poet is urged by Seven Seas to cultivate a sense of belonging and return to his 'home'. He accomplishes this by articulating a deep gratitude for the healing he has received through his poetry.

Interestingly, Walcott makes clear the revelation that poetry offers a new leap beyond the ego. Like Philoctete, Achille and the unnamed narrator in "Arawak Horizon", his submergence into other realities not only inspires revolutionary stratagems against neo-colonial forces that seek to limit the creative imagination and control the mind, but facilitates a deepened line of analysis in reconstructing the frames of Caribbean identity and being through the multifaceted possibilities and poetic pleasures of spirit. The expectation is that spirit symbols, psychic journeying, metamorphosis, clairvoyance, flight, dream transmission and ancestral magic may yield innovative positions of cultural criticism.

The purpose of giving shape to spectral presences that lay immersed in language allows the critic to speak of those repressed cultures without privileging hegemonic reading structures. These alternative modes of

A CARIBBEAN POETICS OF SPIRIT

representation inspire an intent to revise philosophical explorations of specific historic events, Caribbean ontology and freedoms. The impact of such an aesthetic undoubtedly has deep implications for the creative writer, who generates the finest elements of whatever heritage we seek to preserve and pass on to future generations.

This project provides not only a rubric but a critical frame for reading the literary text with a renewed inquiry into the region's resources and philosophies that are embedded in non-traditional epistemological tools and indeed, in the immortal world. It conceives a nuanced understanding of the various ideological agendas that contour the Caribbean imagination and suggests the need for greater attention to the syncretic pathways and folk-based traditions that continue to inform Caribbean consciousness. Such a proposition should promise Caribbean peoples a useful blueprint for engaging the future and for providing healing interventions to the many traumatic eruptions of the past. To catch the wraiths of one's past is to gain hold of one's destiny. One awaits with earnest expectation the next round of contributions to this urgent strand in the tapestry of Caribbean intellectualism.

Afterword

THIS PROJECT HAS INVESTIGATED THE CRISIS OF BEING, becoming and belonging for Caribbean people through the foci of spirit presences drawn from African Caribbean and Indigenous cultures as a powerful but underutilized portal for understanding the social malaise in the region. The literary representations comprise the myriad ways in which the repressed circuits of historical trauma are forced into articulation through language. By an engagement with ghosts and facets of the Caribbean cosmic universe, NourbeSe Philip, Grace Nichols, George Lamming, Erna Brodber, Shani Mootoo, Maryse Condé, Gisèle Pineau, Patricia Powell, Derek Walcott and Wilson Harris have in many ways, broadened the theoretical parameters of Caribbean literature. The texts' polyvocality presents a sustained engagement with alternative ways of thinking about the self and new forms of relations with the past. The cross-section of themes evoked in the fictional constructions of spirit have made possible interventions to ontological self-engineering, thus delineating pathways to symbolic restoration of Caribbean peoples in more inclusive ways.

Moreover, this work has engaged a methodological flexibility commensurate with the thematic and stylistic divergences of each text to open and sustain conversations within contradictions and consequently contributes to the process of shaping the diverse entity that is the Caribbean. The method has proven to be beneficial as it has facilitated the recuperation and implementation of alternative ways of thinking about the myriad signifying practices of a Caribbean poetics of spirit. Each text, in its unique way, shows that the experience of colonization not only created a disjuncture between the colonial past and post-colonial realities in

A CARIBBEAN POETICS OF SPIRIT

the Caribbean world, but also demonstrates how the cosmologies of the ancient world and that of every ethnic migrant group explored in this study, have been pivotal to an emerging new world order. Consequently, the narratives have opened the manifold ways in which to fashion and read the self. The texts in chapter two piloted a potentiating praxis in the quest of reconciling issues of non-belonging and social awkwardness through a refusal to reduce originary violent histories to forgetfulness. By excavating latent memories within the collective unconscious, one is able to envision a reality beyond deterministic cycles of conquest and disempowerment. Such efforts illuminate a viable and interior dimension of Caribbean peoples, which is accessible via the creative imagination.

NourbeSe Philip in *Zong!* and Grace Nichols in *I is a Long Memoried Woman*, have similarly unraveled some of the eruptive forces that impact Caribbean peoples in the contemporary world in the wake of the triangular slave trade. Through an intricate design of language that simulates the horror of the Middle Passage and its aftermath, the poets de-territorialize space and offer an alternative temporality, which work towards initiating dialogue with spectres of blackness that have been denied subjectivity and voice. The axis of memory that is embedded in the land, the sea and folk-based beliefs provide a space of infinite possibility, where one is empowered to chart new beginnings. The power of crisis to push knowledge beyond governing epistemes is widely acknowledged in this chapter.

The notion of belated hauntings is also problematized by Lamming in *Season of Adventure* and Erna Brodber in *The Rainmaker's Mistake*. Both texts speak to the process of moving from ontological erasure into seasons of freedom and individuality. Lamming's and Brodber's shared concern with disempowered Afro-Caribbean nationals and their descendants signal an imperative to assume responsibility for curating therapeutic interventions that address the spirit, soul and body. The strategies of ceremony, liminality, boundary-crossing, psychic journeying, hypnosis, possession and ancestral magic become a way to bring into full focus a resilient sense of Caribbean identity. The centrality of the spiritual in these discourses, greatly suggests its purchase in the project of emancipation.

Chapter five places an onus on assessing an eclectic identity that

AFTERWORD

involves articulations of being migrant, marginalized, exiled and queer, to find out precisely the various manifestations of what it means to be a spectral figure, not only in the here and now but in the past and future. In this chapter, the figure of the 'spectre' is a response to prevailing discursive formations, which deny equal respect and dignity to all. Thus, these new crises of subject formation for Caribbean persons who crave acceptance despite their difference, have been probed to illuminate the often unpleasant and lethal psychic consequences of historical, racial, political and gendered inequalities, which impinge on the emotional health of persons. The selection of stories depicts a refusal of closure, clear endings, certainty and stability to offer a continuous experimentation with unending visitations of violence and mental confusion in the contemporary world. Subsequently, a necessary return to spiritual pathways energizes a quest for autonomy, agency, healing and liberty, which ultimately shapes the psyche and mobilizes people towards collective redress.

It is evident that the tide is high with conversations about the non-human moving beyond the nation space and plantation. The past continues to curve into the present where cycles of abuse, exploitation, resource extraction, the contestation for territory, the deepening effects of climate change, the compromising of our democracy and new totalitarian orders persist in the habits of people and society. History is thus a burden that needs to be worked out. Our cultural workers and writers are conceiving bold ideas to match vicious moments in history; one of the ways in which they are doing it is through the terrain of spirit.

APPENDIX

The expressive features and contexts of spirit may be recognizable to others by way of the social factors that give rise to its formal properties and appeals. For the sake of clarity, I highlight these modes of spirit in which they generally (but not exhaustively) tend to be used in the table below:

Sample Causes/ Initiating Factors	Modality/ Deciphering Praxis	Characteristic(s)	Sample Social, Cultural, Signifying Effectiveness
Essentialism Ontological erasure	*Ritual/ceremony*	Symbolic; formulaic; herb-based; incantatory; action-oriented	Recuperation; cure; empowerment; transcendence; intervention
Abjection Castaways	*Mediums/seers*	Intermediaries; clairaudient; clairvoyant; clairsentient	Warning; service; power display
Latency	*Dreams*	Ceremonially induced; Time-travel	Negotiation
Unjust/ abnormal death Products of a fevered imagination	*Ghosts*	Disembodied; smoke; shadows; apparitions	Surveillance; compel overdue reckoning; haunt; torment; threat; rebuke
Concealed/ unhealed trauma Secret abuse	*Cryptophore*	Entombment	Avoidance; aggression
Entrenched unfreedoms	*Liminal presences / boundary crosser*	Fluid, betwixt worlds	Rapport; encapsulates trajectories of accommodation and mixing
Sedimentation of ethnic cultures Colonial implosion	*Mythic presences*	Archetypes	Elaborates on new forms of historiography; reconnection; potentialities of plural meaning

Table continues on next page

APPENDIX

Sample Causes/ Initiating Factors	Modality/ Deciphering Praxis	Characteristic(s)	Sample Social, Cultural, Signifying Effectiveness
Colonial violence Murder Erasure by imperial archive	*Spirit-imbued hieroglyphs and symbols*	Experimental; linguistic fragmentation	Transmission; bonds ideology to language
Amnesia	*Cultural memory as spirit agent*	Embodiment	Authorization; impartation
Stasis Zombification	*Discursive and artistic divination*	Stitch-work; kinetic and tactile movements	Mending; liberation; prowess
Extermination and genocide	*Postmemory*	Sacred objects; talismanic tools; family albums; maps	Ritual remembrance; cultural assertion

Notes

CHAPTER 1

1. Geist is Proto-Germanic for ghost.

2. Martin Munro, "Introduction," to *The Haunted Tropics*, ed. Munro (Kingston: UWI Press, 2015), vii.

3. Damian Grant, *Realism (The Critical Idiom Reissued)*. (London: Routledge, 2019), 9.

4. Frantz Fanon, *Black Skin, White Masks* (NY: Grove Press, 2008).

5. Caribbean (existential) phenomenology departs from the early structures of pure thought or pure consciousness in order to engage with lived experience. For all intents and purposes of this work, I use the term phenomenology in the tradition of Caribbean existentialism as engaged by Lewis Gordon, Paget Henry, Frantz Fanon and Wilson Harris. See Frantz Fanon, *Black Skin, White Masks* (New York: Grove Press, 2008); Gordon Lewis, *Existence in Black: An Anthology of Black Existential Philosophy* (London: Routledge, 1997); Paget Henry, "African and Afro-Caribbean Existential Philosophies," in *Existence in Black: An Anthology of Black Existential Philosophy* (London: Routledge, 1997), 11–17; Wilson Harris, *The Womb of Space: The Cross-Cultural Imagination* (California: Greenwood, 1983). Although moving to different beats, Fanon, Harris, Henry and Gordon have provided meaningful lines of determination and articulations of Caribbean autonomy outside colonial trends. Lewis Gordon, for example, observes that Caribbean phenomenology and existential thought are not tied to European beliefs and practices. While the terms, in part, are reflective of the history of European literature which bears the names "existentialism" and "phenomenology", Gordon states, "We can regard [the] philosophy of [black] existence . . . as philosophical questions premised upon concerns of freedom, anguish, responsibility, embodied agency, sociality and liberation." See Lewis Gordon, "Introduction," to *Black: An Anthology of Black Existential Philosophy* (London: Routledge, 1997), 3. Opening up the scope for further discussion is Paget Henry, who notes that "Caribbean existential philosophy must be constituted around the systematic formulation and evaluation of our attitudes toward *existence in the region* [. . .]. [This encompasses] our earliest and most basic inherited [and] life-affirming . . . attitudes toward

NOTES

spiritual existence. These attitudes included a very deep respect for the power of deities and ancestors." See Paget Henry in "African and Afro-Caribbean Existential Philosophies," in *Existence in Black: An Anthology of Black Existential Philosophy* (London: Routledge, 1997), 13–14. Henry's definition of Caribbean existential thought offers the generative ground for connecting ideas of being with concerns of meta-physicality and spirituality. Such a premise transcends the limitation of pure consciousness in the Husserlian sense and facilitates a recognition of Caribbean essence, existence and consciousness vis-à-vis the inter-relatedness of plural and cross-cultural experiences. Henry's emphasis is on perception as both a concrete and embodied experience, which is not unlike Wilson Harris's disposition to Caribbean space and existence.

6   Frantz Fanon, *The Wretched of the Earth* (New York: Grove Press, 2007), 57–58.

7   Fanon, *Wretched*, 183.

8   Édouard Glissant, "The Quarrel with History", in *Caribbean Discourse: Selected Essays* (Charlottesville: Virginia University Press, 1989), 62.

9   Syncretism is a form of cross-cultural exchange where old and new traditions merge into a functioning unified entity. For example, some items, common to both Europe and Africa seem to have reinforced each other in the New World and may be called parallel traditions. See George Eaton Simpson in *Religious Cults of the Caribbean: Trinidad, Jamaica and Haiti* (San Juan: Institute of Caribbean Studies, 1970), 126.

10   Edward Baugh, "Maps Made in the Heart," *Journal of West Indian Literature* 18, no. 2 (2010): 18.

11   Baugh, "Maps", 1–19.

12   Peter Burroughs, "Colonial Self-Government," in *British Imperialism in the Nineteenth Century*, ed. Colin C. Eldridge (London: Macmillan, 1989), 41.

13   Burroughs, "Self-Government," 39–64.

14   See Edward Baugh, *West Indian Poetry 1900–1970: A Study in Cultural Decolonization* (Kingston: Savacou Publications, 1970).

15   Richard Allsopp, "The Niger-Congo Languages as Linguistic Source," in *Education Issues in Creole and Creole-Influenced Vernacular Contexts* (Kingston: UWI Press, 2014), 31–42.

16   There are many Francophone scholars and critics who have contributed to the scope of Antillean criticism, including Édouard Glissant (Antillanité), Patrick Chamoiseau (Creolité), Aimé Césaire and Frantz Fanon (Negritude). Yet, while the movements of Antillanité, Creolité and Negritude carry their distinct linguistic, contextual and ideological orientations, the decolonial ethos reflects a transcultural concern with the renovations of Caribbean identity outside of imperialistic trends. See Aimé Césaire, *Discourse on Colonialism*

NOTES

(New York: New York University Press, 2001); Édouard Glissant, *Poetics of Relation*, trans. Betsy Wing (Michigan: Michigan University Press, 1997); Jean Bernabé, Patrick Chamoiseau, Raphaël Confiant, and Mohamed Bouya Taleb-Khyar, Éloge de la Créolité (Paris: Gallimard, 1993).

17　Paget Henry, *Caliban's Reason: Introducing Afro-Caribbean Philosophy*. (New York: Routledge, 2000).

18　Henry, "Introduction," to *Caliban's Reason*, 3–4.

19　Henry, *Caliban's Reason*, 5.

20　Henry, *Caliban's Reason*, 11–69.

21　The erasure of Caribbean ontology by colonial master narratives is conceptualized in Erna Brodber's novel, *Myal*, in which the novelist alludes to the effects (spirit thievery) that the colonial education has on young Ella O'Grady. Ole African's dictate that "the half has never been told" is an ongoing refrain which anticipates the alienating effects of colonial education and other mechanisms of cultural impotence. See Erna Brodber, *Myal* (Illinois: Waveland Press, 2014), 34.

22　Edward Kamau Brathwaite, "The African Presence in Caribbean Literature," *Dedalus* 102, no. 2 (1974): 73–109.

23　Obeah is an important symbol of resistance and credible threat to colonial ideology. It has been a marker of the black folk aesthetic that is now constitutive of Caribbean literary and cultural production. Interestingly, Carnival and Obeah run on parallel lines as there is a spiritual basis for Carnival echoed in the performance of playing mas. Kela Francis observes that mas is an embodiment of spirits whereby "African maskers bring the mysterious world of nature and supernatural into the known and more predictable community of humans, so that the spirits may commune with the people and can cause them to respond in various ways: dancing, drumming, praying, hand-clapping, offering and singing". See Kela Nnarka Francis in "The Spirituality of Carnival: Using Yoruba Cosmology to Read *The Dragon Can't Dance,"International Journal of Art and Art History*, 3 (2015), 63–82. Obeah beliefs and practices became both receptacles of lost African traditions and seeds of new Caribbean ones. It first entered the discourse in response to Tacky's Rebellion in St Mary Parish, Jamaica. Carolyn Cooper contends that it was a Jamaican who conducted a religious ceremony at Bois Caiman in which a freedom covenant was affirmed. This conjurer is an Obeahman. See Carolyn Cooper, "Haiti – the Price of Freedom," *The Gleaner*, 17 January 2010. In this sense, Carnival and Obeah converge within an emancipatory performance of ritual wielded against the dehumanizing impulses of colonialism.

24　Cynric Williams, *Hamel, the Obeah Man* (Ontario: Broadview Editions, 2010).

NOTES

25 Williams, *Hamel*, 41.

26 Diana Paton, *The Cultural Politics of Obeah: Religion, Colonialism and Modernity in the Caribbean Word* (Cambridge: Cambridge University Press, 2015).

27 Eugenia O'Neal, "Credulous Blacks and Faithful Mulattoes," in *Obeah, Race and Racism: Caribbean Witchcraft in the English Imagination* (Kingston: UWI Press, 2020), 312.

28 Herbert de Lisser, *The White Witch of Rosehall* (London: Macmillan Caribbean, 2018).

29 De Lisser, *White Witch*, 129.

30 Edgar Mittelholzer, *With a Carib Eye* (London: Seeker and Warburg, 1958), 23.

31 See Edgar Mittelholzer, *Shadows Move among Them* (Philadelphia: Lippincott, 1951) and *My Bones and My Flute: A Ghost Story in the Old-Fashioned Manner* (London: Secker & Warburg, 1955). In these fictions, Mittelholzer's dystopias disguised as utopias posited the view that the neo-enslaved communities are fully aware of their domination, and in light of their perceived impotence to resist colonial oppression, consciously invented fantasies which further locked them into stasis.

32 Wilson Harris, *Palace of the Peacock* (London: Faber and Faber, 1960).

33 Wilson Harris, "Tradition and the West Indian Novel," in *Tradition, the Writer and Society: Critical Essays* (London: New Beacon, 1967), 32.

34 Wilson Harris, *Tradition*, 32

35 Wilson Harris, "Profiles of Myth and the New World," in *Selected Essays of Wilson Harris: The Unfinished Genesis of the Imagination*, ed. Andrew Bundy (London: Routledge, 1999), 201–11.

36 Sylvia Wynter, "We Must Learn to Sit Down and Talk about a Little Culture," *Jamaica Journal* 2, no, 4 (1968): 23–32.

37 Barbara Webb, "Lo real maravilloso in Caribbean Fiction," in *Myth and History in Caribbean Fiction: Alejo Carpentier, Wilson Harris, and Édouard Glissant* (Massachusetts: University Press of Massachusetts, 1992), 13.

38 Édouard Glissant, "The Open Boat," in *Poetics of Relation*, trans. Betsy Wing (Michigan: University Press of Michigan, 1997), 5.

39 Glissant, *Poetics*, 5.

40 Erica Johnson, *Caribbean Ghostwriting* (Vancouver: Fairleigh Dickinson University Press, 2009).

41 Johnson, "Memorializing the Ghost," *Ghostwriting*, 12.

42 Johnson, "Moi, Tituba," *Ghostwriting*, 79.

43 Carolyn Cooper, "Something Ancestral Recaptured: Spirit possession as trope in Selected Feminist Fictions of the African Diaspora," in *Motherlands: Black*

NOTES

Women's Writing from Africa, the Caribbean and South Asia, ed. Susheila Nasta (London: The Women's Press, 1991), 64–87.

44 Cooper, "Something Ancestral," 64–87.

45 Kamau Brathwaite, *Word Making Man: Poem for Nicolás Guillén in Xaymaca* (Kingston: Savacou Cooperative, 1979), 6.

46 See Joyelle McSweeney, "Poetics, Revelations, and Catastrophes: An Interview with Kamau Brathwaite," *Rain Taxi* (2005): 1–11 and Kamau Brathwaite, "Namsetoura," in *Born to Slow Horses* (Connecticut: Wesleyan University Press, 2005), 118–22.

47 Kamau Brathwaite, "Caliban," in *The Arrivants: A New World Trilogy – Rights of Passage/ Islands/ Masks* (London: Oxford University Press, 1988), 192.

48 Several anthropologists and cultural critics, such as Margarite Fernández Olmos and Lizabeth Paravisini-Gerbert, have explored the portrayals of Caribbean magic and spiritual-ritual systems, such as Obeah, that survived the trans-atlantic journey and which formed part of the cultural heritage of people in the diaspora. These belief systems are tied to the historical ideas of Caribbean self-identification and Caribbean-influenced political movements. See Margarite Fernández Olmos and Lizabeth Paravisini-Gebert, *Sacred Possessions: Vodou, Santería, Obeah, and the Caribbean* (New Jersey: Rutgers University Press, 1997). See also Sheshalatha Reddy's "Inspiriting Flesh/Fleshing Out Spirit" in *British Empire and the Literature of Rebellion: Revolting Bodies, Laboring Subjects* (London: Palgrave Macmillan, 2017), 73–128, in which Reddy parses out the concept of spirit as it interfaces with the troubled history of slavery in the Caribbean. Reddy looks specifically to Jamaican labour struggles and the violent nationalist outworkings of the 1930–1940s which harks back to the Morant Bay rebellion as a potent example of earlier Jamaican labour resistance.

49 Jenny Sharpe, "The Rebels Old Obeah Woman," in *Ghosts of Slavery* (Minnesota: University Press of Minnesota, 2003), 1–44.

50 Kamau Brathwaite, "Veve," in *The Arrivants: A New World Trilogy – Rights of Passage/ Islands/ Masks* (London: Oxford University Press, 1988), 11.

51 Homi Bhabha, "DissemiNation: Time, Narrative and the Margins of the Modern Nation," in *The Location of Culture* (London: Routledge, 2012), 139–70.

52 Derek Walcott, *Omeros* (London: Faber and Faber, 1990).

53 Wilson Harris, "Arawak Horizon," in *The Sleepers of Roraima and Age of the Rainmakers* (London: Peepal Tree, 2014), 153–73.

54 Harris, "Yurokon," in *Sleepers*, 81–104.

55 Harris, "Couvade," in *Sleepers*, 35–58.

56 Harris, "History, Fable and Myth in the Caribbean and Guianas," in *Selected*

NOTES

Essays of Wilson Harris: The Unfinished Genesis of the Imagination, ed. Andrew Bundy (London: Routledge, 1999), 151.

57 Harris, "History," 152–60.

58 Harris, "History," 152.

59 Harris, "History," 157.

60 Erica Johnson, "Introduction," to *Cultural Memory, Memorials, and Reparative Writing* (New York: Springer International Publishing, 2018), 1–2.

61 Christian Lundberg, "Enjoying God's death: The passion of the Christ and the practices of an evangelical public," *Quarterly Journal of Speech* 95, no. 4 (2009): 390.

62 Philip, Marlene NourbeSe, *Zong!* (Connecticut: Wesleyan University Press, 2008).

63 Patricia Powell, *The Fullness of Everything* (London: Peepal Tree, 2009).

64 Marianne Hirsch, "Introduction," to *The Generation of Postmemory: Writing and Visual Culture After the Holocaust* (New York: Columbia University Press, 2012), 5.

65 Hirsch, *Generation of Postmemory*, 5.

66 Elizabeth DeLoughrey and George Handley, "Introduction," to *Postcolonial Ecologies: Literature of the Environment* (London: Oxford University Press, 2011), 4.

67 Sylvia Wynter, "Novel and History, Plot and Plantation." *Savacou* 5, no. 1 (1971): 100.

68 Wynter, "Novel and History," 100.

69 Olive Senior, *Gardening in the Tropics* (Ontario: Insomniac, 1994) and Lorna Goodison, *To Us, All Flowers are Roses: Poems* (Illinois: University of Illinois Press, 1995).

70 Derek Walcott, "The Antilles: Fragments of Epic Memory," in *What the Twilight Says: Essay* (London: Farrar, Straus and Giroux, 1998), 68.

71 Andrew Bundy, "Introduction," to *Selected Essays of Wilson Harris: The Unfinished Genesis of the Imagination*, ed. Andrew Bundy (London: Routledge, 1999), 2–3.

72 Bundy, *Selected Essays*, 10.

73 Edwidge Danticat, *The Farming of Bones: A Novel* (New York: Soho Press, 1998), 85.

74 Kamau Brathwaite, "The Black Angel," in *DreamStories* (New York: Longman, 1994), 28.

75 See examples of the use of circular images in (i) Achille's return to Africa in *Omeros* via a movement through the sea; (ii) the circularity of the cosmos in the long-memoried woman's imagination through contact with plantations in

NOTES

Grace Nichols's poetry; and (iii) the telescopic journeys into caves, waterfalls, brooks and bridges in Harris's Carib fables.

76 Paul Gilroy, "The Black Atlantic as Counterculture of Modernity," in *The Black Atlantic: Modernity and Double Consciousness* (Cambridge, MA: Harvard University Press, 1993), 12.

77 Gilroy, "The Black Atlantic," 12.

78 Derek Walcott, "The Sea is History," in *The Poetry of Derek Walcott 1948-2013* (London: Farrar, Straus and Giroux, 2014), 253-56.

79 Glissant, "The Open Boat," 7.

80 Kamau Brathwaite, "Caribbean Culture: Two Paradigms," in *Missile and Capsule*, ed. Jurgen Martini (Bremen: University Press of Bremen, 1983), 9–54.

81 Kamau Brathwaite, *Sun Poem*, (Oxford: Oxford University Press, 1982), 51.

82 Melvin B. Rahming, "Towards a Critical Theory of Spirit: The Insistent Demands of Erna Brodber's Myal," *Revista/Review Interamericana* I (2001): 8.

83 Wilson Harris, "Author's Note," in *The Whole Armour* and *The Secret Ladder* (London: Faber and Faber, 1973),9.

84 Sandra Pouchet Pacquet, foreword to *The Pleasures of Exile* (Michigan: Michigan University Press, 1992), xii–vx.

85 See Gordon Rohlehr, "Possession as Metaphor: Lamming's *Season of Adventure*," in *The Shape of that Hurt and other Essays* (Port of Spain: Longman Trinidad Limited, 1992), 66–96

86 As delineated in the essay, "What the Twilight Says: An Overture", Derek Walcott employs the use of amber or twilight as a way of interrogating the complex life of the tropics. The in-between state of semi-darkness, a meridian between light and dark, is a baseline of myth. The effect of changing shapes through a play with conflicting images is a method to think through ideas of dual realities and spirit presences. See Walcott, "What the Twilight Says: An Overture," in *What the Twilight Says: Essays* (New York: Farrar, Straus and Giroux, 1998), 3–35.

87 Édouard Glissant, *Poetics of Relation*, trans. Betsy Wing (Michigan: Michigan University Press, 1997).

88 Barbara Lalla, "Notes", in *Defining Jamaican Fiction: Marronage and the Discourse of Survival* (Alabama: University Press of Alabama, 1996), 202.

89 Hsiu-Fang Hsieh and Sarah Shannon, "Three Approaches to Qualitative Content Analysis," *Qualitative Health Research*, vol. 15, no. 9 (2005): 1277–88.

90 Eve Sedgwick, "Paranoid Reading and Reparative Reading, or, You're So Paranoid You Probably Think this Essay is about You," in *Touching Feeling: Affect, Pedagogy, Performativity* (Durham: Duke University Press, 2003), 123–51.

NOTES

CHAPTER 2

1   Wilson Harris, "A Talk on the Subjective Imagination," in *Explorations: A Selection of Talks and Articles, 1966–1981* (Denmark: Dangaroo Press, 1981), 58.

2   Gordon Rohlehr, "Folk Research: Fossil or Living Bone," in *Transgression, Transition, Transformation: Essays in Caribbean Culture* (San Juan: Lexicon, 2007), 380–81.

3   Marianne Hirsch, "Masking the Subject," in *Family Frames: Photography, Narrative, and Postmemory* (New York: CreateSpace Independent Publishing, 2012), 107.

4   Marianne Hirsch, "Introduction," to *The Generation of Postmemory: Writing and Visual Culture After the Holocaust,* (New York: Columbia University Press, 2012), 4–5.

5   It should be noted that while this project acknowledges the diversity of groups (Arawak,Carib, Warrau, for example) that comprise the Indigenous population, it uses the umbrella expression 'Indigenous'. This underscores the necessity of recovering a cultural heritage of adaption to specific geographical zones. For this reason, this study formalizes a critical hypothesis that the First Peoples of Guyana have shared a common origin in the Amazon basin and hence posits a shared culture based on a special relationship with the environment.

6   Hena Maes-Jelinek, "The Whole Armour: A Compassionate Alliance," in *The Labyrinth of Universality: Wilson Harris's Visionary Art of Fiction* (Amsterdam: Rodopi, 2006), 108.

7   Gordon Rohlehr, "National Heritage Library," in *Transgression, Transition, Transformation: Essays in Caribbean Culture* (San Juan: Lexicon, 2007), 389.

8   Rohlehr, "Heritage", 389.

9   Wilson Harris, "Couvade," in *The Sleepers of Roraima and the Age of the Rainmakers* (London: Peepal Tree, 2017), 37.

10   Harris, "Couvade," 46–7.

11   Harris, "Couvade," 43.

12   Harris, "Couvade," 46.

13   Harris, "Couvade," 47.

14   Harris, "Couvade," 57.

15   Harris, "Couvade," 41.

16   Harris, "Couvade," 42.

17   Harris, "Couvade," 41.

18   Harris, "Couvade," 28.

19   Harris, "Couvade," 46.

NOTES

20 Harris, "Couvade," 46.

21 Harris, "Couvade," 46–47.

22 Harris, "Couvade," 55.

23 Harris, "Couvade," 39.

24 Harris, "Couvade," 58.

25 Marianne Hirsch, "Introduction," to *The Generation of Postmemory: Writing and Visual Culture After the Holocaust*, (New York: Columbia University Press, 2012), 5.

26 Wilson Harris, "Amerindian Legacy," in *Selected Essays of Wilson Harris: The Unfinished Genesis of the Imagination*, ed. Andrew Bundy (London: Routledge, 1999), 169.

27 Wilson Harris, "Yurokon," in *The Sleepers of Roraima and the Age of the Rainmakers* (London: Peepal Tree, 2017), 94.

28 Harris, "Yurokon," 90–91.

29 Harris, "The Schizophrenic Sea," in *The Womb of Space: The Cross-Cultural Imagination* (California: Greenwood, 1983), 24.

30 In this lecture, which translates to "The Black Novelist and his People: Notes for a Conference", Glissant uses the image of folds, coils or "replis" to corroborate his projection of a liminal aesthetic that actively participates in a multiplicity of connections through time and space. While the lecture is delivered in French, Michael Dash offers sporadic translations in his oeuvre, *Édouard Glissant: Cambridge Studies in African and Caribbean Literature* (London: Cambridge University Press, 1995). It should also be noted that although Glissant applies the analysis of folds or interstitial zones, with its complex system of layering, to Martiniquan cultural processes of resistance and assimilation, the paradigm can plausibly be extended to reading the mythic and cosmic infrastructure of the Anglophone Caribbean world. Michael Dash fittingly notes in his essay, "A Poetics of Liminality", that Glissant's poetics of liminality reflect "the need to make an epistemological break with the poetics of erasure, practiced by an earlier generation, and [represent] a more deconstructive, less closed model for [reading] Caribbean thought [. . .] time[,] space[,] transcendence [and] transversality". (See J. Michael Dash, "A Poetics of Liminality: Another Caribbean Fin de Siècle," in *The Other American: Caribbean Literature in a New World Context* (Virginia: University Press of Virginia, 1998), 134–58). To be able to re-purpose fiction as a medium through which boundaries of time and space are fluid is at the heart of Harris's writings.

31 Dash, "A Poetics of Liminality: Another Caribbean Fin de Siècle," 150.

32 Dash, "Poetics," 150.

33 Harris, "Yurokon," 90–99.

NOTES

34   Harris, "Yurokon," 87–89.

35   Hena Maes-Jelinek, "From Living Nature to Borderless Culture in Wilson Harris's Work," in *Caribbean Literature and the Environment: Between Nature and Culture*, eds. Elizabeth DeLoughrey et al. (Virginia: University Press of Virginia, 2005), 257.

36   Paget Henry, "Introduction," to *Time, History, and Philosophy in the Works of Wilson Harris* (New York: Columbia University Press, 2016), xii.

37   Harris, "Yurokon," 92–94.

38   Harris, "Yurokon," 89.

39   Harris, "Yurokon," 89.

40   Harris, "Yurokon," 86.

41   Harris, "The Schizophrenic Sea," 24.

42   Harris, "Yurokon," 97.

43   Harris, "Yurokon," 86.

44   Harris, "Yurokon," 99.

45   Wilson Harris, "The Untameable Cosmos," in *The Womb of Space: The Cross-Cultural Imagination* (California: Greenwood, 1983), 39–54.

46   Wilson Harris, "The Whole Armour," in *The Guyana Quartet* (London: Faber and Faber, 1985), 266.

47   Harris, "The Whole Armour," 252.

48   Harris, "The Whole Armour," 252.

49   Harris, "The Whole Armour," 274.

50   Harris, "The Whole Armour," 274.

51   For further readings on the underlying references to female Amazonian warrior traditions, see Adrienne Mayor, *The Amazons: Lives and Legends of Warrior Women Across the Ancient World* (New Jersey: Princeton University Press, 2014) and Richard Reynold, *Superheroes: A Modern Mythology* (Mississippi: University Press of Mississippi, 1993). Magda's agency, independence and witchy powers cobble together the curious rumours and wild gossip about the triumphs of fierce, female warriors in the lower basins of South America. The allusion does not in any way romanticize these mythical traditions, but serves to discomfort or neutralize the hegemonic gaze enacted by monolithic or patriarchal cultural authority and discourses. It should also be noted that Magda is not a model of female perfection. At the very least, her femininity is perplexing. However, her body becomes a space and place of ideological power. As Judith Butler asserts in *Bodies That Matter*, "the fixity of [woman's] body, its contours, its movements, [is] fully . . . rethought along the lines of power". See Judith Butler, "Introduction," to *Bodies that Matter: On the Discursive of Sex* (New York: Routledge, 1993), 2.

NOTES

52 Gregory Shaw, "Time of the Tiger," in *Wilson Harris: The Uncompromising Imagination*, ed. Hena Maes-Jelinek (Denmark: Dangaroo Press, 1991), 107–14.

53 Mark McWatt, "Libidinous Landscapes: Sexual Inscriptions of Place in Guyanese Literature," *Commonwealth: Essays and Studies* vol. 25, no. 2 (2003): 81.

54 Harris, "The Whole Armour," 313.

55 Harris's *Armour* explores notions of threshold space and its association with the violence of colonization and rape. It seems to repeat the metaphorical conflation of land, women and native and circles back to the mythic position of women as threshold figures and emblems of space.

56 Sharon is making love to Cristo in the jungle but is still telepathically connected to Magda's wake.

57 Edouardo Viveiros de Castro, "Cosmological Deixis and Amerindian Perspectivism," *Journal of the Royal Anthropological Institute* vol. 4, no. 3 (1998): 469–72.

58 Harris identifies the character of Magda with uncanny qualities. The evidence is to be found in her description as "a witch" and "a lurking beast". See Harris, "Whole Armour," 321.

59 Harris, "Whole Armour," 334–35.

60 Harris, "Whole Armour," 337–42.

61 See "Whole Armour" in *The Labyrinth of Universality* (Netherlands: Rodopi, 2006), 111–14.

62 Harris, "Whole Armour," 333.

63 Harris, "Whole Armour," 309.

64 Shaw, "Time of the Tiger," 114.

65 Harris, " Whole Armour," 350.

66 Harris, " Whole Armour," 349–50.

67 Harris, " Whole Armour," 351.

CHAPTER 3

1 Jean Wyatt, "Giving Body to the Word: The Maternal Symbolic in Toni Morrison's *Beloved*," *Publications of the Modern Language Association of America*, vol. 108, no. 4 (1993): 474–88.

2 Ron Eyerman, "The Making Collective Identity," in *Cultural Trauma: Slavery and the Formation of African American Identity* (Cambridge: Cambridge University Press, 2002), 61.

3 Erna Brodber, *Myal* (Illinois: Waveland Press, 2014), 34.

4 Paula Morgan, "Re-membering Our Scattered Skeletons," in *The Terror and*

NOTES

the Time: Banal Violence and Trauma in Caribbean Discourse (Kingston: UWI Press, 2015), 32.

5   M. NourbeSe Philip and Setaey Adamu Boateng, *Zong!* (Connecticut: Wesleyan University Press, 2008), 202.

6   Patricia Saunders, "Defending the Dead, Confronting the Archive: A Conversation with M. NourbeSe Philip," *Small Axe* 12 no. 2 (2008): 68.

7   Saidiya Hartman, "Prologue: The Path of Strangers," in *Lose Your Mother: A Journey Along the Atlantic Slave Route*, 1st ed. (London: Farrar Straus and Giroux, 2008), 17.

8   Hannah Lutchmansingh, "Haunted Histories: Spectres of the Middle Passage in Caribbean Literature," *Tout Moun: Caribbean Journal of Cultural Studies* 4, no. 1 (2018): 1-20.

9   Philip and Boateng, *Zong!*, 3.

10   Philip and Boateng, *Zong!*, 18.

11   Philip and Boateng, *Zong!*, 3.

12   Philip and Boateng, *Zong!*, 193–94.

13   Saunders, "Defending the Dead, Confronting the Archive: A Conversation with M. NourbeSe Philip," 78–79.

14   Saunders, "Defending the Dead," 78.

15   Philip and Boateng, *Zong!*, 107–8.

16   Ian Baucom, "Liverpool, a Capital of the Long Twentieth Century," in *Specters of the Atlantic: Finance Capital, Slavery, and the Philosophy of History* (London: Duke University Press, 2007), 31.

17   Philip and Boateng, *Zong!*, xii.

18   Dahud Kehinde Shangodoyin and Ojo Oluwayemisi Oyeronke, "Statistical Inference in Ifa Divination," in *Orisa: Yoruba Gods and Spiritual Identity in Africa and the Diaspora*, eds. Toyin Falola and Ann Genova (Trenton, NJ: Africa World Press, 2005), 77.

19   Philip and Boateng, *Zong!*, 204.

20   Philip and Boateng, *Zong!*, 158.

21   Philip and Boateng, *Zong!*, 61.

22   Philip and Boateng, *Zong!*, 67.

23   Philip and Boateng, *Zong!*, 71.

24   Philip and Boateng, *Zong!*, 59.

25   Philip and Boateng, *Zong!*, 192.

26   Philip and Boateng, *Zong!*, 172.

27   Philip and Boateng, *Zong!*, 204.

28   Jason de Caires Taylor, "Vicissitudes," in *Underwater Sculptures*, June 17, 2013. https://www.underwatersculpture.com/works/underwater/.

NOTES

29 Philip and Boateng, *Zong!*, 126.

30 Saidiya Hartman, "So Many Dungeons," in *Lose Your Mother: A Journey Along the Atlantic Slave Route*, 1st ed. (London: Farrar Straus and Giroux, 2008), 133.

31 Stuart Hall, "Cultural Identity and Diaspora," in *Identity: Community, Culture, Difference*, ed. Jonathan Rutherford (London: Lawrence and Wishart, 1990), 222–37.

32 Kwame Dawes, "Grace Nichols," in *Talk Yuh Talk: Interviews with Anglophone Caribbean Poets* (Virginia: University Press of Virginia, 2000), 138.

33 Grace Nichols, *I Have Crossed An Ocean* (London: Bloodaxe, 2010), 12.

34 Gabriele Griffin, "Writing the Body: Reading Joan Riley, Grace Nichols and Ntozake Shange," in *Black Women's Writing*, ed. Gina Wisker (New York: Martin's Press, 1993), 28.

35 Nichols, *I is a Long Memoried Woman* (London: Karnak House, 1983), with emphasis on the poems, "New Birth", "I Will Enter", "In My Name", "Your Blessing", "Like Clamouring Clamouring Ghosts" and "Drum Spell".

36 Edward Kamau Brathwaite, *Roots* (Havana: Ediciones Casa de la Americas, 1896), 29–30.

37 Brathwaite, "Caribbean Culture: Two Paradigms," in *Missile and Capsule*, ed. J. Martin (Bremen: Bremen University Press, 1983), 9–54.

38 Grace Nichols, "One Continent to Another," in *I is a Long Memoried Woman* (London: Karnak House Pub, 1983), 9.

39 Nichols, "One Continent to Another," 9.

40 Nichols, "One Continent to Another," 9.

41 Wilson Harris, "History, Fable and Myth in the Caribbean and Guianas," in *Selected Essays of Wilson Harris: The Unfinished Genesis of the Imagination*, ed. Andrew Bundy (London: Routledge, 1999), 157.

42 Harris, "History, Fable and Myth in the Caribbean and Guianas," 157.

43 Grace Nichols, "Waterpot," in *I is a Long Memoried Woman* (London: Karnak House Pub, 1983), 17.

44 Nichols, "Waterpot," 18.

45 Grace Nichols, "Days That Fell," in *I is a Long Memoried Woman* (London: Karnak House Pub, 1983), 15.

46 Nichols, "Days That Fell," 15.

47 Nichols, "Days That Fell," 14.

48 Nichols, "Days That Fell," 15.

49 Nichols, "Days That Fell," 14.

50 Michael Bennett and Vanessa Dickerson, "Introduction," to *Recovering the Black Female Body: Self-Representation by African American Women* (New Jersey: Rutgers University Press, 2000), 13.

NOTES

51 Nichols, "Ala," in *I is a Long Memoried Woman*, 27.

52 Nichols, "I Coming Back", in *I is a Long Memoried Woman*, 48.

53 Édouard Glissant, "Cross-Cultural Poetics," in *Caribbean Discourse: Selected Essays* (Charlottesville: Virginia University Press, 1989), 139.

54 Sarah Lawson, "Epic Journeying I: I is a long memoried woman," in *Grace Nichols* (London: Northcote House, 2007), 67.

55 Nichols, "Night is Her Robe," in *I is a Long Memoried Woman*, 52.

56 Nichols, "Yemanji," in *I is a Long Memoried Woman*, 71.

57 Nichols, "Yemanji," 71.

58 Nichols, "I Will Enter," in *I is a Long Memoried Woman*, 69.

59 Nichols, "Of Golden Gods," in *I is a Long Memoried Woman*, 66.

60 Nichols, "Of Golden Gods," 66–67.

61 Nichols, "The Battle With Language," in *Caribbean Women Writers: Essays from the First International Conference*, ed. Selwyn Cudjoe (Massachusetts University Press: 1990), 288.

62 Nichols, "Holding My Beads," in *I is a Long Memoried Woman*, 93.

63 Nichols, "Holding My Beads," 93.

CHAPTER 4

1 George Lamming, *Season of Adventure* (Michigan: University Press of Michigan, 1960).

2 Erna Brodber, *The Rainmaker's Mistake* (London: New Beacon, 2007).

3 Harris, "Phenomenal Legacy," in *Explorations: A selection of talks and articles, 1966–1981* (Denmark: Dangaroo Press, 1981), 43–48.

4 Harris, "History, Fable and Myth in the Caribbean and Guianas," in *Selected Essays of Wilson Harris: The Unfinished Genesis of the Imagination*, eds. Andrew Bundy and Wilson Harris (London: Routledge, 1999), 152–60.

5 Harris, "Profiles of Myth and the New World," in *Selected Essays of Wilson Harris: The Unfinished Genesis of the Imagination*, ed. Andrew Bundy (London: Routledge, 1999), 201–11.

6 Harris, *Tradition, the Writer and Society: Critical Essays* (London: New Beacon, 1967).

7 Gordon Rohlehr, "Folk Research: Fossil or Living Bone," in *Transgression, Transition, Transformation: Essays in Caribbean Culture* (San Juan: Lexicon, 2007), 380–81.

8 Rohlehr, "Dream Journeys," in *Transgression*, 410–55.

9 Rohlehr, "Where is Here? What Jail is This? Who Are We?" in *Transgression*, 457–502.

NOTES

10 Rohlehr, "Possession as Metaphor: Lamming's *Season of Adventure*," in *The Shape of that Hurt and Other Essays* (San Juan: Longman Trinidad Ltd, 1992), 66–96.

11 Silvio Torres-Saillant, "Kamau Brathwaite and the Caribbean World," in *Caribbean Poetics: Toward an Aesthetic of West Indian Literature* (Cambridge: Cambridge University Press, 1997), 137.

12 Harris, *Tradition*, 28.

13 Paula Morgan, "From Apocalypse to Awakenings: Interviews with Gordon Rohlehr," *Tout Moun Journal of Caribbean Studies* 2, no. 1 (2013):14.

14 Barbara Webb, "Conclusion," to *Myth and History in Caribbean Fiction: Alejo Carpentier, Wilson Harris, and Édouard Glissant* (Massachusetts: University Press of Massachusetts, 1992), 149.

15 Harris notes that his concept of the Caribbean unconscious was drawn from his role as surveyor of the Guyanese rainforests and his experiments with language to communicate the unique Caribbean depth and density of experience. See Michael Gilkes, "The Landscape of Dreams," in *The Uncompromising Imagination*, ed. by Hena Maes-Jelinek (Denmark: Dangaroo Press, 1991), 33–35 and Alan Riach, "Interview with Wilson Harris 1990", *The Radical Imagination: Lectures and Talks*, eds. Alan Riach and Mark Williams (Belgium: L3-Liège Language and Literature, 1992), 62.

16 Harris, "History, Fable and Myth in the Caribbean and Guianas," in *Selected Essays of Wilson Harris: The Unfinished Genesis of the Imagination*, ed. Andrew Bundy (London: Routledge, 1999), 156.

17 Harris, "Quetzalcoatl and the Smoking Mirror: Reflections on Originality and Tradition," in *Selected Essays of Wilson Harris*, 184–96.

18 Rohlehr, "Where is Here?", 458.

19 While critics like Sandra Pouchet-Pacquet, Kathleen Deguzman and Glyne Griffith have provided substantial scholarship on Lamming's novel regarding the Caribbean decolonization's fighting phase, particularly focusing on the pathways of folk cultures, one wishes that further emphasis was given to Fola's immersion into a world of spirit. In "Natural Histories of Social Bodies: Rethinking Caribbean and Victorian Realities", for example, Deguzman's views on Caribbean being are contextualized within Victorian realism and spiritual history, which diverges from an articulation of being and becoming that is rooted in the *Caribbean's* ancestral mythologies and cultural practices. To explain *Season of Adventure*'s alternate reality is not only to go against the mainstream of cultural hegemony, but to uncover a highly specialized vocabulary suitable for the exploration of human consciousness as it participates with intimations of its cosmic relatedness. See Glyne Griffith, "Metaphysics and the

NOTES

Other," in *Deconstruction, Imperialism and the West Indian Novel* (Kingston: UWI Press, 1996), 53–81; Kathleen Deguzman, "Natural Histories of Social Bodies: Rethinking Caribbean and Victorian Realisms," *Studies in the Novel* vol. 49, no. 4 (2017):518–37; Sandra Pouchet-Pacquet, *The Novels of George Lamming* (Portsmouth: Heinemann Educational Publishers, 1982); Curdella Forbes, *From Nation to Diaspora: Samuel Selvon, George Lamming and the Cultural Performance of Gender* (Kingston: UWI Press, 2005).

20   Walcott, *Omeros*, 257. See the lines: "There, in miniature, / the world was globed like a fruit, since its texture is/both acid and sweet like a golden *pomme-Cythère*," emphasis mine.

21   An earlier version of my investigation into the interface between ritual and *tonelle* symbology in Lamming's text was published in the *Journal of West Indian Literature*, 27, no. 2 (2019): 29–38.

22   Lamming, *Season of Adventure*, 94.

23   Rohlehr, "Possession as Metaphor: Lamming's *Season of Adventure*," 79.

24   Lamming, *Season of Adventure*, 30.

25   Lamming, *Season of Adventure*, 130.

26   Lamming, *Season of Adventure*, 94.

27   Lamming, *Season of Adventure*, 95.

28   Carolyn Cooper, "Something Ancestral Recaptured: Spirit Possession as Trope in Selected Feminist Fictions of the African Diaspora," in *Motherlands: Black Women's Writing from Africa, the Caribbean and South Asia*, ed. Susheila Nasta (London: The Women's Press, 1991), 64.

29   Lamming, *Season of Adventure*, 84.

30   Rohlehr, "Possession as Metaphor: Lamming's *Season of Adventure*," 76.

31   Lamming, *Season of Adventure*, 150.

32   Lamming, *Season of Adventure*, 173.

33   Lamming, *Season of Adventure*, 175.

34   Olmos Margarite Fernández Olmos and Lizabeth Paravisini-Gebert, "The Afro-Cuban Religious Traditions of Regla de Palo and the Abakuá Secret Society," in *Creole Religions of the Caribbean: An Introduction from Vodou and Santeria to Obeah and Espiritismo* (New York: New York University Press, 2003), 79.

35   Lamming, *Season of Adventure*, 363.

36   Rohlehr, "Possession as Metaphor: Lamming's *Season of Adventure*," 87.

37   Erna Brodber, "History and Social Death," *Caribbean Quarterly* 58, no. 4 (2012): 112.

38   Brodber, *The Rainmaker's Mistake*, 29.

NOTES

39   Shalini Puri, "An 'Other' Realism: Erna Brodber's *Myal*," *ARIEL: A Review of International English Literature* 24, no. 3 (1993): 102–3.

40   Brodber, *The Rainmaker's Mistake*, 7–22.

41   Marie Sairsingh, *Africana Philosophy and the Metaphysics of the "After-Man": Examining Selected Texts by Erna Brodber*, (PhD thesis, Howard University, 2018).

42   Sylvia Wynter's concept of the post-human recognizes blackness as a persistent sign, no matter the class or colour-mixing in African-American literature. See Katherine McKittrick, *Sylvia Wynter: On Being Human as Praxis* (New York and London: Duke University Press, 2015). In an interview with David Scott, Wynter asserts, "The status principle of the society is based on the fact [that] blackness is unalterably a fact of inferiority." See David Scott, "The Re-enchantment of Humanism: An Interview with Sylvia Wynter," *Small Axe* 8, no. 120 (2000): 173–211. Wynter foregrounds the processes by which the West created hierarchies of humankind based on colour and indeed class. Throughout her philosophical discourses, she draws on the principles of African spiritual engendered systems, which is not unlike Lamming's use of the figure of Caliban and Brathwaite's use of Sycorax. However, Wynter's concepts of the post-human are arguably more readily applicable to Africana existentialist theory, as opposed to the vast cross-cultural realities of the Caribbean, particularly in the context of the family of Lace People (an allegory of the First Peoples) in Brodber's *Rainmaker*. More specifically, Wynter's notions of the "after-man" are arguably largely rooted in speculative fiction. Such narratives, while encompassing partial derivations of a Caribbean spirit tradition, set up narrative conventions in relation to utopias, dystopias, alternative planets and generic science fiction that destabilize notions of the human and the natural environment. My analysis diverges since my concern is with the embodied and lived, cultural norms of Caribbean people.

43   Rohlehr, "George Lamming and Kamau Brathwaite," in *Transgression, Transition, Transformation: Essays in Caribbean Culture* (San Juan: Lexicon, 2007), 395.

44   Erna Brodber, "I Dream to Change the World," *Tout Moun Journal of Caribbean Studies* 4, no. 1 (2018): 10.

45   Brodber, *The Rainmaker's Mistake*, 11.

46   See Okoro Damascus and Chu Stan, "A Historical and Socio-Context Analysis of Igbo Worlds," in *African Women and the Shame and Pain of Infertility: An Ethico-cultural Study of Christian Response to Childlessness among the Igbo People of West Africa* (Oregon: Wipf and Stock, 2020), 35. Igwe is the Igbo god of thunder and lightning, whose cosmic force is embodied in the referential framework of Brodber's thunderstorm. It is an example of how African

NOTES

cosmologies may be incorporated into an aesthetic sensibility. This dynamic interaction between social and cosmic processes illustrates the imperative of curating modalities of psychic and artistic independence outside of Western registers.

47 Curdella Forbes, "Erna Brodber's *The Rainmaker's Mistake*," *Postcolonial Text* 5, no. 3 (2010): 1–4.

48 Kelly Baker Josephs, "*The Rainmaker's Mistake* (Review)," *Callaloo* 31, no. 3 (2008): 938–41.

49 Annie Paul, "*The Rainmaker's Mistake*, by Erna Brodber," *Black Rain* (2008): 1–5.

50 Brodber, *The Rainmaker's Mistake*, 16.

51 Brodber, *The Rainmaker's Mistake*, 48 (emphasis added).

52 Wilson Harris, "The Life of Myth and its Possible Bearing on Erna Brodber's Fictions: *Jane and Louisa Will Soon Come Home* and *Myal*," *Kunapipi* 12, no. 3 (1990): 86–92.

53 Brodber, *The Rainmaker's Mistake*, 32.

54 Brodber, *The Rainmaker's Mistake*, 148.

55 Erna Brodber, *Myal* (Illinois: Waveland Press, 2014), 34.

56 Brodber, *The Rainmaker's Mistake*, 137.

57 Brodber, *The Rainmaker's Mistake*, 140.

58 Brodber, *The Rainmaker's Mistake*, 23–30.

59 Neil ten Kortenaar, "Foreign Possessions: Erna Brodber's *Myal*, the Medium, and Her Message," *ARIEL: A Review of International English Literature* 30, no. 4 (1999): 51–54.

60 Eduardo Viveiros, *The Relative Native: Essays on Indigenous Conceptual Worlds* (Chicago: Hau Books, 2015).

61 Alan Kolata, "In the Realm of the Four Quarters," in *America in 1492: The World of the Indian Peoples Before the Arrival of Columbus*, ed. Alvin Josephy Jr (New York: Knopf, 1992), 215–50.

62 John Bierhorst, *The Mythology of South America* (London: Oxford University Press, 2002).

63 Harris, "History, Fable and Myth," 157.

64 Brodber, *The Rainmaker's Mistake*, 150.

CHAPTER 5

1 Eduardo Galeano, "Lust for Gold, Lust for Silver," in *Open Veins of Latin America: Five Centuries of the Pillage of a Continent* (NY: Monthly Review Press, 1997), 2.

NOTES

2   Martin Munro, *The Haunted Tropics: Caribbean Ghost Stories* (Kingston: UWI Press, 2015).

3   Maryse Condé, "The Obeah Man, Obeah," in *Haunted Tropics*, 1–10.

4   Shani Mootoo, "The Bonnaire Silk Cotton Tree," in *Haunted Tropics*, 102–15.

5   Gisèle Pineau, "The Voyage of the Centipede," in *Haunted Tropics*, 49–66.

6   Patricia Powell, *The Fullness of Everything* (London: Peepal Tree, 2009).

7   It should be noted that this reparative approach is not intended to offer utopic or glamourized models of mediation to oppressive systems. Rather, this iteration serves as an invitation for rigorously naming, embodying and curating spaces, which are required to address the greater complexities of Caribbean being. This book thus serves as one instance among many on how we identify and interpret humanity through the multiple significations and nuanced framework of the spectre.

8   Julia Kristeva, "Approaching Abjection," in *Powers of the Horror: An Essay on Abjection*, translated by Leon S. Roudiez (NY: Columbia University Press, 1980), 8.

9   Kristeva, "Abjection," 8.

10   As Glissant observes, "The root is unique, a stock taking all upon itself and killing all around it. In opposition to this . . . [there is] the rhizome, an enmeshed root system, a network spreading either in the ground or in the air, with no predatory rootstock taking over permanently. The notion of the rhizome . . . challenges that of a totalitarian root. Rhizomatic thought is the principle behind what I call the Poetics of Relation, in which each and every identity is extended through a relationship with the Other." See Glissant, "Errantry, Exile," in *Poetics of Relation*, trans. Betsy Wing (Michigan: University Press of Michigan, 1997), 11.

11   David Scott, "The re-enchantment of Humanism: An Interview with Sylvia Wynter," *Small Axe* 8, no. 120, (2000): 136.

12   Eve Kosofsky Sedgwick, "Paranoid Reading and Reparative Reading, or, You're So Paranoid You Probably Think this Essay is about You," in *Touching Feeling: Affect, Pedagogy, Performativity* (London and New York: Duke University Press, 2003), 123–51.

13   Homi K. Bhabha, "DissemiNation: Time, Narrative and the Margins of the Modern Nation," in *The Location of Culture* (New York: Routledge, 1994), 199–244.

14   Gayatri Spivak, "Can the Subaltern Speak?," in *Colonial Discourse and Post-Colonial Theory: A Reader*, ed. Patrick Williams and Laura Chrisman (New York: Columbia University Press, 1994), 66–109.

15   An abridged version of these ideas was published in a collection of essays

NOTES

entitled, *Crime in Selected Caribbean Territories*, edited by Paula Morgan and Dylan Kerrigan in *Caribbean Quarterly: A Journal of Caribbean Culture*. See Hannah Regis, "Not Fit to be Mentioned": Ghosts and Narratives of Criminal Intimacies in Selected Short Stories from The Haunted Tropics: Caribbean Ghost Stories," *Caribbean Quarterly* 66, no. 2 (2020): 177–94.

16   See Robert Young, *Postcolonialism: An Historical Introduction* (New Jersey: John Wiley and Sons, 2016).

17   See VeVe Clark, "'I Have Made Peace with My Island': An Interview with Maryse Condé," *Callaloo* 38, no. 1 (1989): 87–133.

18   Lucía M. Suárez, "Gisele Pineau: Writing the Dimensions of Migration," *World Literature Today* 75, no. 3 (2001): 8–21.

19   Derek Walcott, *Ti-Jean and His Brothers* (Port of Spain: Alexander Street Press, 2003).

20   Mootoo, "The Bonnaire Silk Cotton Tree," 113.

21   Mootoo's reference to J'ouvert recalls the transformative and confrontational effects and potentialities of the Trinidadian Carnival. A larger frame of reference may be derived since in the narrative, the J'ouvert is a form of trans-historical transmission that is re-appropriated by the spectral beings insofar that they materialize their own tragic experiences and historical memory in the mortal world. The grotesqueness that is underpinned in Mootoo's narrative, through the performances of spectral presences amidst the world of the living, makes it possible for us to consider Carnival as a visionary experience and a waking dream for those involved.

22   Mootoo, "The Bonnaire Silk Cotton Tree," 113.

23   Jeannie Thomas, "The Usefulness of Ghost Stories," in *Haunting Experiences: Ghosts in Contemporary Folklore*, ed. Dianne Goldstein and Jeannie Thomas, 1st ed (Colorado: University Press of Colorado, 2007), 26–30.

24   In an interview I conducted with Shani Mootoo in March 2016 in San Fernando, Trinidad, Mootoo suggests that, "By eliding the disappearance of subaltern subjects from mainstream discourse, the immediate world, as reflected in Nandita's encounter, will continue to be a monstrous site of terror – a hellish space of sorts; the story may be read as a metaphor for a system that compresses the contemporary nation space into ethical degeneracy."

25   Christina Sharpe, "Making Monstrous Intimacies: Surviving Slavery, Bearing Freedom," in *Monstrous Intimacies: Making Post-Slavery Subjects* (New York and London: Duke University Press, 2010), 4.

26   Saidiya Hartman, "Introduction," to *Scenes of Subjection: Terror, Slavery, and Self-Making in Nineteenth-Century America* (London: Oxford University Press, 1997), 5.

NOTES

27 Condé, "The Obeahman, Obeahed," 1–3.

28 Joan Dayan, "Dismemberment, Naming, and Divinity," in *Haiti, History, and the Gods* (California: University Press of California, 2008), 37.

29 By incantation and magical potions, Carmélien is able to summon the spirit of Bella and lay claim to it. It is a procedure quite different from communicating with the spirits of ancestors (as in Lamming's *Season of Adventure*) in a reverent way, or in seances, during which priests or attendant mediums are possessed by ancestral energy.

30 The framework of the *kumbla* has been used widely by Caribbean scholars, and while there are layers to its meaning, it is particularly engaged to denote the protective shell of community and the emergence from inside the egg. Much like understanding Erna Brodber's prose, revelations are gleaned from the inside. The *kumbla* is explored as a cocoon or protective womb in which metamorphosis occurs. However, my use of the *kumbla* space in the context of Pineau's narrative considers the dangers of being enclosed and swallowed if one remains within the protective shell for too long. To this extent, the idiom in "Centipede" evokes the stench of a rotten egg that isolates Jessie from the rest of the community because of her stored-up griefs and masked hurts. See Evelyn O'Callaghan's "Interior Schisms Dramatised: The Treatment of the 'Mad'," in *Out of the Kumbla: Caribbean Women and Literature*, eds. Carole Boyce Davies and Elaine Savory Fido (New Jersey: Africa World Press, 1990), 89–110, and Daryl Cumber Dance, "Go Eena Kumbla: A Comparison of Erna Brodber's *Jane and Louisa Will Soon Come Home* and Toni Cade Bambara's *The Salt Eaters*," in *Caribbean Women Writers: Essays from the First International Conference*, ed. Selwyn R. Cudjoe (Massachusetts: University Press of Massachusetts, 1990), 69–84.

31 Pineau, "Voyage," 52.

32 Pineau, "Voyage," 50.

33 Pineau, "Voyage," 53.

34 Pineau, "Voyage," 53.

35 Pineau, "Voyage," 60.

36 Pineau, "Voyage," 60.

37 Pineau, "Voyage," 63–64 (emphasis added).

38 Karla Holloway, "Who's Got the Body?" in *Private Bodies, Public Texts: Race, Gender, and a Cultural Bioethics* (London: Duke University Press, 2011), 107.

39 See Patricia Powell, "A Search for Caribbean Masculinities," *Anthurium: A Caribbean Studies Journal* 10, no. 2, (2013): 1–12.

40 Powell, *The Fullness of Everything*, 123.

41 Although in his adult life, Winston opts for a heterosexual lifestyle, his ado-

NOTES

lescent wrestle with liminality confronts the rigid codes of gender binaries in postcolonial Jamaica. The novel is not a story of transition away from one gender to another but marks a series of passages to a recognition of how the self evolves over time. Powell's *Fullness*, indeed demonstrates how a particular character, in particular locales and eras, experiences the fluidity and fragility of identity.

42   In her other novels, *Me Dying Trial* (1993), *A Small Gathering of Bones* (1994), and *The Pagoda* (1998), Powell explores literary representations of trans and non-normative human experiences, thus throwing light on the concepts of identity, transgression, transformation and social recognition.

43   Powell, *Fullness*, 43.

44   Powell, *Fullness*, 83.

45   Powell, *Fullness*, 9.

46   Powell, *Fullness*, 116.

47   Powell, *Fullness*, 130.

48   Powell, *Fullness*, 111.

49   See Nicolas Abraham and Maria Torok, *The Shell and the Kernel*, Volume 1, edited, translated and introduced by Nicholas T. Rand (Chicago and London: Chicago University Press, 1994), 157–61 and 165–205.

50   Powell, *Fullness*, 148.

51   Powell, *Fullness*, 149.

52   Powell, *Fullness*, 149.

53   Powell, *Fullness*, 42.

54   Haptic criticism focuses on art (including film) that explores a form of bodily contact, specifically through touch between two subjects with the intent of transforming one's perception of the other by channeling or mimicking the other's feelings or emotions. It is used to evoke the power of sensuous closeness. By giving way to ideas of touch and psychic ecstasy, the self in question rushes up to the surface through interaction with another surface. When this happens, there is a process of metamorphosis and deep change. Such an encounter invites processes of trust and makes transformation in intimate contexts possible. See Marks's "Introduction," to *Touch: Sensuous Theory and Multisensory Media* (Minnesota: University Press of Minnesota, 2002), xii.

55   Powell, *Fullness*, 219.

56   Powell, *Fullness*, 219.

57   Powell, *Fullness*, 47.

58   bell hooks, "Critical Thinking," in *Teaching Critical Thinking: Practical Wisdom* (New York: Routledge, 2010), 10.

NOTES

CHAPTER 6

1   Wilson Harris, "Impressions After Seven Years," *New World* 44, no. 1 (1966): 17–20.

2   Walcott has engaged the framework of spirit throughout several of his works to introduce the ideas of simultaneity, hybridity and in-betweenity and also to represent the hazy nature of ancestral memory. In *Another Life* (Colorado: Lynne Rienner, 2004), 71, he writes of "The leaping Caribs [who] whiten,/ in one flash, the instant / the race leapt at Sauteurs . . . / One scream of bounding lace . . . / I am pounding the faces of gods back into the red clay they / leapt from the mattock of heel after heel." Here, the scream of a dying race precedes the poetic undertaking of giving proper burial to the dead by memorializing their lives in confessional fiction. Additionally, in "The Spoiler's Return" (*Collected Poems*, 1948–1984 London: Faber and Faber, 1986), 432–38, he rehearses the trauma of contemporary living and urbanization, as depicted in the spectral presence of Spoiler, who is spatially located at the top of Laventille and who records the deterioration of the city under corrupt systems of governance. Spoiler is a modernization of the wanderer; a ghost who hovers on the edges of society, and keeps record of the human and ecological derelictions of the islands. Similarly, in "The Schooner Flight" (*Collected Poems*, 1948–1984, London: Faber and Faber, 1986), 345–61, Shabine is a metaphoric, spirit presence who oscillates between spaces, dialects and the hallucinatory world of dream and physical sea voyages in his attempt to flee the corrupt islands and his infidelity with Maria Conception.

3   I use the term "root culture" or "soil heritage" to delineate aspects of a sedimented Caribbean history.

4   Wilson Harris, "Arawak Horizon," in *The Sleepers of Roraima and Age of the Rainmakers*, 157.

5   Raja Patteti, "Narratives," in *The Fiction of Wilson Harris: A Study in West Indian Discourse* (Nigeria: Prestige, 2008), 81.

6   Michael Gilkes, "The Landscape of Dreams," in *The Uncompromising Imagination*, ed. Hena Maes-Jelinek (Denmark: Dangaroo Press, 1991), 33–35.

7   Harris, "Arawak Horizon," 158.

8   Harris, "Arawak Horizon," 158.

9   Harris, "Arawak Horizon," 157.

10 Wilson Harris, *Fossil and Psyche* (Arlington: University Press of Texas, 1974), 8–12.

11 Harris, "Arawak Horizon," 158.

12 Harris, "Arawak Horizon," 158.

NOTES

13   In *Tradition, The Writer and Society: Critical Essays*, Harris offers the concept of the mythic imagination. This emerged because of his skepticism of the realistic novel. He also refers to the realist text as the novel of persuasion, in which characters become static or one-dimensional (London: New Beacon, 1967), 30. Outside of these monolinear pathways, Harris strives to immerse the reader in a fluid context in which preconceptions are shed and new ways of seeing are advanced. In the essay "Interior of the Novel: Amerindian/ European/African Relations", he asserts, "Within the art of fiction we are attempting to explore...the 'vacancy' in [words] and nature within which agents appear who are translated one by the other and who . . . reflect a burden to plunge into the unknown, into the translatable, transmutable legacies of history." (Wilson Harris and Hena Maes-Jelinek, *Explorations: A Selection of Talks and Articles, 1966–1981* [Denmark: Dangaroo Press, 1981], 17–18). Harris is referring to the reverberations and all the possibilities inherent in the structure of language. Reminiscent of Harris, Jacques Derrida also notes the anxiety that can arise when readers can no longer find safety in a conforming centre outside of hegemonic reading practices (Derrida, "Structure, Sign and Play in the Discourse of the Human Sciences," in *Writing and Difference* [Chicago: University of Chicago Press, 2001], 352). By accepting a decentred system of language that is opposed to hierarchical modalities of reading and understanding the world, a new and most radical conception of the human and indeed, of society, emerges.

14   Harris, "Arawak Horizon," 159.

15   See Sandra Drake, "Language and Revolutionary Hope," in *The Literate Imagination: Essays on the Novels of Wilson Harris*, ed. by Michael Gilkes (London: Macmillan, 1989). She notes that Harris's metaphoric use of the zemi, dovetails with the structure and themes of alternate and instructive ancestral worlds, non-linear history and the coexisting of ancestral presences within ordinary and corporeal domains.

16   Harris, "Arawak Horizon," 162.

17   Harris, "Arawak Horizon," 159.

18   Gordon Rohlehr, "Round Table: Wilson Harris and Caribbean Literature," in *Theatre of the Arts*, ed. Hena Maes-Jelinek and Bénédicte Ledent (Amsterdam: Rodopi, 2002), 236, emphasis mine.

19   Gregory Shaw, "Language and Revolutionary Hope," in *The Literate Imagination: Essays on the Novels of Wilson Harris*, ed. Michael Gilkes (London: Macmillan, 1989), 147–48.

20   J. Michael Dash, "A Poetics of Liminality: Another Caribbean Fin de Siècle," in

NOTES

The Other America: Caribbean Literature in a New World Context (Virginia: University Press of Virginia, 1998), 134–158.

21   Dash, "Poetics of Liminality," 150.

22   Dash, "Poetics of Liminality," 153.

23   Harris, "Arawak Horizon," 158.

24   Harris, "Arawak Horizon," 168–70.

25   Martin Carter, "Listening to the Land," in *University of Hunger*, ed. Gemma Robinson (London: Bloodaxe, 2006), 72.

26   Harris, "Arawak Horizon," 159.

27   Vidiadhar Surajprasad Naipaul, "Middle Passage," in *The Middle Passage* (New York: Vintage Books, 1996), 27.

28   Harris, "Arawak Horizon," 164.

29   Silvio Torres-Saillant, "Kamau Brathwaite and the Caribbean World," in *Caribbean Poetics: Toward an Aesthetic of West Indian Literature* (Cambridge: Cambridge University Press, 1997), 137–49.

30   Torres-Saillant, "Kamau Brathwaite and the Caribbean World," 149.

31   Harris, "Arawak Horizon," 159.

32   Harris, "Arawak Horizon," 164.

33   Harris, "Arawak Horizon," 170.

34   Kirsten Peterson and Anna Rutherford, "Intimations of the Stranger," in *Wilson Harris: The Uncompromising Imagination*, ed. Hena Maes-Jelinek (Denmark: Dangaroo Press, 1991), 28.

35   Peterson and Rutherford, "Intimations of the Stranger," 28–31.

36   Harris, "Arawak Horizon," 172.

37   Harris, "Arawak Horizon," 157.

38   Derek Walcott, *Omeros* (London: Faber and Faber, 1990), 12.

39   Walcott, *Omeros*, 14.

40   Derek Walcott, "The Antilles: Fragments of Epic Memory," in *What the Twilight Says: Essays* (New York: Farrar, Straus and Giroux, 1998), 70.

41   Walcott, "Antilles," 70.

42   Walcott, *Omeros*, 151.

43   Jean Antoine-Dunne, "Ghostly Echoes," in *Derek Walcott's Love Affair with Film* (London: Peepal Tree, 2017), 163–4.

44   Jean Antoine-Dunne, "Film and the Attack on the Senses," in *Derek Walcott's Love Affair with Film* (London: Peepal Tree, 2017), 30.

45   Walcott, *Omeros*, 12.

46   Walcott, *Omeros*, 4.

47   Walcott, *Omeros*, 295.

48   Walcott, *Omeros*, 66.

NOTES

49   Walcott, *Omeros*, 21.

50   Walcott, *Omeros*, 13.

51   Walcott, *Omeros*, 45.

52   Homi K. Bhabha, "DissemiNation: Time, Narrative and the Margins of the Modern Nation," in *The Location of Culture* (New York: Routledge, 2012), 139–70.

53   Iain Chambers, "Many Voices," in *Mediterranean Crossings: The Politics of an Interrupted Modernity* (London: Duke University Press, 2008), 5.

54   Édouard Glissant, *Poetics of Relation* (Michigan: University Press of Michigan), 1997.

55   Walcott, *Omeros*, 3.

56   Derek Walcott, "What the Twilight Says: An Overture," in *What the Twilight Says: Essays* (New York: Farrar, Straus and Giroux, 1998), 3–35.

57   Jahan Ramazani, "The Wounds of History: Walcott's *Omeros* and the Postcolonial Poetics of Affliction," *Publications of the Modern Language Association* 112, no.3 (1997): 405–17.

58   Mikhail Bakhtin, "Epic and Novel," in *The Dialogic Imagination: Four Essays* (Austin: Texas University Press, 2010), 1–31.

59   Wilson Harris, "Continuity and Discontinuity," in *Selected Essays of Wilson Harris: The Unfinished Genesis of the Imagination,* ed. Andrew Bundy (New York: Routledge, 1999), 176–83.

60   Harris, "Continuity," 176.

61   Bakhtin, "Epic," 31.

62   Walcott, *Omeros*, 3.

63   Walcott, *Omeros*, 8.

64   The name of Achille's boat is also a signifier for the American currency and the way that St Lucian identity is involved in the Western capitalist tourist industry.

65   Walcott, *Omeros*, 6.

66   Walcott, *Omeros*, 8.

67   Walcott, *Omeros*, 291.

68   Walcott, *Omeros*, 319.

69   Walcott, "A Far Cry From Africa," in *Collected Poems, 1948–1984* (London: Faber and Faber, 1986), 17–18.

70   Kamau Brathwaite, *History of the Voice: The Development of Nation Language in Anglophone Caribbean Poetry* (London: New Beacon, 1984), 17.

71   The long-standing debate about the plasticity of the Creole (language) in poetic and narrative expression interconnects with Brathwaite's experimentation in form and language. This is acutely expressed in the metaphor of the coral,

NOTES

which is a signifier of the creation of new civilizations out of the interchanging processes of creolization, as articulated by Brathwaite in *Contradictory Omens: Cultural Diversity and Integration in the Caribbean* (Mona: Savacou Publications, 1974), 17.

72 Walcott, *Omeros*, 136.

73 Walcott, *Omeros*, 137.

74 Walcott, *Omeros*, 37.

75 Walcott, *Omeros*, 142.

76 This movement between worlds prevents Achille from perceiving either Africa or St Lucia as utopic. It is an understanding of the grapple for 'belonging', which Walcott comments on: "There is a duty in every son to become his own man. The son severs himself from the father. The Caribbean very often refuses to cut the umbilical cord to confront its own stature. So a lot of people exploit an idea of Africa out of both the wrong kind of pride and the wrong kind of heroic idealism." See Edward Hirsh, "The Art of Poetry," in *Critical Perspectives on Derek Walcott*, ed. Robert D. Hamner (Colorado: Lynne Rienner, 1997), 79.

77 Jean Antoine-Dunne, "Making New," in *Derek Walcott's Love Affair with Film* (London: Peepal Tree, 2017), 178–81.

78 Walcott, *Omeros*, 276.

79 Walcott, *Omeros*, 88–89.

80 Walcott, *Omeros*, 89.

81 Walcott, *Omeros*, 227–66.

82 Walcott, *Omeros*, 19.

83 Walcott, *Omeros*, 239.

84 Walcott, *Omeros*, 242.

85 Walcott, *Omeros*, 246.

86 Walcott, *Omeros*, 246.

87 Walcott, *Omeros*, 240.

88 Walcott, *Omeros*, 248.

89 Walcott, *Omeros*, 294.

Bibliography

Abraham, Nicolas, and Maria Torok. *The Shell and the Kernel*. Edited, translated and introduced by Nicholas T. Rand. Volume 1. Chicago and London: Chicago University Press, 1994.

Allsopp, Richard. "The Niger-Congo Languages as Linguistic Source." In *Education Issues in Creole and Creole-Influenced Vernacular Contexts*, 31–42, edited by Ian Robertson and Hazel Simmons-McDonald. Kingston: UWI Press, 2014.

Antoine-Dunne, Jean. "Film and the attack on the Senses." In *Derek Walcott's Love Affair with Film*, 30. London: Peepal Tree, 2017.

———. "Ghostly Echoes." In *Derek Walcott's Love Affair with Film*, 163–4. London: Peepal Tree, 2017.

———. "Making New." In *Derek Walcott's Love Affair with Film*, 178–81. London: Peepal Tree, 2017.

Bakhtin, Mikhail. "Epic and Novel." In *The Dialogic Imagination: Four Essays*, 1–31. Austin: Texas University Press, 2010.

Baucom, Ian. "Liverpool, a Capital of the Long Twentieth Century." In *Specters of the Atlantic: Finance Capital, Slavery, and the Philosophy of History*, 31. London: Duke University Press, 2007.

Baugh, Edward. "Maps Made in the Heart." In *Journal of West Indian Literature* 18, no. 2 (2010): 18.

———.*West Indian Poetry 1900–1970: A Study in Cultural Decolonization*. Kingston: Savacou Publications, 1970.

Bennett, Michael, and Vanessa Dickerson. "Introduction." In *Recovering the Black Female Body: Self-Representation by African American Women*, 13. New Jersey: Rutgers University Press, 2000.

Bernabé, Jean, Patrick Chamoiseau, Raphaël Confiant, and Mohamed Bouya Taleb-Khyar. Éloge de la Créolité. Paris: Gallimard, 1993.

Bhaba, Homi. "DissemiNation: Time, Narrative and the Margins of the Modern Nation." In *The Location of Culture*, 139–244. London: Routledge, 2012.

Bierhorst, John. *The Mythology of South America*. London: Oxford University Press, 2002.

BIBLIOGRAPHY

Brathwaite, Kamau. *Barabajan Poems*, 1492–1992. Mona: Savacou Publications, 1994.

———. "Caliban." In *The Arrivants: A New World Trilogy – Rights of Passage/Islands/ Masks*, 191–95. London: Oxford University Press, 1981.

———. "Caribbean Culture: Two Paradigms." In *Missile and Capsule*, 9–54, edited by Jurgen Martini. Bremen: University Press of Bremen, 1983.

———. *Contradictory Omens: Cultural Diversity and Integration in the Caribbean*. Mona: Savacou Publications, 1974.

———. *History of the Voice: The Development of Nation Language in Anglophone Caribbean Poetry*. London: New Beacon, 1984.

———. "Namsetoura." In *Born to Slow Horses*, 118–22. Connecticut: Wesleyan University Press, 2005.

———. *Roots*. Havana: Ediciones Casa de las Americas, 1896.

———. *Sun Poem*. 51. Oxford: Oxford University Press, 1982.

———. "The African Presence in Caribbean Literature." In *Dedalus* 102, no. 2 (1974): 73–109.

———. "The Black Angel." In *Dream Stories*, 28. New York: Longman, 1994.

———. "Veve." In *The Arrivants: A New World Trilogy – Rights of Passage/ Islands/ Masks*, 11. London: Oxford University Press, 1988.

———. *Word Making Man: Poem for Nicolás Guillén in Xaymaca*. Kingston: Savacou Cooperative, 1979.

Brodber, Erna. "History and Social Death." In *Caribbean Quarterly* 58, no. 4 (2012): 112.

———. "I Dream to Change the World." In *Tout Moun Journal of Caribbean Studies* 4, no. 1 (2018): 10.

———. *Myal*. Illinois: Waveland Press, 2014.

———. *The Rainmaker's Mistake*. London: New Beacon, 2007.

Bundy, Andrew. "Introduction." In *Selected Essays of Wilson Harris: The Unfinished Genesis of the Imagination*, 3–10, edited by Andrew Bundy. London: Routledge, 1999.

Burroughs, Peter. "Colonial Self-Government." In *British Imperialism in the Nineteenth Century*, edited by Colin. C. Edridge, 39–64. London: Macmillan, 1989.

Butler, Judith. "Introduction." In *Bodies that Matter: On the Discursive of Sex*, 2. New York: Routledge, 1993.

Carter, Martin. "Listening to the Land," In *University of Hunger*, edited by Gemma Robinson, 72. London: Bloodaxe, 2006.

Césaire, Aimé. *Discourse on Colonialism*. New York: New York University Press, 2001.

Chambers, Iian. "Many Voices." In *Mediterranean Crossings: The Politics of an Interrupted Modernity*, 5. London: Duke University Press, 2008.

BIBLIOGRAPHY

Clark, Vèvè. "'I Have Made Peace with My Island': An Interview with Maryse Condé." In *Callaloo* 38, no. 1 (1989): 87–133.

Condé, Maryse. "The Obeah Man, Obeahed." In *The Haunted Tropics: Caribbean Ghost Stories*, 1–10. Kingston: UWI Press, 2015.

Cooper, Carolyn. "Haiti – the Price of Freedom." *The Gleaner*, 17 January 2010.

———. "Something Ancestral Recaptured: Spirit possession as trope in Selected Feminist Fictions of the African Diaspora." In *Motherlands: Black Women's Writing from Africa, the Caribbean and South Asia*, edited by Sushiela Nasta, 64–87. London: The Women's Press, 1991.

Craig, John. *A New Universal Etymological and Pronouncing Dictionary of the English Language, Embracing All the Terms Used in Art, Science and Literature*. New York: H.G. Collins, 1846.

Damascus, Okoro, and Chu Stan. "A Historical and Socio-Context Analysis of Igbo Worlds." In *African Women and the Shame and Pain of Infertility: An Ethico-cultural Study of Christian Response to Childlessness among the Igbo People of West Africa*, 35.Oregon: Wipf and Stock, 2020.

Dance, Daryl Cumber. "Go Eena Kumbla: A Comparison of Erna Brodber's *Jane and Louisa Will Soon Come Home* and Toni Cade Bambara's *The Salt Eaters*." In *Caribbean Women Writers: Essays from the First International Conference*, 69–84, edited by Selwyn R. Cudjoe. Massachusetts: University Press of Massachusetts, 1990.

Danticat, Edwidge. *The Farming of Bones: A Novel*. New York: Soho Press, 1998.

Dash, Michael. "A Poetics of Liminality: Another Caribbean Fin de Siècle." In *The Other America: Caribbean Literature in a New World Context*, 134–58. Virginia: University Press of Virginia, 1998.

———. *Édouard Glissant: Cambridge Studies in African and Caribbean Literature*. London: Cambridge University Press, 1995.

Dawes, Kwame. "Grace Nichols." In *Talk Yuh Talk: Interviews with Anglophone Caribbean Poets*, 138. Virginia: University Press of Virginia, 2000.

Dayan, Joan. "Dismemberment, Naming, and Divinity." In *Haiti, History, and the Gods*, 37. California: University Press of California, 2008.

Deguzman, Kathleen. "Natural Histories of Social Bodies: Rethinking Caribbean and Victorian Realisms." In *Studies in the Novel* 49, no. 4 (2017): 518–37.

De Lisser, Herbert. *The White Witch of Rosehall*. London: Macmillan Caribbean, 2018.

DeLoughrey, Elizabeth, and George Handley. "Introduction." In *Postcolonial Ecologies: Literature of the Environment*, s4. London: Oxford University Press, 2011.

Derrida, Jacques. "Apparition of the Unapparent: The Phenomenological Conjuring Trick." In *Specters of Marx: the State of the Debt, the Work of Mourning and the New International*, 156–61. New York: Peggy Kamuf Routledge, 1994.

BIBLIOGRAPHY

———. "Structure, Sign and Play in the Discourse of the Human Sciences." In *Writing and Difference*, 352. Chicago: University of Chicago Press, 2001.

Drake, Sandra. "Language and Revolutionary Hope." In *The Literate Imagination: Essays on the Novels of Wilson Harris*, edited by Michael Gilkes. London: Macmillan, 1989.

Eyerman, Ron. "The Making Collective Identity." In *Cultural Trauma: Slavery and the Formation of African American Identity*, 61. Cambridge: Cambridge University Press, 2002.

Fanon, Frantz. *Black Skin, White Masks*. New York: Grove Press, 2008.

———. *The Wretched of the Earth*. New York: Grove Press, 2007.

Forbes, Curdella. "Erna Brodber's The Rainmaker's Mistake." In *Postcolonial Text* 5, no. 3 (2010): 1–4.

———. *From Nation to Diaspora: Samuel Selvon, George Lamming and the Cultural Performance of Gender*. Kingston: UWI Press, 2005.

Francis, Kela. "The Spirituality of Carnival: Using Yoruba Cosmology to Read *The Dragon Can't Dance*", *International Journal of Art and Art History* 3, no.1, (2015): 63–82.

Galeano, Eduardo. "Lust for Gold, Lust for Silver." In *Open Veins of Latin America: Five Centuries of the Pillage of a Continent*, 2. New York: Monthly Review Press, 1997.

Gilkes, Michael. "The Landscape of Dreams." In *The Uncompromising Imagination*, edited by Hena Maes-Jelinek, 33–35. Denmark: Dangaroo Press, 1991.

Gilroy, Paul. *The Black Atlantic: Modernity and Double Consciousness*. Cambridge MA: Harvard University Press, 1993.

Glissant, Édouard. "Cross-Cultural Poetics." In *Caribbean Discourse: Selected Essays*, 139. Charlottesville: Virginia University Press, 1989.

———. "Errantry, Exile." In *Poetics of Relation*, 11. Translated by Betsy Wing. Michigan: University Press of Michigan, 1997.

———. *Poetics of Relation*. Translated by Betsy Wing. Michigan: Michigan University Press, 1997.

———. "The Open Boat." In *Poetics of Relation*, 5–7. Translated by Betsy Wing. Michigan: Michigan University Press, 1997.

———. "The Quarrel with History." In *Caribbean Discourse: Selected Essays*, 62. Charlottesville: Virginia University Press, 1989.

Goodison, Lorna. *To Us, All Flowers Are Roses: Poems*. Illinois: University of Illinois Press, 1995.

Gordon, Avery. *Ghostly Matters: Haunting and the Sociological Imagination*. Minnesota: University Press of Minnesota, 2008.

Grant, Damian. *Realism (The Critical Idiom Reissued)*. London: Routledge, 2019.

BIBLIOGRAPHY

Griffin, Gabriele. "Writing the Body: Reading Joan Riley, Grace Nichols and Ntozake-Shange." In *Black Women's Writing*, edited by Gina Wisker, 28. New York: St. Martin's Press, 1993.

Griffith, Glyne. "Metaphysics and the Other." In *Deconstruction, Imperialism and the West Indian Novel*, 53–81. Kingston: UWI Press, 1996.

Hall, Stuart. "Cultural Identity and Diaspora." In *Identity: Community, Culture, Difference*, edited by Jonathan Rutherford, 222–37. London: Lawrence and Wishart, 1990.

Harris, Wilson. "Amerindian Legacy." In *Selected Essays of Wilson Harris: The Unfinished Genesis of the Imagination*, edited by Andrew Bundy, 169. London: Routledge, 1999.

———. "Arawak Horizon." In *The Sleepers of Roraima and Age of the Rainmakers*, 153–73. London: Peepal Tree, 2014.

———. "A Talk on the Subjective Imagination." In *Explorations: A Selection of Talks and Articles, 1966–1981*, 58. Denmark: Dangaroo Press, 1981.

———. "Author's Note." In *The Whole Armour* and *The Secret Ladder*, 9. London: Faber and Faber, 1973.

———. "Continuity and Discontinuity." In *Selected Essays of Wilson Harris: The Unfinished Genesis of the Imagination*, edited by Andrew Bundy, 176–83. New York: Routledge, 1999.

———. "Couvade." In *The Sleepers of Roraima and Age of the Rainmakers*, 35–58. London: Peepal Tree, 2014.

———. *Fossil and Psyche*. Arlington: University Press of Texas, 1974.

———, and Hena Maes-Jelinek. "Interior of the Novel: Amerindian/European/African Relations." In *Explorations: A Selection of Talks and Articles, 1966–1981*, 17–18. Denmark: Dangaroo Press, 1981.

———. "History, Fable and Myth in the Caribbean and Guianas." In *Selected Essays of Wilson Harris: The Unfinished Genesis of the Imagination*, edited by Andrew Bundy, 151–60. London: Routledge, 1999.

———. "Impressions After Seven Years." In *New World* 44, no. 1 (1966): 17–20.

———. *Palace of the Peacock*. London: Faber and Faber, 1960.

———. "Phenomenal Legacy." In *Explorations: A selection of talks and articles, 1966–1981*, 43–48. Denmark: Dangaroo Press, 1981.

———. "Profiles of Myth and the New World." In *Selected Essays of Wilson Harris: The Unfinished Genesis of the Imagination*, edited by Andrew Bundy, 201–11. London: Routledge, 1999.

———. "Quetzalcoatl and the Smoking Mirror: Reflections on Originality and Tradition." In *Selected Essays of Wilson Harris: The Unfinished Genesis of the Imagination*, edited by Andrew Bundy, 186–96. London: Routledge, 1999.

BIBLIOGRAPHY

———. "The Life of Myth and its Possible Bearing on Erna Brodber's Fictions: *Jane and Louisa Will Soon Come Home* and *Myal*." In *Kunapipi* 12, no.3 (1990): 86–92.

———. "The Schizophrenic Sea." In *The Womb of Space: The Cross-Cultural Imagination*, 24. California: Greenwood, 1983.

———. "The Untameable Cosmos." In *The Womb of Space: The Cross-Cultural Imagination*, 39–54. California: Greenwood, 1983.

———. "The Whole Armour." In *The Guyana Quartet*, 252–351. London: Faber and Faber, 1985.

———. *The Womb of Space: The Cross-Cultural Imagination*. California: Greenwood, 1983.

———. "Tradition and the West Indian Novel." In *Tradition, the Writer and Society: Critical Essays*, 28–32. London: New Beacon, 1967.

———. *Tradition, the Writer and Society: Critical Essays*. London: New Beacon, 1967.

———. "Yurokon." In *The Sleepers of Roraima and Age of the Rainmakers*, 81–104. London: Peepal Tree, 2014.

Hartman, Saidiya. "Introduction." In *Scenes of Subjection: Terror, Slavery, and Self-Making in Nineteenth-Century America*, 5. London: Oxford University Press, 1997.

———. "Prologue: The Path of Strangers." In *Lose Your Mother: A Journey Along the Atlantic Slave Route*, 17. 1st ed. London: Farrar Straus and Giroux, 2008.

———. "So Many Dungeons." In *Lose Your Mother: A Journey Along the Atlantic Slave Route*, 133. 1st ed. London: Farrar Straus and Giroux, 2008.

Henry, Paget. "African and Afro-Caribbean Existential Philosophies." In *Existence in Black: An Anthology of Black Existential Philosophy*, 11–17. London: Routledge, 1997.

———. *Caliban's Reason: Introducing Afro Caribbean Philosophy*. New York: Routledge, 2000.

———. "Introduction." In *Caliban's Reason: Introducing Afro Caribbean Philosophy*, 3–13. New York: Routledge, 2000.

———. "Introduction." In *Time, History, and Philosophy in the Works of Wilson Harris*, xii. New York: Columbia University Press, 2016.

Hirsch, Marianne. "Introduction." In *The Generation of Postmemory: Writing and Visual Culture After the Holocaust*, 4–5. New York: Columbia University Press, 2012.

———. "Masking the Subject." In *Family Frames: Photography, Narrative, and Postmemory*, 107. New York: CreateSpace Independent Publishing, 2012.

Hirsh, Edward. "The Art of Poetry." In *Critical Perspectives on Derek Walcott*, edited by Robert D. Hamner, 79. Colorado: Lynne Rienner Publishers, 1997.

Hodge, Merle. "Challenges of the struggle for sovereignty: Changing the world versus writing stories." In *Caribbean Women Writers: Essays From the First International*

BIBLIOGRAPHY

Conference, edited by Selwyn Cudjoe, 202–8. Massachusetts: University Press of Massachusetts, 1990.

Holloway, Karla. "Who's Got the Body?" In *Private Bodies, Public Texts: Race, Gender, and a Cultural Bioethics*, 107. London: Duke University Press, 2011.

hooks, bell. "Critical Thinking." In *Teaching Critical Thinking: Practical Wisdom*, 10. New York: Routledge, 2010.

Hsieh, Hsiu-Fang, and Sarah Shannon. "Three Approaches to Qualitative Content Analysis." In *Qualitative Health Research* 15, no. 9 (2005): 1277–88.

Johnson, Erica. "A Brief Introduction." In *Cultural Memory, Memorials, and Reparative Writing*, 1–2. New York: Springer International Publishing, 2018.

———. *Caribbean Ghostwriting*. Vancouver: Fairleigh Dickinson University Press, 2009.

———. "Memorializing the Ghost." In *Caribbean Ghostwriting*, 12. Vancouver: Fairleigh Dickinson University Press, 2009.

———. "Moi, Tituba." In *Caribbean Ghostwriting*, 79. Vancouver: Fairleigh Dickinson University Press, 2009.

Josephs, Kelly Baker. "The Rainmaker's Mistake (Review)." In *Callaloo* 31, no. 3 (2008): 938–41.

Kolata, Alan. "In the Realm of the Four Quarters." In *America in 1492: The World of the Indian Peoples Before the Arrival of Columbus*, edited by Alvin Josephy Jr, 215–50. New York: Knopf, 1992.

Kortenaar, Neil ten. "Foreign Possessions: Erna Brodber's *Myal*, the Medium, and Her Message." In *ARIEL: A Review of International English Literature* 30, no. 4 (1999): 51–54.

Kristeva, Julia. "Approaching Abjection." In *Powers of the Horror: An Essay on Abjection*, 8. Translated by Leon S. Roudiez. New York: Columbia University Press, 1980.

Lalla, Barbara. "Notes." In *Defining Jamaican Fiction: Marronage and the Discourse of Survival*, 202. Alabama: University Press of Alabama, 1996.

Lamming, George. *Season of Adventure*. Michigan: University Press of Michigan, 1960.

Lawson, Sarah. "Epic Journeying I: I is a Long Memoried Woman." In *Grace Nichols*, 67. London: Northcote House, 2007.

Levine, Lawrence W. *Black Culture and Black Consciousness: Afro-American Folk Thought from Slavery to Freedom*. Oxford: Oxford University Press, 2007.

Lewis, Gordon. *Existence in Black: An Anthology of Black Existential Philosophy*. London: Routledge, 1997.

Lundberg, Christian. "Enjoying God's death: The passion of the Christ and the practices of an evangelical public." In *Quarterly Journal of Speech* 95, no. 4 (2009): 390.

Lutchmansingh, Hannah. "Haunted Histories: Spectres of the Middle Passage in Caribbean Literature." In *Tout Moun: Caribbean Journal of Cultural Studies* 4, no. 1 (2018): 1–20.

Maes-Jelinek, Hena. "From Living Nature to Borderless Culture in Wilson Harris's Work." In *Caribbean Literature and the Environment: Between Nature and Culture*, edited by Elizabeth DeLoughrey et al, 257. Virginia: University Press of Virginia, 2005.

———. "The Whole Armour: A Compassionate Alliance." In *The Labyrinth of Universality: Wilson Harris's Visionary Art of Fiction*, 108–14. Amsterdam: Rodopi, 2006.

Marks, Laura. "Introduction." In *Touch: Sensuous Theory and Multisensory Media*, xii. Minnesota: University Press of Minnesota, 2002.

Mayor, Adrienne. *The Amazons: Lives and Legends of Warrior Women Across the Ancient World*. New Jersey: Princeton University Press, 2014.

McKittrick, Katherine. *Sylvia Wynter: On Being Human as Praxis*. New York and London: Duke University Press, 2015.

McSweeney, Joyelle. "Poetics, Revelations, and Catastrophes: An Interview with Kamau Brathwaite." In *Rain Taxi*. www.raintaxi.com. 2005.

McWatt, Mark. "Libidinous Landscapes: Sexual Inscriptions of Place in Guyanese Literature." In *Commonwealth: Essays and Studies* 25, no. 2 (2003): 81.

Mittelholzer, Edgar. *My Bones and My Flute: A Ghost Story in the Old-Fashioned Manner*. London: Secker and Warburg, 1955.

———. *Shadows Move Among Them*. Philadelphia: Lippincott, 1951.

———. *With a Carib Eye*. London: Seeker and Warburg, 1958.

Moore, Megan. "Texts." In *Philosophy and Practice in Writing a History of Ancient Israel*, 92. London: T and T Clark International, 2006.

Mootoo, Shani. "The Bonnaire Silk Cotton Tree." In *The Haunted Tropics: Caribbean Ghost Stories*, 102–15. Kingston: UWI Press, 2015.

Morgan, Paula. "From Apocalypse to Awakenings: Interviews with Gordon Rohlehr." In *Tout Moun Journal of Caribbean Studies* 2, no. 1 (2013): 14.

———. "Re-membering Our Scattered Skeletons." In *The Terror and the Time: Banal Violence and Trauma in Caribbean Discourse*, 32. Kingston: UWI Press, 2015.

Munro, Martin. "Introduction." In *The Haunted Tropics*, edited by Martin Munro, vii. Kingston: UWI Press, 2015.

———. *The Haunted Tropics: Caribbean Ghost Stories*. Kingston: UWI Press, 2015.

Naipaul, Vidiadhar Surujpersad. "Middle Passage." In *The Middle Passage*, 27. New York: Vintage Books, 1996.

Nichols, Grace. "Ala." In *I is a Long Memoried Woman*, 27. London: Karnak House, 1983.

BIBLIOGRAPHY

———. "Days That Fell." In *I is a Long Memoried Woman*, 14–15. London: Karnak House, 1983.

———. "Holding My Beads." In *I is a Long Memoried Woman*, 93. London: Karnak House, 1983.

———. "I Coming Back." In *I is a Long Memoried Woman*, 48. London: Karnak House, 1983.

———. *I Have Crossed An Ocean*. London: Bloodaxe, 2010.

———. *I is a Long Memoried Woman*. London: Karnak House, 1983.

———. "I Will Enter." In *I is a Long Memoried Woman*, 69. London: Karnak House, 1983.

———. "Night is Her Robe." In *I is a Long Memoried Woman*, 52. London: Karnak House, 1983.

———. "Of Golden Gods." In *I is a Long Memoried Woman*, 66–67. London: Karnak House, 1983.

———. "One Continent to Another." In *I is a Long Memoried Woman*, 9. London: Karnak House, 1983.

———. "The Battle With Language." In *Caribbean Women Writers: Essays from the First International Conference*, edited by Selwyn Cudjoe, 288. Massachusetts University Press: 1990.

———. "Waterpot." In *I is a Long Memoried Woman*, 17–18. London: Karnak House, 1983.

———. "Yemanji." In *I is a Long Memoried Woman*, 71. London: Karnak House, 1983.

Norton, David. *A History of the English Bible as Literature*. Cambridge: Cambridge University Press, 2000.

O'Callaghan, Evelyn. "Interior Schisms Dramatised: The Treatment of the 'Mad'." In *Out of the Kumbla: Caribbean Women and Literature*, edited by Carole Boyce Davies and Elaine Savory Fido, 89–110. New Jersey: Africa World Press, 1990.

Olmos, Margarite Fernández, and Lizabeth Paravisini-Gebert. "The Afro Cuban Religious Traditions of Regla de Palo and the Abakuá Secret Society." In *Creole Religions of the Caribbean: An Introduction from Vodou and Santeria to Obeah and Espiritismo*, 79. New York: New York University Press, 2003.

———. *Sacred Possessions: Vodou, Santería, Obeah, and the Caribbean*. New Jersey: Rutgers University Press, 1997.

O'Neal, Eugenia. "Credulous Blacks and Faithful Mulattoes." In *Obeah, Race and Racism: Caribbean Witchcraft in the English Imagination*, 312. Kingston: UWI Press, 2020.

Pacquet, Sandra Pouchet. "Foreword." In *The Pleasures of Exile*, by George Lamming, xii–vx. Michigan: University of Michigan Press, 1992.

BIBLIOGRAPHY

———. *The Novels of George Lamming*. Portsmouth: Heinemann Educational Publishers, 1982.

Patteti, Raja. "Narratives." In *The Fiction of Wilson Harris: A Study in West Indian Discourse*, 81. Nigeria: Prestige, 2008.

Paton, Diana. *The Cultural Politics of Obeah: Religion, Colonialism and Modernity in the Caribbean World*. Cambridge: Cambridge University Press, 2015.

Paul, Annie. "The Rainmaker's Mistake, by Erna Brodber." In *Black Rain* (2008): 1–5.

Peterson, Kirsten, and Anna Rutherford. "Intimations of the Stranger." In *Wilson Harris: The Uncompromising Imagination*, 28–31, edited by Hena Maes-Jelinek. Denmark: Dangaroo Press, 1991.

Philip, Marlene NourbeSe, and Setaey Adamu Boateng. *Zong!* Connecticut: Wesleyan University Press, 2008.

Pineau, Gisèle. "The Voyage of the Centipede." In *The Haunted Tropics: Caribbean Ghost Stories*, 49–66. Kingston: UWI Press, 2015.

Powell, Patricia. "A Search for Caribbean Masculinities." In *Anthurium: A Caribbean Studies Journal* 10, no. 2, (2013): 1–12.

———. *The Fullness of Everything*. London: Peepal Tree, 2009.

Puri, Shalini. "An 'Other' Realism: Erna Brodber's *Myal*." In *ARIEL: A Review of International English Literature* 24, no. 3 (1993): 102–3.

Rahming, Melvin B. "Towards a Critical Theory of Spirit: The Insistent Demands of Erna Brodber's *Myal*." In *Revista/Review Interamericana* 1, (2001): 8.

Ramazani, Jahan. "The Wounds of History: Walcott's Omeros and the Postcolonial Poetics of Affliction." In *Publications of the Modern Language Association* 112, no. 3 (1997): 405–17.

Reddy, Sheshalatha. "Inspiriting Flesh/Fleshing Out Spirit." In *British Empire and the Literature of Rebellion: Revolting Bodies, Laboring Subjects*, 73–128. London: Palgrave Macmillan, 2017.

Regis, Hannah. "Not Fit to be Mentioned: Ghosts and Narratives of Criminal Intimacies in Selected Short Stories from *The Haunted Tropics: Caribbean Ghost Stories*." In *Caribbean Quarterly* 66, no. 2 (2020): 117–194.

———. "Myth, Ancestors and Ritual." *Journal of West Indian Literature* 27, no 2 (2019): 29–38.

Rennert, Hellmut. *Essays on Twentieth-century German Drama and Theater: An American Reception 1977–1999*. NY: Peter Lang, 2004.

Reynold, Richard. *Superheroes: A Modern Mythology*. Mississippi: University Press of Mississippi, 1993.

Riach, Alan. "Interview with Wilson Harris (1990)." In *The Radical Imagination: Lectures and Talks*, 62, edited by Alan Riach and Mark Williams. Belgium: L3-Liège Language and Literature, 1992.

BIBLIOGRAPHY

Roh, Franz. "Magic Realism: Post-Impressionism." In *Magical Realism: Theory, History, Community*, 16, edited by Wendy B. Faris and Zamora Parkinson. Durham: Duke University Press, 1995.

Rohlehr, Gordon. "Dream Journeys." In *Transgression, Transition, Transformation: Essays in Caribbean Culture*, 410–55. San Juan: Lexicon, 2007.

———. "Folk Research: Fossil or Living Bone." In *Transgression, Transition, Transformation: Essays in Caribbean Culture*, 380–81. San Juan: Lexicon, 2007.

———. "George Lamming and Kamau Brathwaite." In *Transgression, Transition, Transformation: Essays in Caribbean Culture*, 395. San Juan: Lexicon, 2007.

———. "National Heritage Library." In *Transgression, Transition, Transformation: Essays in Caribbean Culture*, 389. San Juan: Lexicon, 2007.

———. "Possession as Metaphor: Lamming's Season of Adventure." In *The Shape of that Hurt and other Essays*, 66–96. POS: Longman Trinidad Limited, 1992.

———. "Round Table: Wilson Harris and Caribbean Literature." In *Theatre of the Arts*, 236, edited by Hena Maes-Jelinek and Bénédicte Ledent. Amsterdam: Rodopi, 2002.

———. "Where is Here? What Jail is This? Who Are We?" In *Transgression, Transition, Transformation: Essays in Caribbean Culture*, 457–502. San Juan: Lexicon Trinidad, 2007.

Said, Edward. "Introduction." In *Orientalism*, 1–31. London: Penguin Books, 2019.

Sairsingh, Marie. *Africana Philosophy and the Metaphysics of the "After-Man": Examining Selected Texts by Erna Brodber*. PhD thesis: Howard University, 2018.

Saunders, Patricia. "Defending the Dead, Confronting the Archive: A Conversation with M. NourbeSe Philip." In *Small Axe* vol. 12 no. 2 (2008): 68–79.

Scott, David. "The re-enchantment of Humanism: An Interview with Sylvia Wynter." In *Small Axe* 8, no. 120 (2000): 136–211.

Sedgwick, Eve. "Paranoid Reading and Reparative Reading, or, You're So Paranoid You Probably Think this Essay is about You." In *Touching Feeling: Affect, Pedagogy, Performativity*, 123–51. Durham: Duke University Press, 2003.

Senior, Olive. *Gardening in the Tropics*. Ontario: Insomniac, 1994.

Shangodoyin, Dahud Kehinde, and Ojo Oluwayemisi Oyeronke. "Statistical Inference in Ifa Divination." In *Orisa: Yoruba Gods and Spiritual Identity in Africa and the Diaspora*, 77, edited by Toyin Falola and Ann Genova. Trenton, NJ: Africa World Press, 2005.

Sharpe, Christina. "Making Monstrous Intimacies Surviving Slavery, Bearing Freedom." In *Monstrous Intimacies: Making Post-Slavery Subjects*, 4. NY and London: Duke University Press, 2010.

Sharpe, Jenny. "The Rebels Old Obeah Woman." In *Ghosts of Slavery*, 1–44. Minnesota: University Press of Minnesota, 2003.

BIBLIOGRAPHY

Shaw, Gregory. "Language and Revolutionary Hope." In *The Literate Imagination: Essays on the Novels of Wilson Harris*, 147–48, edited by Michael Gilkes. London: Macmillan, 1989.

———. "Time of the Tiger." In *Wilson Harris: The Uncompromising Imagination*, 107–14, edited by Hena Maes-Jelinek. Denmark: Dangaroo Press, 1991.

Simpson, George. "The Shango Cult in Nigeria and in Trinidad." In *Religious Cults of the Caribbean: Trinidad, Jamaica and Haiti*. San Juan: Institute of Caribbean Studies, 1970, 126.

Spivak, Gayatri. "Can the Subaltern Speak?" In *Colonial Discourse and Post-Colonial Theory: A Reader*, 66–109, edited by Patrick Williams and Laura Chrisman. New York: Columbia University Press, 1994.

Suárez, Lucía M. "Gisele Pineau: Writing the Dimensions of Migration." In *World Literature Today* 75, no. 3 (2001): 8–21.

Sukenik, Eleazar. *The Earliest Records of Christianity*. New Jersey: Gorgias Press, 2008.

Taylor, Jason de Caires. "Vicissitudes." In *Underwater Sculptures*. Last modified 17 June 2013. https://www.underwatersculpture.com/works/underwater/.

Thomas, Jeannie. "The Usefulness of Ghost Stories." In *Haunting Experiences: Ghosts in Contemporary Folklore*, 26–30, edited by Dianne Goldstein and Jeannie Thomas. 1st ed. Colorado: University Press of Colorado, 2007.

Torres-Saillant, Silvio. "Kamau Brathwaite and the Caribbean World." In *Caribbean Poetics: Toward an Aesthetic of West Indian Literature*, 137–49. Cambridge: Cambridge University Press, 1997.

Viveiros de Castro, Edouardo. "Cosmological Deixis and Amerindian Perspectivism." In *The Journal of the Royal Anthropological Institute* 4, no. 3 (1998): 469–72.

———. *The Relative Native: Essays on Indigenous Conceptual Worlds*. Chicago: Hau Books, 2015.

Walcott, Derek. "A Far Cry From Africa." In *Collected Poems, 1948–1984*, 17–18. London: Faber and Faber, 1986.

———. *Another Life*. Colorado: Lynne Rienner, 2004.

———. *Omeros*. London: Faber and Faber, 1990.

———. "The Antilles: Fragments of Epic Memory." In *What the Twilight Says: Essay*, 68–70. London: Farrar, Straus and Giroux, 1998.

———. "The Schooner's Flight." In *Collected Poems 1948–1984*, 345–61. London: Faber and Faber, 1986.

———. "The Sea is History." In *The Poetry of Derek Walcott 1948–2013*, 253–56. London: Farrar, Straus and Giroux, 2014.

———. "The Spoiler's Return." In *Collected Poems 1948–1984*, 432–38. London: Faber and Faber, 1986.

BIBLIOGRAPHY

———. *Ti-Jean and His Brothers*. Port of Spain: Alexander Street Press, 2003.

———."What the Twilight Says: An Overture." In *What the Twilight Says: Essays*, 3–35. New York: Farrar, Straus and Giroux, 1998.

Webb, Barbara. "Conclusion." In *Myth and History in Caribbean Fiction: Alejo Carpentier, Wilson Harris, and Édouard Glissant*, 149. Massachusetts: University Press of Massachusetts, 1992.

———. "Lo real maravilloso in Caribbean Fiction." In *Myth and History in Caribbean Fiction: Alejo Carpentier, Wilson Harris, and Édouard Glissant*, 13. Massachusetts: University Press of Massachusetts, 1992.

Williams, Cynric. *Hamel, the Obeah Man*. Ontario: Broadview Editions, 2010.

Wyatt, Jean. "Giving Body to the Word: The Maternal Symbolic in Toni Morrison's *Beloved*." In *Publications of the Modern Language Association of America* 108, no. 4 (1993): 474–88.

Wynter, Sylvia. "Novel and History, Plot and Plantation." *Savacou* 5, no. 1 (1971): 95–100.

———. "We Must Learn to Sit Down and Talk about a Little Culture." In *Jamaica Journal* 2, no. 4 (1968): 23–32.

Young, Robert. *Postcolonialism: An Historical Introduction*. New Jersey: John Wiley and Sons, 2016.

Index

"n" denotes notes; "t" denotes table in appendix

abject bodies, 109, 114

abjection, as initiating factor for mediums/seers, 175t; concept of, 110

absent present, concept of, 113, 117, 134

abuse, theme of 126

affect, definition of, 22

affective filiations, 22–24

Africana philosophy, Caribbean literature and, 99

Africans: ancestors, 161; animism, 158; cosmologies, 193–94; diaspora, 35; spiritual engendered systems, 193 n42; syncretism, 9–10

African-Caribbean: diaspora, 26–27, 101, 166; heritage, 2–3, 9; iconography, 105; nationals, 172; spiritual practices, 119; voice of, 159–60

agency, trope of, 81, 83

"Ala" (Nichols), 80

Allsopp, Richard, 8

alterity, 127

alternative medicine, 166

alternative temporality, 172

Amazonian women, myth of the, 54, 186 n51

Amazonian myths, 106

Amerindian myths, 53

amnesia, 176t

Anansi, 18, 21, 77

ancestors, 37, 43, 69, 86–108; importance of in the Black diaspora, 85; reunion with, 120; summoning of, 17

ancestral cosmologies, 146

ancestral magic, 132

ancestral names, 160

ancestral powers, 167

ancestral traditions: loss of, 149; contemporary relevance of, 37, 166

ancestral veneration, 16–19, 93

Anglophone Caribbean writers, 6–8

Annie Palmer (White Witch of Rosehall), 10–11

anthropomorphized scapes, 26–31

anti-colonial praxis, 4–8

Antoine-Dunne, Jean, 152, 153, 162

"Arawak Horizon" (Harris), 36, 136–49, 153, 154; as allegory for historical genocide, 138; liminal spaces, 144–45; natural elements and rebirth, 148–49; numerals, use of, 148; spatializing effects of colonial history, 137; runes, 140, 146; shamanic rites, 147; spirit realm, 139–40; symbolism of the womb, 139–40; zemi, 143

Arawak myths, 53, 138

Arawaks, 58; historical genocide of, 138

archive as mortuary, 66

archival gaps, 64

arranged marriages, 118

artist/writer, responsibilities of, 117

Aruac people (St Lucia), 157

Baker-Josephs, Kelly, 101

Bakhtin, Mikhail, 155–56

Baucom, Ian (*Spectres of the Atlantic*), 68–69

Baugh, Edward, on Caribbean humanism, 5

beads of African ancestors, 84–85

belonging, 203 n75

Bhabha, Homi, 20; on the interstice, 111; on liminality, 154

Bierhorst, John, 106

biopiracy, 27

black female body, commodification of, 117

blackness, 193 n42

black radicalism and re-envisioning of black ontology, 99

Black Stalin, 8

border discourse (Chambers), 154

body, the: and the divine, 132; abuse and healing of, 134

bolom (unborn figure), 115

bone-flute, 47, 51–52

bones, symbol of, 150–51

"Bonnaire Silk Cotton Tree, The" (Mootoo), 109, 110, 114–17

boundary crossers, 175t

Brand, Dionne, 15

Brathwaite, Edward Kamau, 8, 9, 29, 32; Afro-Caribbean voice, 159; geo-psyche, 18; Legba figure, 20; metaphorical language, 202 n70; tidalectics, 30, 76

Brodber, Erna, 2–3, 171; cross-cultural narratives, use of, 106–7; cultural myth, syncretization of, 106–7; embodiment, technique of, 105; *kumbla*, 197 n30; *Myal*, 31–32, 35, 65, 179 n21; *The Rainmaker's Mistake*, 96–108, 172; myth-making, 102–3; reassembling of the African diaspora, 101, theme of violence in, 98; yam motif, 97–100

Bundy, A.J., 28

bush baby, 47

Butler, Judith, 186 n51

cannibalism, 47, 50–51

Caribbean consciousness, literary text and, 170

Caribbean epistemology, radical change in, 110

Caribbean (existential) phenomenology, 4, 177–78 n5

Caribbean ghost genre, 113

Caribbean histories, tapestry of, 99

Caribbean identity, 43–44, 56, 158, 169, 171; and centrality of the spiritual, 172. *See also* identity

Caribbean linguistic heterogeneity, 112

Caribbean literature, 2–3

Caribbean myth, as analytical tool, 14; *douendom*, 115

Caribbean mythic imagination, 89

Caribbean native mythology, 107

INDEX

Caribbean natural world, 145–46

Caribbean ontology, 87, 110, 170, 195 n7

Caribbean philosophy, 9

Caribbean poetics of spirit, 9–12, 136–70, 171

Caribbean spectrality, 36, 117

Caribbean spectrality in literature: affective filiations, 22–24; ancestral veneration, 16–19; anthropomorphized scapes, 26–31; cultural memory, 22–24; ghosts and haunting, 15–16; liminality and limbo, 20–22; magical spaces, 26–31; mythic imagination 12–14; polyphony, 31–33; postmemory, 24–25; psychological phenomena, 22–24; ritual, 16–19; spectral presence, 25–26; tricksters, conduits and mediumship, 19–20; vestigial presences, 12–14

Caribbean literature, critical framework for reading, 170

Caribbean unconscious, concept of (Harris), 89

Caribbean metaphysical universe, 90

Caribbean womanhood, 167

Caribbean writing: innovations by Harris, 142; innovations by Walcott, 162, 164; and collective redress, 173

Caribs, ancestral culture of, 40–47, 58

Carnival, 10; and Obeah, 179 n23; Trinidadian, 196 n21

Carter, Martin ("Listening to the Land"), 146

castaways, as initiating factors for mediums/seers, 175t

Catholic Church, 166

caves, symbolism of, 140–41

centipede, metaphor of the, 125–26

Ceremony of Souls, 17, 32, 90, 93

ceremony/ritual, 175t

Chambers, Iain, 154

chattel slavery, 117

child abuse, 120, 126

Christian missionaries, 11

church hymns, as used in healing process, 132

circular images, 44, 161

class, binaries of, 126

Cliff, Michelle, 15

collective community, 84

collective identities, 57

collective memory, 113

collective social action, 61

colonial brainwashing, 9–10

colonial discourse, 154

colonial experience: dehumanization and, 86; haunting associated with, 14–16, 137-38; overcoming, 51–52, 86, 88, 96, 109; writing to undo, 109, 171–72

colonial grand narrative of the Caribbean, dismantling of, 74

colonial implosion as factor for mythic presences, 175t

colonial literature, negative impact of, 3–4

colonial memory, 115

colonial pedagogical indoctrination, 92

colonial taboos, inheritance of, 127–28

colonial violence/murder, 176t

commodification of the female body, 117

community, 48, 56–57, 59; as organic

INDEX

concept, 38; in Brodber's work, 102–3

Condé, Maryse, 3, 6, 8, 15, 35, 112, 134, 171; "The Obeahman, Obeahed", 109, 113, 117–20

Congo drum, 95–96

coning, 132

Cooper, Carolyn, 17, 93, 179 n23

corpses as metaphor, 113

cosmologies of the ancient world, 172

cosmo-spirituality, reliance on by Harris and Walcott, 137

cosmos, metaphor of, 49

couvade, custom of, 39–40

"Couvade" (Harris), 21, 24–25, 38–47, 52, 53, 58, 59, 61

creativity: and the divine, 134; and healing, 133

Creole languages, 8, 202 n70

creolization, syncretism within, 5

cryptophore, 36, 175t

cultural ecology, 28

cultural memory, 22–24, 137, 176t

cultural resistance, 166

culture of terminality, 37

Dabydeen, David, 29

D'Aguiar, Fred, 29

Danticat, Edwidge, 29

Dash, J. Michael, 144, 185 n30

"Days that Fell" (Nichols), 79

death, as metaphor, 113

de Lisser, Herbert (*The White Witch of Rosehall*), 10–11

DeLoughrey, Elizabeth, 26

Derrida, Jacques, 200 n13

disembodied presence, 113

divination, 176t

divine, ants as messengers of the,

167; association between the sensual and, 132

divine possession, 93

douendom, 115

Drake, Sandra, 200 n15

"Dream Journeys", (Rohlehr), 87

dream ritual, 41–42

dreams, 41, 53, 175t

dream universe, Harris's use of, 138–39

duppies, 114; agency of, 116

ecological imperialism, 27

environment. *See* nature

epic, genre of the, 155–56

epic stratagems, 89

erasure by imperial archive, 176t

essentialism, as initiating factor for ritual/ceremony, 175t

ethnic culture, sedimentation of as factor for mythic presences, 175t

exaqua, 65

exile, 173

existentialism. *See* Caribbean existential phenomenology

experiential humanism, 126

Eyerman, Ron, 64

fables, 44

family dysfunction, 120–21, 125, 126, 129–32

family, interpretations of, 61

family secrets, 120

Fanon, Frantz, 4–5; existentialism of, 177–78 n5

Faustian bargain, 114

female body: commodification of the, 117; suppression of, 120

female, aggressions against, 113

INDEX

female power, 186 n51; 186 n55
female suffering, 8
female interiority, 118
Fernandez Olmos, Margarite, 26–27
fiction: new understandings through, 126; critical reflection through, 116; ontological retrieval through, 112
First Peoples, 2, 34, 38, 46, 56, 59, 153; of Guyana, 184 n5; historical genocide of, 138. *See also under* Indigenous
folds, metaphor of, 48
folk aesthetics, 87
folklore, 19–20
"Folk Research: Fossil or Living Bone" (Rohlehr), 87
folkways, 133
Forbes, Curdella, 101
forgiveness, 133
France, influence of on Condé, 112–13; influence of on Pineau, 113
Francophone writers, 6–8, 178–79 n16
freedom, concept of, 86–108, 169–70, 172; in *The Rainmaker's Mistake*, 101–2
futurity, 111

gender: binaries of, 126; haunting effects of violence relating to, 8; and identity, 198 n41; 198 n43
generational haunting, 37
generational trauma, 24, 63, 127
genocide/extermination, 176t
geography of the Caribbean, 149–50
geo-psyche, 18
"George Lamming and Kamau Brathwaite", (Rohlehr), 87
ghost dreaming, 94

ghost narrative, 113; function of, 117
ghost fictions, violence in, 120
ghosts, 15–16, 115, 142, 149, 155, 175t; and colonialism, 1–2; and forgiveness, 133
ghouls, 110
Gilroy, Paul, 29–30
Glissant, Édouard, 5, 9, 14, 30, 32, 34; "The Black Novelist and his People: Notes for a Conference", 185 n30; "Cross-Cultural Poetics", 81–82; "Poetics of Relation", 110; rhizomatic thought, 195 n10
Gordon, Lewis, existentialism of, 177–78 n5
Grant, Damian *(Realism)*, 3
graphics, symbolic use of by Harris, 142
Gregson vs Gilbert (1783), 65–67, 81
griot, 169
Greek mythologies, merging of Caribbean and, 159
Griffin, Gabriele, 75
Guadeloupe: Condé in, 113; influence of on Pineau, 113; in "The Voyage of the Centipede", 120
Guyana, creative discourses of, 88
Guyanese landscape, 28–29, 47, 51; importance of for Harris, 136

Haiti, Voodoo in, 12
Hall, Stuart, 74
Handley, George B., 26
haptic rituals, 132
haptic criticism, 198 n54
Harris, Wilson, 3, 9, 32, 34, 162, 171; *The Age of Rainmakers*, 141; contrasted with work of Rohlehr, 88; divergence with Walcott, 153;

223

dream universe, 138–39; the epic, 156; existentialism of, 177–78 n5; *Fossil and Psyche*, 140–41; imaginative fiction of, 147–48; importance of landscape for, 136; Indigenous ancestors, 37–62; limbo, 87; language and graphic writing, 142; liminality, 21, 144, 185 n30; magical spaces, 28–29; metaphor and symbolism, use of, 141; mythic imagination, 12–14, 87, 200 n13; narrative hybridity of, 138; nature, use of, 49–50; *Palace of the Peacock*, 12, 96; polyphony, 32, 33; possession, 87, 143–44; postmemory, 24–25, 37; "The Schizophrenic Sea", 48, 51; *The Sleepers of Roraima*, 37; "The Subjective Imagination", 37; symbology of, 147; *Tradition, the Writer and Society*, 140; zemi, 200 n15. *See also* "Arawak Horizon"; "Couvade"; *Whole Armour, The*; "Yurokon"

Hartman, Saidiya, 65
haunted bodies, 137
haunted histories, 63–85
haunted texts, 112
Haunted Tropics: Caribbean Ghost Stories, The (Munro, ed.), 1–2, 109
haunting, 15–16, 172; border discourse and, 154; of the modern landscape, 116. *See also* generational haunting; haunted bodies; haunting histories
healing, theme of, 133, 134
healing practices, 99, 132, 165–66
healing strategies, 135, 149; through language, 152
heteronormativity, 127
Henry, Paget, 9, 177 n5

hieroglyphs/symbols, 176t
Hirsch, Marianne, 24, 34, 37
historical genocide of First Peoples, 138
historical grief, 63
historical materialism, negative impact of, 3–4
"History, Fable and Myth in the Caribbean and Guianas" (Harris), 87
"Holding My Beads" (Nichols), 84
Holloway, Karla, 126
homoerotic discourses, exploration of in *The Fullness of Everything*, 128
homophobia, 127
hooks, bell, on critical thinking, 134
hounfort, 17, 93
hybridity, 114, 134
hyper-masculinity, 128

"I Coming Back" (Nichols), 81
identity, 111, 113–13, 148, 198 n41; name-changing and, 105; national, 154; reinventions of, 128; theme of, 97–98; Walcott and, 161. *See also* Caribbean identity
Ifa divination rituals, 69
Igbo girls, beads of, 84–85
I Have Crossed An Ocean (Nichols), 75
I is a Long Memoried Woman (Grace Nichols), 73–85; Anansi, 77–78; limbo as conceptual tool, 77–78; reconstructing history, 76; resistance, acts of, 78; traumatic memory, 74, 77; trope of memory, 73; water as symbol, 74–75

INDEX

illusion, trope of, 57–58

imaginative fiction, Harris's writing as, 147–48

immigration, as self-saving act, 128

incest, 120

Indigenous, explication of use of term, 44, 184 n5

Indigenous cosmovisions, 37–62

Indigenous fables, 44–46

Indigenous genocide, 117

Indigenous healing rituals, 44–45. *See also* healing practices

Indigenous heritage, 2–3, 9

Indigenous holocaust, Caribbean, 38, 109, 142, 146

Indigenous, nature-based language, 149

Indigenous mysticism, 57

Indigenous mythologies, 38, 57, 142; re-writing Caribbean history using, 39

Indigenous postmemory, 37–62

Indigenous praxes, 141

Indigenous traditions, 146

individuality, 172; interpretations of, 61

initiation rites, 59

intergenerational transmission, 37

intersections, 134

interstice, 111, 145

Ismond, Patricia, 155

"I Will Enter", 83

Jamaican masculinity, ideals of, 127

James, C.L.R, 96

Jewish Holocaust, 24

Johnson, Erica *(Caribbean Ghostwriting)*, 14; *(Cultural Memory, Memorial and Reparative Writing)*, 22

journeying motif, 102–3

jumbies, 110, 114–15

justice, abandonment of, 114; returning of, 117

Keens-Douglas, Paul, 8

Kolata, Alan, 106

knowledge systems, 141

Kristeva, Julia, 36; concept of abjection, 110

kumbla, 120, 197 n30

ladder, as spatial metaphor, 47–48

la diablesse, 57

Lalla, Barbara, 33

Lamming, George, 2–3, 17, 32, 35, 171; *Season of Adventure,* 86–108, 172

landscapes, 42; as divine, 168; assaulted by Europeans, 140. *See also* anthropomorphized scapes; Guyanese landscape; living landscape; magical spaces

language, use of by Walcott, 149–50, 152

La Soufrière volcano, 152, 165

latency; as cause of dreams, 175t; intergenerational traumatic, 37

Lawson, Sarah, 82

Legba figure, 20, 94

limbo, 20–22, 77

liminality, 20–22, 154; as a conceptual framework, 111; life in, 118–19

liminal presences, 175t

liminal spaces, 144–45

literary text and Caribbean consciousness, 170

living landscape, 18; images of, 153

Lundberg, Christian, 22

225

Maes-Jelinek, Hena, 49
magical rites, 117; functionality of, 133. *See also* ancestral magic
magical spaces, 26–31, 162
marginalization, 110, 126, 173
marginal lives, 114
mas, 179 n23
masculinity, ritualized modes of, 126, 127, 129
masquerade, trope of, 57–58
massacre aboard the *Zong*, 65–67
material world, relations between immaterial and, 1–2
McCoppin, Rachel, 26
McKittrick, Katherine, 27
McSweeney, Joyelle, 18
mediums/seers, 175t
memory: and ancestors, 69; archaeology of, 67; Caribbean space as vessel of, 146, 150; and the colonial experience, 143; and ghostwriting, 15–16; historical, 63, 151; intrusions of, 121; ocean as space of, 72; painful, 123; repression of from childhood, 113, 127; transgenerational, 51; trope of, 73
mental illness, 120, 123–24, 126
metamorphosis, 38, 58, 144, 154
metaphor, use of by Walcott, 155
metensomatosis, 39
Middle Passage, 29, 73, 161–62, 172; spectres of the, 63–85, 83; and Brathwaite's tidalectics, 76
Milky Way myth, 53
migration, 173
Mittelholzer, Edgar, 11–12, 180 n31
mixed heritage, 2–3
"monstrous intimacies", 117
Mootoo, Shani, 3, 35, 112, 134, 171,

196 n21, 196 n24; abject, concept of, 110; "The Bonnaire Silk Cotton Tree", 109, 110, 114–17
Morgan, Paula, 65
mortician, symbolism of occupation of, 129–31
multiple consciousness, use of, 125
myal, 31
mysticism, 119–20
myth, 39, 86–108
myth creations of Central and South American cultures, 106
mythic images, 60
mythic imagination: 12–14; contrasted with realism, 200 n13; in work of Erna Brodber, 96, 102; in work of George Lamming, 89, 90; in work of Grace Nichols, 74; in work of Wilson Harris, 12–14, 39, 42, 52, 87–88, 200 n13
mythic innovations, 90
mythic memory, 151
mythic presences, 175t
mythic time, 63, 87, 145
Munro, Martin *(The Haunted Tropics: Caribbean Ghost Stories)*, 1–2
murder, 65

Naipaul, V.S., 146
name-changing, shifting identities through, 105
names, importance of, 45, 160
Nanny of the Maroons, 19–20
narrative style, fluidity in, 123
nationalist discourses of freedom, 86–87
nationhood, 108
nation, interpretation of, 61
nation language (Walcott), 159–60

INDEX

natural elements, Indigenous presence in the, 49

natural phenomena, spiritual and cultural interpretations of, 101

nature, Harris's use of, 49–50, 58, 139, 145

necromancer, 117

necrophilia as metaphor, 113

neo-capitalist orders, 109

Nichols, Grace, 2–3, 29, 34–35, 63, 73, 74, 77, 81, 84, 85, 171, 172; remembrance and reparations, 64; use of dreams, 75–76; use of syncretic magic, 82

"Night Is Her Robe" (Nichols), 82

nightmare, confronting trauma in, 122, 128–29

nonhistory, 5

nonlinearity, narrative style as, 123

Obeah, 10–11, 82, 119, 167, 179 n23

Obeah man, 120

Obeah woman, 92

obsession, 117–18

"Of Golden Gods" (Nichols), 83–84

Omeros (Walcott), 19, 20, 36, 149–69; analogy with Greek mythologies, 152, 159; circularity, use of images of, 155; griot, 169; healing practices, 165–68; liminality, 154–55; living landscape, 153; loss of ancestral traditions, 149; memory, 166; merging of realms, 158–59; metrical form used, 151–52; natural and supernatural worlds, 168–69; rebirth, 162; representation of names, 161; return to Africa, 158–61; self-discovery in, 162; sunrise metaphor, 155; symbolism of the bird, 158;

symbolism of the quilt, 162–64; symbolism of sea and coral, 150; symbolism of trees, 157-58; use of orthography, 151

O'Neal, Eugenia, 10

"One Continent/to Another" (Nichols), 77–78

ontological erasure, as initiating factor for ritual/ceremony, 175t

ontologies. *See* ways of being

oral culture, 161

Orion legend, 53

Orinoco creation myths, 106

Orisha priestess, 91–92

otherness and the other, 114, 135

outcasts, 122

paedophilia, 126–27

Paravisini-Gerbert, Lizabeth, 26–27

parental guilt, 131

Paton, Diana, 10

patriarchy, hegemony of, 120

Patterson, Orlando, and chattel slavery, 100

Patteti, Raja, 138

Paul, Annie, 101

Peet (character in *The Whole Armour*), 55–56

"Phenomenal Legacy" (Harris), 87

phenomenology. *See* Caribbean (existential) phenomenology

Philip, Marlene NourbeSe, 2, 3, 23, 29, 34–35, 63, 66, 68, 69, 70, 71, 72, 171, 172; reparation theme presented, 70; use of ritual and mourning, 73; *(Zong!)*, 63–75; *Zong* Massacre, 64–65, 70, 151

Pineau, Gisèle, 3, 6, 8, 23, 35, 112, 134,

171, 197 n30; "The Voyage of the Centipede", 109, 113, 120–26
plantations, 27
poetics of liminality, 185 n30
poetics of spirit. *See* Caribbean poetics of spirit
polyphony, 31–33
polyvocality, 171
Pomeroon People (Guyana), 38, 52–61
Port-of-Spain forest, 114
possession, 90–91. *See also* spirit possession
"Possession as Metaphor", (Rohlehr), 87
post-colonial discourse, 141
post-colonialism, 112
post-human, concept of, 193 n42
postmemory, 37, 176t
Powell, Patricia, 3, 23, 35, 36, 112, 134, 171; *The Fullness of Everything*, 109, 126–34, 163
power, theme of abuse of, 117
"Possession as Metaphor: Lamming's Season of Adventure" (Rohlehr), 90
postmemory, 24–25, 37–62
Pragnell, Alfred, 8
products of a fevered imagination, ghosts as, 175t
"Profiles of Myth and the New World", (Harris)
psychological phenomena, 22–24
Puri, Shalini, 98

qualitative content analysis, 33–34
queerness, 173

race, 126
radical openness, 134
Ramazani, Jahan, 155

Rahming, Melvin, 31
Rainmaker's Mistake, The (Brodber), 96–108; an allegory of colonialism, 96; connection between environment and Caribbean people, 101; diasporic fissures and journeys, 102–3; education, role of, 107–8; healing, 99, 105; identity, 98, 108; loss of ancestral memory, 104; sea corpse trope, 103; spiritual awakening of community, 100–1, 108; struggles in post-emancipation, 97; submerged history, theme of, 103–4, 108; time-lapse occurrence, 101; use of polyphony, 105–6, 107; yam motif, 98–99
Ramleela, 27–28
reading strategies, questioning of, 111. *See also* reparative reading
realism, 3, 13, 191 n19; challenging of, 113; contrasted with Brodber's narratives, 103; contrasted with mythic imagination, 200 n13
rebirth, theme of, 38
reconciliation, theme of, 38
reincarnation trope, 48–49
remembrance: of the Middle Passage, 77; and reparations, 64
remembering, process of, 65, 79, 112, 148, 152–53, 172. *See also* memory
reparations and remembrance, 64
reparative reading, 33–34, 111, 195 n7
reparatory project, 97
repressed trauma, 123
representation, alternative modes of, 169–70
restless souls, 15
restoration, 131
rhizome, image of, 154

INDEX

rhizomatic thought (Glissant), 195
n110

ritual, 16–19, 38, 86–108, 175t; and
remembering, 73, 148; and touch,
132

ritual music, 95–96

Rohlehr, Gordon, 32, 37, 87, 143; contrasted with work of Harris, 88; folk
aesthetics and myth, 87–89

root culture, 199 n3

Rudder, David, 8

runes, 140, 141, 153

Sairsingh, Marie, 99

Salkey, Andrew, 8

Saunders, Patricia, 65, 68

scapegoating, 122

science worker, irrelevancy of, 119

Scott, David, 110

sea, symbolism of, 65

Season of Adventure (Lamming),
88–96; African-derived cosmologies in, 91; colonial epistemologies
contested, 88; denial of ancestral
memory, 92; divine possession, 93;
drumming, 95; ghost dreaming,
94; possession, 90; spiritual journey in, 92–93

Sedgwick, Eve Kosofsky, 34; reparative reading, 111

seers/mediums, 175t

self-discovery, journey of, 58, 162

self-imposed exile, 122

Senior, Olive, 27

sensual, association between the
divine and, 132

sexual violation, 77, 117–20

shamanistic practice, 163

shamanistic rites, 147

Shango-Obeah complex, 11–12

Sharpe, Christina, 117

Sharpe, Jenny, 15, 19

Shaw, Gregory, 144

slave ship *(Zong)*, murder of Africans
aboard, 65

slavery, 117

social remembering, 112. *See also*
remembering, process of

soil heritage, 199 n3

soucouyant, 57

spectrality, 1–3, 173; and post-colonial
concepts, 111–12

spectral presences, 25–26; and
alternative modes of representation, 169–70; and envisioning of
redemptive potentials, 134–35; of
First Peoples, 59; in J'ouvert, 196
n21; past and present, 153; in "The
Voyage of the Centipede", 121,
124–25

Spectres of the Atlantic (Baucom),
68–69

spirit narratives, 99–100

spirit possession, Harris's use of,
143–44

spirit presences: comfort from, 133;
representations of, 5–6; 16, 19, 72,
81, 95, 108, 133, 149, 171, 183 n86;
within language, 169–70; textual
representation of, 108

spirit realm, 139

spirits, definition of, 1–2

spirit summoning, 197 n29

spiritual arts, function of, 119

spiritual freedom, 60

spiritual journey, 92–93

spiritual quest, 59, 144

spiritual revelation, 41–42

INDEX

spirituality: Caribbean poetics of, 6; as human and mystical, 132

spirit women, 83

spirit world, communication with, 52

Spivak, Gayatri, 111

spousal abuse, 118

steelband drum, 95

stick fighting, 10

St Lucia, 162; Aruac people of, 157

St Lucian identity, 202 n63

subaltern subjects, 111, 196 n24

subjectivities, 134

subjugation, state of, 119

submerged history, theme of, 103–4

submission, theme of, 117

sunrise metaphor in *Omeros*, 155

supernatural: encounters and repressed memories, 120–21; ritualistic pathways of, 131–32; worlds, 168–69

Swanzy, Henry, 8

syncretic iconography, Afro-Caribbean, 105

syncretism, 5, 30, 82, 166, 178 n9; misrepresentations of, 9–12

Taino, 83

Taylor, Jason de Caires *(Vicissitudes)*, 71

telepathic abilities, 121

Thomas, Jeannie, 117

threshold zones, 154

time: decolonial reading of, 149; unsettling of, 123

tonelle, 89, 93–94, 102

Torres-Saillant, Silvio, 87, 147

Tradition, the Writer and Society, (Harris), 87

transatlantic journey, 29

transatlantic slave trade, 63

trans-Caribbean connections, 113

trauma, 24, 122; culturally transmitted, 64; and secret abuse as initiating factors for cryptophore; theme of, 126, 146

trickster, 78, 114, 133

Trinidad, 12; creative discourses of, 88; Port-of-Spain forest, 114; wilderness of, 110

twilight, metaphor of, 155–56

twilight poetics, 32, 183 n86

unborn figure *(bolom)*, 115

uncanny environments, 137

underwater museums, 71

unfreedoms as cause of liminal presences/boundary crossers, 175t

unjust/abnormal death, as initiating factor for ghosts, 175t

unspeakable discourses, 109–35

vestigial presences, 12–14

vicarious traumatization, 24

victimization, sense of, 121

violence: theme of, 69, 117, 125–26, 157, 165, 172; repressed, 120–21

visions of the dead, 124

Viveiros de Castro, Eduardo, 106

Voodoo, 10, 82

Vodun, 11, 119; drums of, 95

voyeurism, 117–18

wake-work, 67, 73

Walcott, Derek: 3, 27–28, 30, 91, 162, 171; ancestral memory, 199 n2; belonging, 203 n75; Caribbean identity, 169; critique of capitalism, 157; divergence with Harris, 153; the epic, 156–57; *Ti Jean and His Brothers*, 115; use of metaphor, 155; "What the Twilight Says: An Overture", 32, 155, 183 n86; writing style, 149–50, 161, 164. *See* also *Omeros*

"Waterpot" (Nichols), 78–79

water, symbolism of, 67, 74

water divination, 147

ways of being, 5–6

ways of knowing, 9

Webb, Barbara, 14, 89

Western literary traditions, destabilization of, 88

Western materialism, issues with, 3–4

"Where is Here? What Jail is This? Who are We?" (Rohlehr), 87

Whole Armour, The (Harris), 38–39, 52–61, 187 n55, 187 n58; Amazonian warrior queen archetype, 54–56; themes of deception and illusion, 55; tropes of illusion and masquerade, 57–58; use of dreams in, 53; wilderness journey as spiritual awakening, 58–59

Wiccan spirituality, 132

Williams, Cynric *(Hamel, the Obeah Man)*, 10

Williams, Eric, 96

witch, use of by Rohlehr, 91

womb, symbolism of the, 39, 44, 77, 102, 139–40

women: aggressions against, 113; as objects of sexual plunder, 126

women-centred cultural activities, 82

writing compared with sewing, 164–65

Wyatt, Jean, 63

Wynter, Sylvia, 9, 27, 110; on blackness, 99, 193 n42

yam motif, 98–100

"Yemanji" (Nichols), 82–83

Yoruba lexical items, 70–72

Young, Robert, 112

"Yurokon" (Harris), 21, 24, 25, 38, 46–53, 58, 61

zemi, 143, 200 n15

zombies, 110

zombification: and stasis as factors for divination, 176t; as metaphor, 113, 117–20

Zong! (Philip), 22, 23, 63–85; absence as metaphor, 67; Ghanaian musical influence on, 68; oral traditions as influence, 69; remembrance of the dead, 73; Yoruba lexical items, 70